"*John Frame's Selected Shorter Wr*[...] ways. For one, much of it reads [...] tions than a compilation of theological essays. The highly practical nature of the work is likely due to the fact that now, reaching the end of his teaching career, Frame wants to impart 'what are the most important thoughts I would like to leave to the next generation.' The section on the use of Scripture in preaching is a virtual necessity for students of preaching. Next, since these are Frame's 'most important thoughts,' I find myself savoring each word, even more so than when reading his other works. Everything the apostle Paul wrote is vitally important. But when I read Paul's parting words to the Ephesian elders (Acts 20), I want to pay special attention, because here I'm exposed to some of his chief concerns. Finally, anyone who has read Frame's Theology of Lordship series may have picked up on the way in which the theologian can crystallize and clarify a vital thought in a digression that can occur much later and under different subject headings. *Selected Shorter Writings* serves to elucidate a considerable number of subjects in Frame's previously written works. It provides his clearest and most succinct explanation of perspectivalism."

—**John Barber**, Pastor, Cornerstone Presbyterian Church, Palm Beach Gardens, Florida; Adjunct Professor, Fine Arts, Saints Bible Institute, San Lorenzo, Italy

"In the tradition of John Calvin (*Tracts and Treatises*), Jonathan Edwards (*Miscellanies*), and B. B. Warfield (*Selected Shorter Writings*), Frame has now published his own *Selected Shorter Writings, Volume 1*. As a seminary professor for more than four decades, he has distinguished himself as a prolific author and one of America's foremost theologians and philosophers. Before this book was published, most of these rare theological, philosophical, and practical gems had been hidden away in his electronic files or posted on websites and blogs not widely known to the public. Do yourself a favor and mine the rich truths in these winsome and provocative essays (written in Frame's inimitable style of robust charity) on a wide array of important topics. I highly recommend it!"

—**Steven L. Childers**, Associate Professor of Practical Theology, Reformed Theological Seminary, Orlando; President and CEO, Global Church Advancement

"John wrote this book so that the average person could understand it, which is a concept introduced by the apostle Paul but little employed ever since. It's like the nine-hundred-pound gorilla wrestling with a newborn and restraining himself: John could do a number on us intellectually, but he prefers to communicate for the sake of the kingdom of God."

—**Andrée Seu Peterson**, Senior Writer, *WORLD* magazine

"John Frame is certainly one of those 'dangerous theologians.' Of course, that means he is mild and loving, even as he confronts error boldly and builds the necessary biblical-theological frameworks for our times. He covers many important topics with our necessary standards for accounting (cf. Heb. 4:12–13). We see more of the sea lanes traversed as he pursues that Great White Whale of biblical truth applied!"

—**Andrew J. Peterson**, President, Reformed Theological Seminary, Global Education

"In comparison with the 'feast' of John Frame's major works, these are the 'nuggets.' They still offer vintage Frame, and I heartily recommend them for their wisdom, balance, and incisiveness. Some have a more personal, informal tone, and will usefully complement Frame's major writings, especially for those who want to understand the connection of his writings to the person behind them."

—**Vern S. Poythress**, Professor of New Testament Interpretation, Westminster Theological Seminary; Editor, *Westminster Theological Journal*

"This book is a veritable cornucopia of Frame's theology, and one will find here appetizing personal information no less than rigorously biblical analysis. Frame is not afraid to slay sacred cows ('narrative theology,' the centrality of justification by faith alone, politically liberal evangelical-ism, N. T. Wright's bibliology) if he believes they don't pass biblical muster. Whether you have never read Frame before or have read all that he's written to date, this book will inform, intrigue, encourage, edify, rouse, and convict you."

—**P. Andrew Sandlin**, President, Center for Cultural Leadership; Senior Pastor, Cornerstone Bible Church, Santa Cruz, California

"Dr. Frame has produced a series of theological articles that will encourage the reader to consider more carefully the correct understanding of various Christian ideas encountered in the progress of dogmatic thought. Dr. Frame is committed to being biblical, with a focus on being balanced in one's theological perspective. For Professor Frame, being biblically balanced expresses his goal of a lifetime of teaching theology. He has sought not only to express orthodox doctrine from a biblical perspective, but also to convey a theology that is capable of affecting a Christian's total world and life view. Theology is not an abstract study. Understanding theology not only requires us to correctly understand the propositional truth of Scripture, but also seeks to engage each believer in his or her daily walk with Christ. This excellent book is a must-read for those who seek to be challenged in understanding the biblical and theological issues that face the church of Jesus Christ today."

—**Kenneth Gary Talbot**, President, Whitefield Theological Seminary

JOHN FRAME'S
SELECTED
SHORTER WRITINGS

JOHN FRAME'S
SELECTED
SHORTER WRITINGS

VOLUME 1

JOHN M. FRAME

P&R PUBLISHING

P.O. BOX 817 • PHILLIPSBURG • NEW JERSEY 08865-0817

Printed in the United States of America

ISBN: 978-1-59638-731-7 (pbk.)
ISBN: 978-1-59638-732-4 (ePub)
ISBN: 978-1-59638-733-1 (Mobi)

Library of Congress Cataloging-in-Publication Data

Frame, John M., 1939-
  [Essays. Selections]
  John Frame's selected shorter writings / John M. Frame.
      pages cm
  Includes bibliographical references and index.
  Volume 1: ISBN 978-1-59638-731-7 (pbk.)
  Volume 2: ISBN 978-1-62995-078-5 (pbk.)
  1. Reformed Church--Doctrines. 2. Theology, Doctrinal. 3. Theology--Methodology.
I. Title.
  BX9422.3.F725 2013
  230'.42--dc23
                                    2013018973

To Vern, Richard, and Andrée
dangerous theologians all

For the word of God is living and active, sharper than any two-edged sword, piercing to the division of soul and of spirit, of joints and of marrow, and discerning the thoughts and intentions of the heart. And no creature is hidden from his sight, but all are naked and exposed to the eyes of him to whom we must give account. (Heb. 4:12–13)

Contents

PART 5: PERSONAL

Foreword

JOHN M. FRAME (b. 1939) is a Calvinist theologian and American philosopher especially known for his work in systematic theology, Christian apologetics, and ethics. In the tradition of John Calvin (*Tracts and Treatises*),[1] Jonathan Edwards (*Miscellanies*),[2] B. B. Warfield (*Selected Shorter Writings*),[3] and Herman Bavinck (*Selected Shorter Works*),[4] Frame has now published his own *Selected Shorter Writings, Volume 1.*

Similar to those who have benefited only from J. I. Packer's more well-known books such as *Knowing God*,[5] but have never tapped the riches of his lesser-known writings (e.g., his *Introductory Essay to John Owen's The Death of Death in the Death of Christ*[6]), those who have benefited only from Frame's more well-known books can now mine the riches of his lesser-known, shorter writings.

Before publication of this book, most of these rare theological and philosophical gems had been hidden away as Frame's book appendices or as electronic files or articles posted on websites and blogs not widely known to the public. This book, however, is not merely a compilation of appendices and articles. Instead, these chapters are mostly unpublished

1. John Calvin and Henry Beveridge, *Tracts and Treatises of John Calvin* (Eugene, OR: Wipf and Stock, 2004).
2. Jonathan Edwards, *The Works of Jonathan Edwards*, vol. 13, *The Miscellanies: A–500*, ed. Thomas A. Schafer (New Haven, CT: Yale University Press, 1994); vol. 18, *The Miscellanies: 501–832*, ed. Ava Chamberlain (New Haven, CT: Yale University Press, 2000); vol. 20, *The Miscellanies: 833–1152*, ed. Amy Plantinga Pauw (New Haven, CT: Yale University Press, 2002); vol. 23, *The Miscellanies: 1153–1360*, ed. Douglas A. Sweeney (New Haven, CT: Yale University Press, 2004).
3. Benjamin Breckinridge Warfield, *Selected Shorter Writings*, ed. John Meeter (Phillipsburg, NJ: P&R Publishing, 2001).
4. Herman Bavinck, *Selected Shorter Works* (Portland, OR: Monergism Books, 2011).
5. J. I. Packer, *Knowing God*, 20th anniversary ed. (InterVarsity Press, 1993).
6. John Owen, *The Death of Death in the Death of Christ: A Treatise in Which the Whole Controversy about Universal Redemption Is Fully Discussed* (London: Banner of Truth, 1959).

essays of Frame's thought as part of the culmination of a remarkable career as an author and a teacher of theology and philosophy.

Building on his education at Princeton, Westminster Seminary, and Yale, Frame distinguished himself as an outstanding theologian during thirty-one years on the faculty of Westminster Theological Seminary in Philadelphia and California. Since 2000, he has been on the faculty of Reformed Theological Seminary in Orlando as professor of systematic theology and philosophy. He teaches apologetics, systematic theology, ethics, and history of philosophy and Christian thought.

During his decades as a seminary professor, Frame has distinguished himself as a prolific author, publishing books and articles not only in the areas of apologetics, theology, and ethics, but also in worship, film, music, and other media. Among his larger theological works is his highly acclaimed and award-winning Theology of Lordship series, including *The Doctrine of the Knowledge of God* (1987),[7] *The Doctrine of God* (2002),[8] *The Doctrine of the Christian Life* (2008),[9] and *The Doctrine of the Word of God* (2010).[10]

Frame is especially noted for his work in epistemology and presuppositional apologetics. He is considered one of the foremost interpreters and critics of the thought of the late Christian apologist Cornelius Van Til, whom he studied under at Westminster Seminary. In Frame's first book, *The Doctrine of the Knowledge of God* (1987), he elaborates his Christian epistemology (which he calls *triperspectivalism*) and argues that in order to appreciate the richness of attaining true knowledge, a person must understand that knowledge always involves the integration of three perspectives: the normative, situational, and existential.

His triperspectivalism has made a profound impact on church leaders today, including his practical application of Christ's offices as Prophet (normative), Priest (existential), and King (situational) to all of life and ministry. Frame's passion to see the lordship of the triune God in every sphere of thought and life is contagious. And this needed

---

7. John M. Frame, *The Doctrine of the Knowledge of God* (Phillipsburg, NJ: Presbyterian and Reformed, 1987).

8. John M. Frame, *The Doctrine of God* (Phillipsburg, NJ: P&R Publishing, 2002).

9. John M. Frame, *The Doctrine of the Christian Life* (Phillipsburg, NJ: P&R Publishing, 2008).

10. John M. Frame, *The Doctrine of the Word of God* (Phillipsburg, NJ: P&R Publishing, 2010).

contagion is now spreading to multitudes of Christians and church leaders at a critical time.

Frame believes that those with Reformed and evangelical convictions are at risk of being marginalized in our generation because some Reformed leaders, both inside and outside the academy, espouse unbiblical views of such critical areas as worship, evangelism, Christian spirituality, church planting, missions, and the relationship of the church and culture.[11]

But the good news is that God is raising up a new generation of church leaders and other Christians who are stemming this tide by standing for a robust Reformed theology that includes a biblical view of all these practical areas of ministry. And the theology and philosophy of John Frame is at the forefront, influencing this resurgence of biblical Calvinism among a new generation of church leaders.[12]

Frame represents a historic stream of biblical and philosophical thought[13] deeply rooted in the best foundational contributions of Athanasius, Augustine, Anselm, and Aquinas. In his writings you'll also find the biblical riches rediscovered by the church in the Protestant Reformation by Martin Luther and John Calvin, as well as the reshaping of those biblical truths in the seventeenth century by the English Puritans.

Frame's thought also reflects the Dutch Calvinism of Abraham Kuyper and Herman Bavinck and the Princeton theology of Charles Hodge, B. B. Warfield, and J. Gresham Machen. He writes, "I yield to no one in admiration of three brilliant and godly men, friends of one another, who set the highest standards for Reformed theology in the 1900s: B. B. Warfield, Abraham Kuyper, and Herman Bavinck."[14]

A handful of professors profoundly shaped his thought while he was in seminary, including John Murray, Cornelius Van Til, Ed Clowney, and Norm Shepherd. The three authors he resorts to most often today

11. John M. Frame, *The Escondido Theology: A Reformed Response to Two Kingdom Theology* (Lakeland, FL: Whitefield Media Productions, 2011).

12. David Van Biema, "The New Calvinism—10 Ideas Changing the World Right Now," *Time*, March 12, 2009.

13. See the appendix at the end of this book for a list of the one hundred works that have most influenced John Frame's thought, by the authors referred to in these next few paragraphs.

14. John M. Frame, *Backgrounds to My Thought*, available at http://www.frame-poythress .org/about/john-frame-full-bio/ (accessed May 16, 2013).

are Murray, Van Til, and Clowney.[15] Van Til became the greatest single influence on Frame's apologetics and theology. Other significant influences on his theology include G. C. Berkouwer, R. John Rushdoony, Meredith Kline, and J. I. Packer.

Frame's understanding of philosophy has been shaped not only by many of the authors listed above but also by the writings of Plato, Immanuel Kant, and Ludwig Wittgenstein. His emphasis on the importance of not only knowledge and behavior in the Christian life, but also heart affections, is drawn significantly from the writings of Blaise Pascal and Jonathan Edwards (often through the works of John Gerstner and John Piper as Edwards's contemporary advocates).

Although Frame's primary understanding of Christian apologetics and evangelism has been shaped by Van Til, others have deepened and broadened that understanding, including C. S. Lewis, Francis Schaeffer, Gordon Clark, C. John (Jack) Miller, and Vern Poythress (one of his many students whom he now refers to as his teachers).

As a result of integrating these diverse schools of thought over decades, John Frame is a rare biblical scholar who has a passion not only for people to gain a biblical understanding of theology, philosophy, apologetics, and ethics, but also for people to learn how to apply these disciplines to practical ministries such as worship, evangelism, discipleship, church planting, and missions. That's because, to John Frame, "theology is application."[16]

Frame is marked by both genuine humility and great courage. Knowing that he might be accused of being a theological liberal, he continues to stand against fractured denominationalism, and to fight for greater ecumenical unity in the church.

Knowing that he might be accused of being a theological fundamentalist, he continues to stand against moderate views of Scripture, and to fight for an infallible, inerrant Bible.

Knowing that he might be accused of being a cultural transformationist (and triumphalist), he continues to stand against pessimistic

---

15. Ibid.
16. Frame, *Doctrine of the Knowledge of God*, 1–100.

theological dualism that wrongly separates the church and culture, and to fight for the optimistic, biblical social engagement of Christians as witnesses to the lordship of Christ over all areas of public life.

Knowing that he might be accused of being a cultural isolationist (and pessimist), he continues to stand against theological views of God's kingdom that wrongly equate the priority of the institutional church ministries of the Word and social action, and to fight for understanding the primary purpose of the institutional church as making disciples of all nations through prioritizing the ministries of evangelism and the Word.

Knowing that he might be accused of being a traditionalist, he continues to stand against rapidly emerging, individualistic expressions of "Churchless Christianity," and to fight for the biblical necessity for all Christians to come under the spiritual authority and care of a local church body, through which they prioritize the regular, corporate ministries of the Word, sacrament, and prayer.

Knowing that he might be accused of being a pietist (and revivalist), he continues to stand against theological views that wrongly emphasize the communal dimensions of Christianity at the expense of the personal, and to fight for the biblical validity and need for all Christians to pursue holiness through personal spiritual disciplines such as regular Bible reading, prayer, and fasting.

Knowing that he might be accused of being an out-of-touch, ivory-tower academic, he continues to stand against the trend of church leaders' not receiving seminary training, and to fight for the importance of well-educated church leaders.

Knowing that he might be accused of being opposed to traditional seminary training, he continues to stand against the inherent problems with the traditional seminary model, and to fight for more innovative, practical, church-based seminary training models.

At Reformed Theological Seminary in Orlando (RTS-O), where John and I have served together as resident faculty members for thirteen years, we have heard a description over the years of those who are Reformed (Calvinistic) in theology as being on a theological continuum that ranges from the broadly evangelical (BE) on the one end to the truly Reformed (TR) on the other.

BEs are those who normally emphasize their evangelical theological convictions more strongly than their Reformed convictions. And at the other end of the continuum, TRs normally emphasize their Reformed theological convictions more strongly than their evangelical convictions. So what is John Frame—a BE or a TR? He is neither. Frame is in a completely different category called WR—"Winsomely Reformed." Someone who is WR cannot be identified as normally being at any one particular point on this Calvinistic continuum between the BEs and the TRs. That's because a WR has the unique capacity to function wisely and well anywhere across the doctrinally diverse continuum of evangelicalism—yet still hold strongly to his theologically Reformed convictions.

John Frame is the epitome of someone who is WR. This is why it's been so difficult for people to categorize him. In some contexts, he will overtly emphasize his Reformed convictions. But in other contexts, he will intentionally emphasize only his broader evangelical convictions. This confusing behavior is not because he is fearful or compromising his beliefs, but because he has learned to base his words and emphases on what is most appropriate in each unique context. Frame has a strong commitment to evangelical theology in general and to Reformed theology in particular, coupled with godly wisdom to know in which context and to what extent one or the other should be emphasized.

One would understandably think that a scholar with Frame's intellectual rigor and theological acumen would likely carry with him an aura of haughtiness. Instead, as one who has had an office next to him since 2000, I can tell you firsthand that John is a man marked by a rare blend of remarkable intellect and authentic humility.[17] He is a model of living out what he writes about in his popular booklet *Studying Theology as a Servant of Jesus*[18] (his grandfatherly advice written originally for incoming students at RTS-O).[19]

17. With his nearly five decades of participation in seminary convocation and commencement ceremonies, I know of no one who has worn academic regalia more often, and holds wearing it in more disdain, than Frame.

18. John M. Frame, *Studying Theology as a Servant of Jesus* (Orlando: Reformed Theological Seminary, 2002).

19. As one of the "Fathers" (older professors) at RTS-O, Frame has also had a significant personal influence on all the "Brothers" (younger professors—including me). For instance,

Those who engage John in theological or philosophical debate (and there are many) experience his charitable and fair spirit—his genuine willingness to take a serious look at both sides of an issue. He's well known for treating an opposing view graciously and respectfully, even while deconstructing it.

Many don't know that John is also a classically trained musician (piano and organ) and a critic of film, music, and other media. His passion for and writings on worship and music have provoked controversy, especially in Reformed circles, because he regards contemporary worship music, and even liturgical dance, as biblically permissible and even enjoyable in worship.

John often confuses people because on a Sunday he can enjoy leading a new church plant in informal worship by playing an electric keyboard as part of a contemporary music ensemble. Then on Wednesday of the same week, he can greatly enjoy leading the seminary community in formal worship by playing a sixteenth-century hymn on the majestic, custom-built organ in the RTS-O chapel.

Chapter 38 of this book is titled "Twenty-five Random Things That Nobody Knows about Me." This list came from a Facebook game that his students "dragged [him] into." What I love about this final chapter is that it gives you a glimpse into the personal life of this renowned theologian and philosopher. Here are a few of my favorite things:

- #3: I was always the last guy chosen for sports teams, and with good reason.
- #4: We listened faithfully to Pittsburgh Pirate games from 1950–56, when the team had the worst record in baseball.
- #18: My priorities for ministry were (a) missions, (b) pastorate, (c) academic theology. A visit to mission fields in 1960 ruled out (a). A year and two summers of pastoral experience ruled out (b). So I embraced (c) by default, as God's calling.

---

almost every time I see him, he asks me the same question: "Tell me again, how's your book coming along?"

- #23: I did not marry until I was forty-five. God was preparing someone special.
- #24: In 1999, I led a worship team of myself, a saxophonist, and a trombonist. The other two musicians were in their late seventies, but we really rocked.

John has shared with me how he is sometimes concerned about spending so much time in the privacy of his office writing, rather than being more actively involved in public ministry. So I have often reminded him that there's nothing more practical than sound theology. I've seen firsthand how his theological writings are having a significant practical impact on the lives and ministries of Christian leaders around the world.

John is much more than a theologian, philosopher, and apologist. He is also a loving husband to Mary, father to his grown children, and grandfather to his rapidly growing gaggle of grandchildren. He is a humble and quiet man who prefers writing in the solitude of his office to coming into the public limelight.

All this is to say that it's worth your time to read through these rare theological and philosophical gems in Frame's *Selected Shorter Writings, Volume 1*. Here you will find his "Primer on Perspectivalism"—a clear, concise summary of triperspectivalism that will enhance your knowledge of God, yourself, others, and the world. Other chapters include foundational topics such as these: "What the Bible Is About: One Thing and Three Things," "The Gospel and the Scriptures," "Introduction to the Reformed Faith," and "The Main Thing."

Then enter more deeply into Frame's ongoing humble but bold dialogues by reading essays such as "Reformed and Evangelicals Together," "Is Justification by Faith Alone the Article on Which the Church Stands or Falls?," "N. T. Wright and the Authority of Scripture," "Cultural Transformation and the Local Church," "The Bible and Joe the Plumber," and, of course, the rest of the "Twenty-five Random Things That Nobody Knows about Me."

If you're new to reading the works of John Frame (or theological works in general), let me strongly encourage you to take the time to explore his other writings. Here are just a few introductory readings I recommend that you consider to begin priming your theological pump:

- *Salvation Belongs to the Lord*[20]—a brief mini-systematic theology that is easily accessible to the average reader.
- *Studying Theology as a Servant of Jesus*—practical advice for incoming seminary students and all new students of theology.
- Browse his website, http://www.frame-poythress.org, where you'll find many of his writings. He shares this website with Vern Poythress, Calvinistic theologian, philosopher, New Testament scholar, and one of his former students.

Whether or not you're new to reading Frame's theological works, sooner or later you must own and begin making regular use of his magnum opus—*Systematic Theology: An Introduction to Christian Belief*.[21] This remarkably accessible and practical work is the culmination of his nearly fifty years of studying, writing, teaching, and applying the Word of God to all aspects of life.

I am extremely grateful to God for this man and his ministry. This is why I so strongly promote the reading of his books and articles in all my seminary classes and at the church leadership training events where I speak and teach in North America and abroad. It is a great privilege for me to commend this book to you. Here you'll find a wide array of important topics written in Frame's inimitable style of robust charity. Enjoy mining the rich truths in these winsome and provocative essays!

Steve Childers
Associate Professor of Practical Theology
Reformed Theological Seminary-Orlando
President & CEO, Global Church Advancement

20. John M. Frame, *Salvation Belongs to the Lord: An Introduction to Systematic Theology* (Phillipsburg, NJ: P&R Publishing, 2006).
21. John M. Frame, *Systematic Theology: An Introduction to Christian Belief* (Phillipsburg, NJ: P&R Publishing, 2013).

Preface

THIS IS A book consisting of short articles on various subjects. I think of this book as something like Jonathan Edwards's *Miscellanies* or the two volumes of B. B. Warfield's *Selected Shorter Writings*. Not that I expect these essays to be as valuable as those of Edwards and Warfield, but I think of this book as part of that genre.

My original working title was *Theological Appendices*, mocking myself a bit. My larger works, the Theology of Lordship series, have been laden with "appendices"—shorter articles supplementing the larger treatments. Now I write a book consisting only of appendices, in this case appendices to my own career as a teacher of theology. But my publisher, P&R, has chosen to echo Warfield by calling this book *Selected Shorter Writings*. Indeed, I'm hoping further to parallel Warfield by publishing a second volume of these essays.

Although there are recurring themes through this series of essays, and one will often supplement the discussion in another, I think of these essays as independent. So there will sometimes be overlap between the content of one and that of another. I've thought it more important to preserve the integrity of each essay than to try to combine them all into a regular book.

Most of the essays have not been published or posted before, but a few of them have been. My article "N. T. Wright and the Authority of Scripture" was published in *Did God Really Say?*,[1] but I thought it could use some additional exposure. "A Primer on Perspectivalism" has been on the Frame-Poythress website for a while, but I am hoping its publication here will bring it a larger readership. Similarly with "Introduction to the Reformed Faith." "Twenty-five Random Things" originated on Facebook.

Thanks again to P&R Publishing for its willingness to publish my work, and especially to John J. Hughes and Karen L. Magnuson, who edited the volume.

1. David B. Garner, ed., *Did God Really Say? Affirming the Truthfulness and Trustworthiness of Scripture* (Phillipsburg, NJ: P&R Publishing, 2012), 107–27.

Abbreviations

AGG	John M. Frame, *Apologetics to the Glory of God: An Introduction* (Phillipsburg, NJ: P&R Publishing, 1994)
CVT	John M. Frame, *Cornelius Van Til: An Analysis of His Thought* (Phillipsburg, NJ: P&R Publishing, 1995)
DCL	John M. Frame, *The Doctrine of the Christian Life* (Phillipsburg, NJ: P&R Publishing, 2008)
DG	John M. Frame, *The Doctrine of God* (Phillipsburg, NJ: P&R Publishing, 2002)
DKG	John M. Frame, *The Doctrine of the Knowledge of God* (Phillipsburg, NJ: Presbyterian and Reformed, 1987)
DWG	John M. Frame, *The Doctrine of the Word of God* (Phillipsburg, NJ: P&R Publishing, 2010)
ESV	English Standard Version
KJV	King James Version
LW	N. T. Wright, *The Last Word: Scripture and the Authority of God* (San Francisco: HarperSanFrancisco, 2005)
NKJV	New King James Version
NT	New Testament
OT	Old Testament
SBL	John M. Frame, *Salvation Belongs to the Lord* (Phillipsburg, NJ: P&R Publishing, 2006)
SC	N. T. Wright, *Simply Christian: Why Christianity Makes Sense* (San Francisco: HarperSanFrancisco, 2006)

ST	John M. Frame, *Systematic Theology* (Phillipsburg, NJ: P&R Publishing, 2013)
VE	*Vox Evangelica*
WCF	Westminster Confession of Faith
WLC	Westminster Larger Catechism
WSC	Westminster Shorter Catechism
WTJ	*Westminster Theological Journal*

PART 1

Theology and Theological Method

1

A Primer on Perspectivalism

PERSPECTIVALISM is a name that has come to refer to some aspects of my theological method and that of my friend and colleague Vern Poythress. We have set it forth especially in Poythress's *Symphonic Theology*[1] and Frame's *DKG*, and we have applied this method in a number of other writings.

Recently, someone asked whether there were an article-length introduction to perspectivalism, and I had to admit that there was not. There are some *fairly* concise introductions,[2] but nothing of "article length." Seeing that as a genuine need, I will try to meet it here.[3]

Perspectivalism in General

I employ perspectivalisms of two kinds: as a general concept, and as a more specific method. The general concept is simply that because

---

1. Phillipsburg, NJ: Presbyterian and Reformed, 1987, also available at http://www.frame-poythress.org/poythress_books.htm.

2. Poythress's *Symphonic Theology* is more concise, certainly, than my *DKG*. The student of perspectivalism might also look at my short book *Perspectives on the Word of God* (Eugene, OR: Wipf and Stock, 1999), also available at http://reformedperspectives.org (search under this title). Chapters 3 and 4 of my *DCL* introduce the subject as it pertains to ethics, and the first seven chapters of my *DG* develop an exegetical argument for the concept of divine lordship that underlies this approach. There is also an old lecture of mine, "Epistemological Perspectives and Evangelical Apologetics," from 1982, given before the Evangelical Theological Society, that introduces these concepts as they pertain to apologetics. It is available at http://www.frame-poythress.org/frame_articles/1982Epistemological.html. And my student and good friend Joe Torres has summarized my approach in a Wikipedia article about me: http://en.wikipedia.org/wiki/John_Frame. Cf. also mini-descriptions and defenses of the concept in *DG*, app. C, 767–68, and in my article "Machen's Warrior Children," in *Alister E. McGrath and Evangelical Theology*, ed. Sung Wook Chung (Grand Rapids: Baker Academic, 2003), also available at http://www.frame-poythress.org/frame_articles/2003Machen.htm.

3. I absolutely forbid anyone to call it "Perspectivalism for Dummies."

we are not God, because we are finite, not infinite, we cannot know everything at a glance, and therefore our knowledge is limited to one perspective or another.

God knows absolutely everything, because he planned everything, made everything, and determines what happens in the world he made. So we describe him as omniscient. One interesting implication of God's omniscience is that he not only knows all the facts about himself and the world, but also knows how everything appears from every possible perspective. If a fly were on my office wall, my typing would look very different to that fly from the way it looks to me. But God knows not only everything about my typing, but also how that typing appears to the fly on the wall. Indeed, because God knows hypothetical situations as well as actualities, God knows exhaustively what a fly in that position would experience—*if* such a fly were present, even if it is not. God's knowledge, then, is not only omniscient, but omniperspectival. God knows from his own infinite perspective; but that infinite perspective includes a knowledge of all created perspectives, possible and actual.

But we are different. We are finite, and our knowledge is finite. I can know the world only from the limited perspective of my own body and mind. The effects of this finitude, and even more of sin, should caution us against cocksureness in our claims to knowledge. I am not saying that we should doubt everything. Certainly my limited perspective gives me no excuse to doubt that I have five fingers, or that $2 + 2 = 4$, or that God exists.[4] Our finitude does not imply that all our knowledge is erroneous, or that certainty is impossible.[5] But we do, in most situations, need to guard against mistakes.

One way to increase our knowledge and our level of certainty is by supplementing our own perspectives with those of others. When our own resources fail us, we can consult friends, authorities, books, and so on. We can travel to other places, visit people of other cultures.

4. Romans 1:18–32 teaches that the existence of the God of Scripture is clear, even known, to all human beings. Thus the profession of agnosticism or atheism, or the acknowledgment of a different God, is the repression of knowledge. People disbelieve, though they know better.

5. How certainty can be obtained is discussed in my *DKG*. See also my article "Certainty" at http://www.frame-poythress.org/frame_articles/2005Certainty.htm, chapter 41 on "Assurance" in *DWG*, and corresponding chapters in my *ST*.

Even to get a good understanding of a tree, we need to walk around it, look at it from many angles.

It often happens that someone's idea will seem ridiculous when we first encounter it; but when we try to understand where that person is coming from, what considerations have led him to his idea, then our evaluation of it changes. In such a case, we are trying to see the issue from his perspective, and that perspective enriches our own.

In one sense, of course, it is impossible to transcend one's own perspective. Even when we move around a tree, or consult a friend, or travel to another culture, we are still viewing reality through our own senses and brains. Yet it is possible for the perspectives of others to change our perspective, to make us see differently.

This does not mean, of course, that all ideas are equally true, or equally false. It does not mean that as our perspective grows larger, we inevitably agree with everybody else. I do think that a broadening of perspective usually leads to a greater appreciation of the viewpoints of others. But sometimes a growth in perspective has the opposite effect: it convinces us that the view we are investigating is simply wrong. There is nothing about perspectivalism that eliminates the distinctions between right and wrong, true and false. So perspectivalism is not relativistic, as is sometimes charged.[6]

Rather, it presupposes absolutism. To say that our own views are finite is to contrast them with the absolute, infinite viewpoint of God himself. And we are able to consult God and, through his Word and prayer, in some measure to access his infinite perspective. I say "in some measure." We will never have God's exhaustive knowledge of reality (not even in heaven). And we will never know the world in the same way God knows it, for to do that we would have to be God. But when God speaks to us in Scripture and grants us wisdom in response to prayer, the human knowledge we obtain is warranted by his own exhaustive

---

6. It is somewhat unfortunate that the name *perspectivalism* has been attached to the view I am advocating. I'm not sure who is responsible for the name; maybe I am. But the philosopher Friedrich Nietzsche sometimes described his own view as *perspectivism* (note the different spelling), and in my judgment Nietzsche's perspectivism is indeed relativist, though there is some wisdom to be gained from his observations. The same may be said of the perspectivalism (he did use the *-al* suffix) of Charles Sanders Peirce.

perspective, the perspective that includes all other perspectives. For example, Scripture tells me that God created the heavens and the earth. That knowledge can never be invalidated by any other perspective. It is true from any possible perspective.[7]

Again, it is not that we come to look at things from God's perspective rather than our own. We are not God, so we cannot see things as he does. And we can never step out of our own skin, so to speak, and set aside the perspective of our own thoughts and bodies. But as we can enrich our perspective by looking at things from different angles (a tree, in the example above), by consulting other people, and by observing other places and cultures, much more can we enrich it by consulting God's perspective.

In this sense, the truth in one perspective includes the truth of all the others, including God's. To maximize my own knowledge, I need the knowledge of everyone else, especially that of God. So to see everything perfectly from my own perspective involves seeing everything from everyone else's perspective, and from God's. In that sense, finite perspectives are dependent on God's and interdependent on one another's. My perspective should ideally include yours, and vice versa. An exhaustive view of the universe from my perspective (if that were possible, which it is not) would have to be enriched by yours and everyone else's, including that of God, and, indeed, that of the fly on my wall. So my perspective must include yours, and yours must include mine. In that sense, all finite perspectives are *interdependent*. God's perspective is independent in a way that our perspectives are not, for God governs all perspectives. But even his knowledge, as we have seen, includes a knowledge of all finite perspectives. And all finite perspectives must, to attain truth, "think God's thoughts after him."[8] So in one sense, all perspectives coincide.

---

7. I am here, of course, simplifying the hermeneutical issue. Surely we do make mistakes in biblical interpretation, and those mistakes, like others, can be alleviated by broader perspectives. But the ultimate goal of hermeneutics is, with the above qualifications, to attain the divine perspective. I believe that, at least with relatively simple texts such as Genesis 1:1, the church has attained that perspective. But more must be said, of course, and I address some of those issues in *DWG*. See also Vern S. Poythress, *God-Centered Biblical Interpretation* (Phillipsburg, NJ: P&R Publishing, 1999).

8. I have discussed at length in *DKG*, 18–40, and in *CVT*, 97–113, how the so-called "contents" of God's mind differ from the "contents" of man's. This difficult question was debated

Each, when fully informed, includes all the knowledge found in every other. There is one truth, and each perspective is merely an angle from which that truth can be viewed.

We will never achieve perfect knowledge of that one truth, but we advance toward it step by step. That advance always involves enriching our present perspectives by referring to those of others. The work of attaining knowledge, therefore, is always communal. And inevitably it involves reference to the perfect, exhaustive perspective of God, insofar as he has revealed it to us.

Often, however, God's revelation to us of his own perspective is itself multiperspectival in structure. He has, for example, given us four gospels, rather than one. It is important for us to hear the story of Jesus from four different perspectives. God's perspective, in this case, embraces those of the four gospel writers. His infinite perspective validates those four human perspectives and commends them to all of us. Similarly, God has given us both Kings and Chronicles, though these books overlap in many ways. He has also given us both a prose account (Ex. 12–14) and a poetic account (Ex. 15:1–18) of his deliverance of Israel from Egypt. Many of the psalms, too, give us poetic accounts of what other Scriptures present in prose narrative. There are two givings of the law (Ex. 20:1–17; Deut. 5:1–21). Paul often repeats his ideas (as Rom. 12 and 1 Cor. 12), adding and subtracting matters of interest, varying their contexts.

Scripture, of course, is written by human authors together with the divine Author. God reveals himself by inspiring human beings. He generally does not dictate, but rather enables them to write consistently with their own gifts, education, and personalities, that is, their own perspectives. And by such divine enablement, each author writes exactly

during the controversy in the 1940s between Cornelius Van Til and Gordon H. Clark. My own view is that whatever is in God's mind inevitably differs from everything in a man's, for God's mind is the ultimate Creator of the human mind, as well as its criterion of truth and its sustenance. Even in the area of thought and knowledge, therefore, the Creator-creature distinction is inviolate. This does not imply, however, that God and man cannot know the same propositions. The common expression "think God's thoughts after him" should be understood to express both the continuities ("think God's thoughts") and the discontinuities ("after him") between God's knowledge and ours.

what God wants him to write. And God often determines that his truth
is best conveyed by multiple human perspectives rather than just one.
In Scripture, all those human perspectives convey truth, and all are
warranted by God's infinite perspective, though none is identical with
that divine perspective. This is what we should expect, since God has
created us as people who learn through multiperspectival experience.

Triperspectivalism

Now, if perspectivalism is true in general, it is an important part
of human knowledge to focus on specific differences of perspective.
So, for example, NT scholars often give attention to the samenesses and
differences of the four Gospels. This is a legitimate study, though it is
often done without adequate regard to the unity of Scripture. In my
DCL, I argue that the Ten Commandments provide ten perspectives
on human life. It is not that each commandment deals with a *part* of
Christian ethics; rather, each commandment deals with the whole, from
a particular perspective. We might call such an approach to Christian
ethics *decaperspectivalism*.

But Poythress and I emphasize especially the importance of a set
of threefold distinctions, or triads, that have come to be known as *triperspectivalism*. Many people have seen a certain mystery in the number
three. But in Scripture there is a pervasive pattern of threefold distinctions that, though mysterious, provide us with considerable illumination.

The Trinity

The greatest mystery in Scripture and Christian theology is, of
course, the mystery of the Holy Trinity.[9] We worship one God, but
that one God is three persons, Father, Son, and Holy Spirit. The three
persons are one God, not many. The nature of each person is divine.
Each person has all the divine attributes, and in every act of God the

---

9. For a much more thorough account of the doctrine of the Trinity and its biblical basis,
see my *DG*, 619–735. See also Poythress's application of this doctrine to logic and epistemology
in "Reforming Ontology and Logic in the Light of the Trinity: An Application of Van Til's
Idea of Analogy," *WTJ* 57, 1 (1995): 187–219, also available at http://www.frame-poythress
.org/poythress_articles/1995Reforming.htm.

three persons equally participate. The three persons are equal in honor and glory; they are equally (and uniquely) the object of our worship.

The three persons, however, are not identical to one another. They are in various ways distinct. Theologians have explored concepts such as *eternal generation* and *eternal procession*: the Father eternally begets the Son, not the other way around, and the Spirit proceeds from the Father and Son, not the other way around. The Bible also records divine acts that are specific to one of the persons or another. It was the Son, not the Father or Spirit, who became incarnate, died for our sins, and rose again. It is the Father, not the Son or Spirit, who effectually calls us into fellowship with himself. And it is the Spirit, not the Father or Son, who regenerates believers and gives them gifts to serve in the church. Still, even in these actions, all three of the persons are active. Although the Son, not the Father, became incarnate, the Father was present with him in his incarnate life. And although the Son, not the Father, died on the cross, the Father was active in the atonement, giving him up for us all (Rom. 8:32). To summarize: even in the distinct actions of each person, the other persons are involved. Or, as Scripture sometimes puts it, the Father and Spirit are "in" the Son; the Son is "in" the Father; and the Spirit is the Spirit of the Son and of the Father.[10]

It is tempting, therefore, for us to formulate the doctrine of the Trinity by saying that the three persons are "perspectives" on the Godhead and on one another. But that would be misleading. *Perspective* does not exhaust the ways in which the three persons are distinct. To say that the three persons are merely perspectives on the Godhead would be a Sabellian position, the idea that the differences of the persons are merely differences in the way we look at the one God. Such an approach would reduce the Trinitarian distinctions to distinctions within our own subjectivity. That certainly is not right.

It is correct to say that the three persons are really persons. They interact with one another in ways similar to the ways in which human beings interact with one another. They talk together, plan together, express love for one another. So their relation is far more than merely perspectival.

10. This mutual indwelling of the persons in one another is called *circumincessio* or *perichoresis*.

But if the three persons are not *mere* perspectives on the Godhead, they nevertheless *are* perspectives. They are more than perspectives, but not less. For as I have indicated, each of the three persons bears the whole divine nature, with all the divine attributes. Each is *in* each of the others. So you cannot fully know the Son without knowing the Father and Spirit, and so on. Although the three persons are distinct, our knowledge of each involves knowledge of the others, so that for us knowledge of the Father coincides with knowledge of the Son and Spirit.

Let us now explore a bit more fully the nature of our human perspectival knowledge of the three persons of the Trinity. Although all three persons are active in every act of God,[11] there seems to be a general division of labor among the persons in the work of redemption. The Father establishes the eternal plan of salvation, the Son executes it, and the Spirit applies it to people. It was the Father who sent the Son to redeem us, the Son who accomplished redemption, and the Spirit who applies the benefits of Christ's atonement to believers. Recall John Murray's book *Redemption Accomplished and Applied*:[12] under "redemption accomplished," Murray discusses the atonement, completed once for all. Under "redemption applied," he discusses the *ordo salutis*, the ways in which the Spirit applies the work of Christ to believers (effectual calling, regeneration, conversion, justification, etc.).

Generalizing, we gather that the Father is the supreme *authority*, the Son the *executive power*, and the Spirit the divine *presence* who dwells in and with God's people.

Now, of course, redemption is meaningless without all three of these aspects. Without an authoritative plan, an effectual accomplishment, and a gracious application, none of these has meaning. The application is necessarily the application of Christ's finished work according to the divine plan. The atonement is necessarily the fulfillment of the Father's plan, and without the Spirit's work it does not save. So the plan is not efficacious without the atonement and the application.

---

11. That is to say, every act *ad extra*, every act that has some reference to the creation. There are also divine acts *ad intra*, acts within the divine nature itself, such as the Father's begetting the Son, which are *not* acts in which three persons cooperate, but acts of one person alone.

12. Grand Rapids: Eerdmans, 1955.

So we cannot know any of these adequately without knowing the others. Although the three are distinguishable, our knowledge of each is a perspective on the others and on the whole. To know the Spirit's work, we must see it as an application of the Son's work by the Father's plan. Similarly with knowing the work of the Father and Son.

So our *knowledge* of the work of the three persons is perspectival. In a sense, these divine works are also perspectival in their *nature*. Although they are distinguishable, it is important to realize that the divine plan includes the atonement and its application; the atonement is the out-working of the plan and the event to be applied; and the application is the application of the plan and the atonement. As is the Trinity itself, these divine acts are mysteriously one and many.

Divine Lordship

So we have a general distinction in God's redemption between authority, power, and presence. Each of these is a necessary aspect of divine redemption, and none of them makes sense without the others. Each includes the others in one sense. These same concepts appear in an analysis of divine lordship.[13]

By *Lord* I refer to the mysterious name of Exodus 3:14–15, read *Yahweh* by scholars, but LORD in most English translations. With its Hebrew synonym *Adon* and its Greek equivalent *kurios*, it is found over seven thousand times in Scripture, mostly as a name of God and often applied to Jesus Christ. It is central in the biblical story. God says that this is his memorial name forever (Ex. 3:15), and he performs many mighty works so that people "shall know that I am the LORD" (e.g., Ex. 14:4). The fundamental confessions of faith of both Testaments (Deut. 6:4–5; Rom. 10:9–10; 1 Cor. 12:3; Phil. 2:11) are confessions of lordship. One may say that the basic message of the OT is "God is LORD" and that the basic message of the NT is "Jesus Christ is Lord."

In passages such as Exodus 3:20; 33:19; 34:6–7; and Isaiah 40–66, which underscore and expound the lordship of God, three themes appear

---

13. In my writing, the most extensive exegetical account of divine lordship is found in the first seven chapters of *DG*.

prominently: the Lord is (1) the One who *controls* all things by his mighty power; (2) the One who speaks with absolute *authority*, rightly requiring all to obey, and (3) the One who gives himself to his people in covenant intimacy: "I will take you to be my people, and I will be your God" (Ex. 6:7). I call the third concept *presence* because God often expresses it by saying, "I will be with you" (e.g., Isa. 43:2), and he makes that presence tangible in such theophanies as the cloud and fire that led Israel through the wilderness, the *shekinah* glory that dwelt in the tabernacle and temple, the incarnation of Christ, and the Holy Spirit's indwelling of believers.

Again, the three concepts are perspectivally related. Each implies the others and involves the others.

The Decalogue is a good example of this threefold structure.[14] It begins with God's identifying himself by his name, LORD. Then there is a brief account (called by scholars a *historical prologue*) of God's past benefits to Israel ("who brought you out of the land of Egypt, out of the house of slavery"). The historical prologue displays God's gracious power, his *control* over events on Israel's behalf. Then there are commands, which display his *authority*. Mixed with the commands, there are sanctions: blessings for obedience and curses for disobedience. This indicates the *presence* of the Lord to continue administering the covenant with Israel.

Revelation

Scripture teaches a corresponding threefold structure in divine revelation. There is "general" revelation, God's revelation in creation (Ps. 19:1; Rom. 1). Then there is "special" revelation, God's revelation in words, through a direct voice (Ex. 19–20), prophets (Deut. 18), apostles (John 14:26), and writing (Ex. 31:18; Josh. 1:8; 2 Tim. 3:16). A third form of revelation is described in Matthew 11:27 and Ephesians 1:17 in which

---

14. I follow Meredith Kline's argument that the Decalogue, and Deuteronomy as well, have the literary structure of covenant documents. *Covenant*, of course, is the fundamental relation between Yahweh and Israel, and the *new covenant* is the fundamental relation between Christ and the redeemed. *Lord* denotes the relation of a covenant head to his vassals. So lordship and covenant go together.

God reveals Christ to a person's heart. This is sometimes described as *illumination*, or as the *internal testimony of the Holy Spirit*. I sometimes call it *existential revelation*.

God reveals himself as Lord. So his revelation parallels his lordship attributes. General revelation particularly manifests his control, for his power is exhaustive and universal, so that everything reveals him. Special revelation corresponds especially to his authority, for when God speaks to us, his words serve as ultimate norm for those who hear. Existential revelation is a form of God's presence with his human creatures.

The Bible is the written form of God's special revelation. (Other forms include God's oral speech through theophany, prophets, and apostles.) The Bible plays a special role, for it serves as the covenant document, the ultimate governing constitution of God's people (see texts above). As such, we may not question or disobey what it says.[15]

The Offices of Christ

The Reformed confessions and other theological documents often discuss the three offices of Christ as Prophet, Priest, and King. These offices reflect the same categories we have seen earlier. His kingship represents his *control*, his prophetic office his *authority* as the Word of God, and his priesthood his work on behalf of his people in history, what we have called his *presence*.

Since believers are united with Christ, many have drawn analogies between these offices and the status of believers. We, too, are prophets in the sense that we bear the gospel message to the world. We are kings in that "all things are ours" (cf. 1 Cor. 3:21–23). And we are priests in the sense of 1 Peter 2:9 (what the Reformers called "the priesthood of all believers"). In turn, these offices have been seen as models for church officers: the teaching elder (1 Tim. 5:17) represents especially God's authority, the ruling elder (same verse) God's control, and the deacon the priestly ministry of mercy. As perspectives, none of these gifts can function adequately without the others. But sometimes one or another is more prominent. Indeed, there are sometimes imbalances in churches

---

15. I have developed this understanding of revelation in more detail in *DWG*.

that have too much emphasis on teaching, discipline, or mercy at the expense of the others.[16]

Aspects of Salvation

Salvation involves: (1) God's acting mightily in history to redeem his people, his controlling power expressing itself in grace. The historical prologue of the Decalogue is a good example of this. This historical action is what we earlier called *redemption accomplished*. (2) God's speaking an authoritative word to proclaim this grace and to indicate his people's continuing obligations to him. Theologically speaking, this is the "law of God." (3) God's coming to be among and within his people. This is "redemption applied." Again, three aspects, corresponding to the three lordship attributes. None of these functions without the others. So each is a perspective on the whole process of salvation. Again, there are dangers in overemphasizing one of these over against the others.

Human Knowledge of God

A biblical epistemology will also acknowledge these three elements. Secular epistemologies have found it difficult to relate sense experience, reason, and feelings in their accounts of human knowledge. They have also been perplexed by the relation of the subject (the knower), the object (what the knower knows), and the norms or rules of knowledge (logic, reason, etc.).

In Scripture, sense experience (as in 1 John 1:1–3) presents us with the truth. But that truth must be understood in the light of God's norms, his verbal revelation. And the knower must not resist the truth. He or she must be in proper shape to receive it (Rom. 1).

So God has placed the knowing subject into fruitful contact with the objects of knowledge, with the mediation of God's revealed norms for knowledge, particularly the primacy of his revelation.

Here the object is the world as God has made it and controls it; the norm is God's authoritative revelation; and the subject is the person

---

16. See Jim Fitzgerald, *Triplex: The Three Faces of Leadership* (available for Kindle by Amazon Digital Services, 2010).

who lives in the presence of God. Sense experience connects us with the world, but only if the self is able to make such connections governed by God's Word.

So the three aspects of knowledge correspond to the attributes of God's lordship. The object is the world as God's *control* has made it and maintained it. The norm is God's *authority* for human knowledge. And the subject is the knower, standing in the *presence* of God.

These three aspects of knowledge are perspectival. You can't have one without the others, and with each, you will have the others. Every item of true human knowledge is the application of God's authoritative norm to a fact of creation, by a person in God's image. Take away one of those, and there is no knowledge at all.

So I distinguish three perspectives of knowledge. In the *normative perspective*, we ask the question, "What do God's norms direct us to believe?" In the *situational perspective*, we ask, "What are the facts?" In the *existential perspective*, we ask, "What belief is most satisfying to a believing heart?" Given the view of knowledge outlined above, the answers to these three questions coincide. But it is sometimes useful to distinguish these questions so as to give us multiple angles of inquiry. Each question helps us to answer the others.

The normative perspective, therefore, contains all reality, for all reality is God's general revelation to us. Similarly, the situational contains all reality, our whole environment. And the existential perspective also contains everything, namely, all our experience.

In an important sense, then, the normative perspective includes the situational and existential. To think according to God's norms is to take every fact (situational) and every experience (existential) into account. It is also true that the situational perspective includes the normative (for norms are facts) and the existential (for experiences are facts). And the existential includes the normative and the situational, for the norms and facts are aspects of our experience.

What role, then, does the Bible play in our knowledge of God and of his world? As we have seen, the Bible is the covenant constitution of the people of God, the highest authority, which we may not question. Thus, it is natural to consider it part of the normative perspective. But it is also part of our situation (the fact that illumines all other facts) and of our experience (the experience that illumines all others). So the Bible should not be identified with the normative perspective or vice versa. Each perspective includes everything, as we have seen. But the Bible is a particular fact that governs all perspectives and determines how we should use them.

Our *understanding* of the Bible is multiperspectival. To comprehend the Bible, we must understand it in its historical environment (situational) and we must understand its relevance to us today (situational and existential). But once we come to a prayerful, thoughtful, settled understanding of Scripture's teaching, that teaching must take precedence over knowledge from any other source.

Remember: the normative, situational, and existential perspectives are mutually dependent, and so relative to one another. So some critics of perspectivalism sometimes think that this approach makes the Bible relative to other forms of knowledge. But that is an error. The Bible is not the normative perspective (or the situational or the existential). It is a particular object within all three perspectives given to us by God to serve as the ultimate standard of human thought and life.[17]

Ethics

The same perspectives govern the quest for ethical knowledge, the knowledge of right and wrong.[18] As secular epistemology has been divided along three lines corresponding with these perspectives, so secular ethics has been existential (basing ethical judgments on feelings), teleological (focusing on happiness), or deontological (focusing on duties). I see these as existential, situational, and normative, respectively. These fail in various ways to account for the nature of ethical decisions. One major problem is that most ethicists try to separate these three perspectives from one another.

A biblical ethic will include all three perspectives. Normatively, we seek to obey God's authoritative Word, his law. Situationally, we

---

17. The preceding section summarizes the epistemology expounded at greater length in *DKG*. I have also reformulated this material for the section on the knowledge of God in my *ST*.

18. I have discussed the ethical implications of the perspectives especially in chapters 3–4 of *DCL*, and in my short book *Perspectives on the Word of God*.

seek to apply that law to situations (which are themselves revelation of a sort—general revelation) so as to maximize divine blessing, the highest happiness. Existentially, we seek the inner satisfaction of living as God designed us to live, in his presence. These are perspectives. Each involves the others. But each serves as a check and balance against our misunderstandings of the others.

These perspectives are similar to the secular ethical approaches of deontologism (normative), teleologism-utilitarianism (situational), and subjectivism (existential). But while these secular methods are inconsistent with one another, the three Christian perspectives complement one another. If someone denies the biblical God, he has no reason to think that his norms (deontological), his goals (teleological), and his feelings (subjectivist) will cohere; so he must choose one over the other in case of conflict. But in Christian ethics, the divinely revealed norm fits our situation, because God has defined the norm and made the world to cohere with it. And he has made us in his image to live in the world he has made, under the norms he has determined.

Other Triads

Once you get started thinking this way, threefold distinctions may pop up regularly in your mind. One thinks of the distinction in theology between justification (normative), adoption (situational), and sanctification (existential); the image of God as physical, judicial, and moral (Meredith Kline in *Images of the Spirit*[19]); and so forth. In Appendix A of my *DG*, I mention thirty-six of these, some rather tongue-in-cheek, and in *SBL* and *ST* I find such triads scattered through the whole corpus of Reformed systematic theology.

And in the exploration of the world, of natural revelation, there are also triads of interest. Vern Poythress's first book, *Philosophy, Science, and the Sovereignty of God*,[20] explores how Kenneth Pike's tagmemic linguistics relates to all this, such as the distinction between particle,

19. Grand Rapids: Baker, 1980.
20. Nutley, NJ: Presbyterian and Reformed, 1976. See also Poythress's more recent *In the Beginning Was the Word* (Wheaton, IL: Crossway, 2009), which deals comprehensively with language and its relation to God.

wave, and field. The old philosophical distinction between self, world, and God (*God* here being understood as a divine revelation) is another familiar triad that ties in with our analysis.

Conclusions

How is perspectivalism useful? There are some moments when I think it is a kind of deep structure of the universe and of Bible truth. Other times (most times) I think of it more modestly, as a pedagogical device. Certainly, as a pedagogical device, it gives students some hooks on which to hang bits of theological knowledge—or, to change the metaphor, some string by which to tie things together. But I think it is of even more practical significance.

For one thing, I think it resolves a lot of traditional theological arguments, such as whether redemptive history (the situation) is more important than the divine law (normative) or believing subjectivity. You need each one to appreciate the others. That fact has implications for preaching, evangelism, and our personal appropriation of Scripture.

Second, it encourages us toward balance. Preaching that focuses all the time on law (normative) and not grace (situational) will be corrected by an understanding of the true relation between these, and vice versa. People who emphasize the objective (normative and situational) while disparaging human experience and feelings (existential) can be corrected by a multiperspectival understanding, and vice versa. Perspectivalism is a way of checking ourselves. If a pastor develops a ministry that focuses on norms and situations, he may need to supplement it with something that does justice to the existential perspective, and so on. If a congregation has a lot of prophetic gifts, but few kingly or priestly, perhaps it needs to seek leadership in the other two areas.

So I think that perspectivalism is an encouragement to the unity of the church. *Sometimes* our divisions of theology and practice are differences of perspective, of balance, rather than differences over the essentials of faith.[21] So perspectivalism will help us better to appreciate one another, and to appreciate the diversity of God's work among us.

---

21. See my "Machen's Warrior Children," referenced earlier, and *Evangelical Reunion* (Grand Rapids: Baker, 1991), also available at http://www.frame-poythress.org/frame_books.htm. See also the essay "Reformed and Evangelicals Together" in the present volume.

2

What the Bible Is About:
One Thing and Three Things

THE BIBLE, of course, is a book about God. But God is triune: Father, Son, and Spirit. The purpose of the Bible, like God himself, is both one and many. People seeking to reduce the Bible to "one" thing will be frustrated and disappointed. Similarly, people who see the Bible as a heap of miscellaneous things, a cultural detritus, will never find in it what has fascinated people for centuries.

Triune God, three subject matters in one: (1) a unique worldview, (2) a redemptive history, (3) a new and abundant way of life. Although all three persons of the Trinity are involved with each of these subjects, the first is especially the province of the Father, the second of the Son, the third of the Spirit.

The unique worldview is the biblical Creator-creature distinction. It is the conviction that reality is not all the same, but there are two distinct levels of being: the Creator and the creature.[1]

1. Cornelius Van Til typically walked into each of his apologetics classes and drew two circles on the blackboard: a large upper one representing God, and a small lower one representing the creation. The root of error, he said, is to regard the two levels as the same—in power or authority. Recently, Peter R. Jones has stressed this distinction in his differentiation between *one-ism* and *two-ism*. The former is the belief that all reality is on the same plane, as in what used to be called *New Age* thought and as Jones now calls *neo-pagan spirituality*. The slogan of one-ism might be: "If you want to find God, look deep inside yourself . . . and you will find him there, and you will find that you are him and he is you." Two-ism is the worldview of Van Til and of the Bible. God and his creation are not the same: he is Lord, and we are made to serve and worship him. See Peter R. Jones, *One or Two* (Escondido, CA: Main Entry Editions, 2010).

19

The redemptive history is the biblical narrative, the story of creation, fall, and redemption by Jesus Christ.

The new and abundant life is first the orientation of our hearts toward God,[2] and then the biblical ethic, the way we live.

Three Subjects and Three Persons

In the biblical worldview, God the Father is prominent. Of course, all three persons of the Trinity are involved in creation. And as Van Til emphasized, there is something philosophically important in the fact that the world is both one and many, because God is both one and many. But when Scripture speaks of the Son and the Spirit, it speaks of them as persons sent by the Father. The plan behind creation and providence, as with the plan of redemption, is the Father's plan. The Son and Spirit affirm that plan and carry it out.

In redemptive history, God the Son is prominent. Of course, it is the Father who sent his Son to redeem his people. And it is the Spirit who came upon the virgin Mary so that she could bring forth Jesus. And it is the Spirit who enables his people to receive him into their hearts. But the work of the Spirit is not to draw attention to himself, but to bear witness of Jesus the Son, who took on flesh, died for sinners, was raised from the dead, and ascended into heaven.

In the Christian life, God the Spirit is prominent. Of course, it is the Father and Son who send him to us, and it is his witness to them that brings us new life. But the new life is our union with Christ by the Spirit.

Three Subjects and Three Perspectives

Like the Trinity, these three subject matters are not separate from one another. Each involves the others, and neither can be understood apart from the others. Some Bible passages focus on one or the other, such as Genesis 1:1, which simply states the biblical worldview. But even Genesis 1:1 must be seen in the light of other passages, such as 2 Corin-

---

2. To unfallen Adam, that orientation was a natural endowment of his creation in God's image. To sinners, that orientation is a gift of God's grace through Christ, applied by the Holy Spirit.

thians 4:6 and 5:17, which present the Creator-creature distinction as an analogy of redemption:

> For God, who said, "Let light shine out of darkness," has shone in our hearts to give the light of the knowledge of the glory of God in the face of Jesus Christ. (2 Cor. 4:6)

> Therefore, if anyone is in Christ, he is a new creation. The old has passed away; behold, the new has come. (2 Cor. 5:17)

We don't rightly understand Genesis 1:1 if we don't see the analogy to redemption: creation from nothing is like life from death, and vice versa.

In the history of religion, there is one major rival to the biblical doctrine of salvation. In the biblical doctrine, our problem is ethical: we have sinned and fall short of God's glory. In the rival doctrine, our problem is metaphysical: we are finite and need to become infinite, human and need to become God. Of course, the biblical worldview makes the rival doctrine impossible: we can never become God. Our need is to be personally reconciled with God. But this implies that salvation is historical, not metaphysical. History is the realm of interpersonal relationships. So the biblical worldview is appropriate only to the biblical doctrine of redemption, and vice versa. The Creator-creature distinction means that our relationship with God is historical. Sin comes through a historical transgression, and salvation comes through a historical reconciliation between the Creator and the creature.

The Christian life in the Spirit is also a unique match for the Christian worldview and the biblical redemptive history. We saw in 2 Corinthians 4:6 and 5:17 how creation is analogous to regeneration. God gives new life to his people as he gives being to the universe: sovereignly. The universe does not make itself, and those who are dead in sin do not regenerate themselves. Creation and the new life come by grace. And God gives the grace of the new life based on the historical reconciliation brought about by Jesus on the cross.

My conclusion is that you cannot fully understand the biblical worldview until you see how it is related to the rest of the biblical content—the history of redemption and the Christian life. Indeed, you cannot fully understand any of these without the others.

Each Subject in All of Scripture

So every passage of Scripture teaches us about all three subjects. Genesis 1:1 teaches us the biblical worldview. It also presents the first event of biblical history, the prologue to fall and redemption. And it presents a powerful analogy to the new life.

The narrative/historical parts of Scripture focus on, of course, redemptive history. But they presuppose the biblical worldview and will make no sense to people who deny that worldview. Redemptive history presents God as an actor on the world stage, bringing things to pass according to his will. But if you hold a worldview that says miracles are impossible, that the universe is a singular, closed system of law (or of chance), then redemptive history is unbelievable.

The wisdom literature and the ethical parts of the NT letters focus on the Christian life. But they, too, presuppose the biblical worldview, for the Christian life is a life in union with Christ through the Spirit, as a child of the Father. And they presuppose redemptive history, because the Christian overcomes sin only through the power of the cross.

So each passage of Scripture speaks to all three subject areas. And all of Scripture is about all three. To understand the biblical worldview, you need to read the entire Bible, for the whole Bible describes life in a world created by God. So the whole Bible is about God's relation to the world. And it is about redemptive history. As Jesus taught, all of Scripture testifies of him (Luke 24:27; John 5:39). And all of Scripture is also about the Christian life:

> All Scripture is breathed out by God and profitable for teaching, for reproof, for correction, and for training in righteousness, that the man of God may be competent, equipped for every good work. (2 Tim. 3:16–17)

Threefold Preaching and Teaching

So it would seem that you should not preach one of these subjects without the other two. But here we must qualify the symmetry. The fact is, you cannot teach everything at once. Scripture itself doesn't try to teach everything at once, though every passage about one subject has implications for the others. As we have seen, some passages focus on worldview, others on redemptive history, still others on the Christian life. Scripture doesn't repeat the same thing over and over again. Nor does it emphasize the same thing over and over again. Passages of Scripture vary as to their focus on one or more of the three major emphases, and also as to the many subemphases within those.

The preaching and teaching ministry of the church should seek to give the congregation a "balanced diet," as Scripture itself does. The congregation needs to understand the three major foci of God's Word. This doesn't mean that every sermon must mechanically repeat the three major subject matters again and again. Nor should we attempt to make sure that there is a perfectly equal distribution of material along the three lines. In Scripture itself, there is no mechanical quantification of subject matters.

To some extent, the choice of emphasis in a sermon depends on the present needs of the people, just as the teaching of Jesus and Paul takes account of the needs of its hearers or readers.

There are, of course, certain kinds of needs that arise specifically because of unbalanced emphases in preaching. If the people of a congregation are becoming Christian philosophers, preoccupied with nothing but worldview, then a change in emphasis is in order. Same for "redemptive history" buffs who come up with bizarre ways of "finding Christ in Scripture." And same for those who want everything to be practical and who don't care to go deeply into biblical doctrine.[3]

---

3. These imbalances are related to the distinction that many have made (I can't remember who started it) between *piets, Kuyps,* and *docts* in the Reformed community. Piets (pietists) are concerned mainly about their personal subjective relationship to God. Kuyps (Kuyperians) are concerned about changing society to the glory of God. Docts (doctrinalists)

Such imbalances are easier to see in others than in ourselves. We easily find such imbalances in Christians of other traditions, or who went to different seminaries from ours, or who don't use our buzzwords.

But honestly, I have never heard a single preacher, including myself, who in my estimation maintained a perfect balance. Our indwelling sin leads us to set our own agendas ahead of an honest rendering of the biblical text, ahead of an honest ministry to the needs of our hearers. This is not to say that the task of preaching is hopeless, or that we cannot make progress in our attempts to teach the Bible. This is part of the spiritual warfare, and God has given us the resources to prevail. But those who prevail most are those who are most honest about themselves, the most open to recognize their own self-righteousness.

The Structure of Systematic Theology

These three emphases correspond to traditional divisions within systematic theology. Worldview is the main concern of the doctrine of God. The history of redemption is the focus of Christology and the doctrine of the atonement. The Christian life is the province both of the traditional *ordo salutis* (calling, regeneration, conversion, etc.) and of Christian ethics (the application of the law as gratitude for God's grace).

The doctrine of the Word of God, focusing on the doctrine of Scripture, incorporates all three emphases. It is part of worldview, the doctrine of God, since the Word is the divine *logos*. It is part of the history of redemption, the canon by which God governs his covenant community. And it is part of the Christian life, God's sufficient Word to each believer.

Morals for Preachers

We often hear that every sermon needs to be worldview-conscious, redemptive-historical, and/or practical. (In the present Reformed

---

are concerned with maintaining the pure doctrine of the confessions. In my terminology, these concerns are existential, situational, and normative, respectively, and in terms of the present essay they correspond somewhat with Christian life, redemptive history, and worldview, respectively.

community, the redemptive-history buffs are ascendant, but there are protests from the other perspectives.) Actually, there should be a balanced diet of all three emphases in the church—like proteins, fats, and carbs. But as Scripture itself shows us, there are many ways to exhibit these three emphases, and they need not be rivals to one another. And there need be no more battles in the church over emphasis.

3

The Gospel and the Scriptures

IT IS DISTRESSING that after two thousand years, Christians are still arguing about what the gospel is and what role it should play in the life of the church. The debate goes on—between Protestants, Catholics, and Eastern Orthodox, and between different varieties of Protestants. Even within the Reformed branch of Protestantism, my own doctrinal home, there are continued debates. There are questions about the doctrine of justification, focused on the work of Norman Shepherd, N. T. Wright, the Federal Vision movement, and others. There is also debate about the distinction between law and gospel and how that distinction is relevant to ministry. And there is the question of how and to what extent the gospel, however defined, should be "central" in the ministry of the church.

This essay won't try to clear up all the confusion, but I hope it may point out some profitable directions that future discussion might take, and may settle a few issues for those who share some basic assumptions with me about these subjects.

Gospel generally refers to the content of the apostolic preaching, following Jesus' ascension to glory. Paul refers to it with different levels of specificity:

1. In 1 Corinthians 2:2, Paul tells the church, "I decided to know nothing among you except Jesus Christ and him crucified." We may regard this as a summary of the gospel, for Paul indicates that it is the *entire* content of his preaching. But clearly the content of the gospel can be spelled out at greater length, for Paul himself presents longer summaries

elsewhere. Still, this formulation is important for many reasons, among them that it is the most concise formulation of the gospel in Scripture.

2. A somewhat less concise summary is found in 1 Corinthians 15:1–4, where Paul, responding to questions about the resurrection, says:

> Now I would remind you, brothers, of the gospel I preached to you, which you received, in which you stand, and by which you are being saved, if you hold fast to the word I preached to you—unless you believed in vain.
>
> For I delivered to you as of first importance what I also received: that Christ died for our sins in accordance with the Scriptures, that he was buried, that he was raised on the third day in accordance with the Scriptures.

Paul goes on to mention Jesus' resurrection appearances. He aims to convince the Corinthians that the resurrection of Christ is a central part of the apostolic message, and it is by that message that they are being saved.

3. A still lengthier summary is Paul's entire letter to the Romans. In that letter, Paul aims to set forth his gospel to the Roman Christians, to prepare them for his personal visit (Rom. 1:15). He summarizes:

> For I am not ashamed of the gospel, for it is the power of God for salvation to everyone who believes, to the Jew first and also to the Greek. For in it the righteousness of God is revealed from faith for faith, as it is written, "The righteous shall live by faith." (Rom. 1:16–17)

In Romans, Paul speaks of human sin, the hopelessness of seeking salvation through human works (chaps. 1–3), and therefore the necessity of receiving salvation from God apart from works through the grace of Christ (chaps. 3–5). Through Christ believers are justified. But the gospel of Romans also includes a message of sanctification. Since believers are united to Christ in his death and resurrection, they are no longer slaves of sin. They can live holy lives (chaps. 6–8). After a discussion of the reason for Israel's unbelief (God's sovereign choice) in chapters 9–11, Paul describes the nature of the believer's new holy life in chapters 12–15.

So understood, the gospel of Romans encompasses the entire scope of Christian theology and ethics.[1] It also contains references to the OT background of the gospel, particularly the sin of Adam (chap. 5), the faith of Abraham (chap. 4), and the experience of Israel (chaps. 9–11).

4. *Gospel* also refers to each of the four books at the beginning of our NT that present the story of Jesus' incarnation, ministry, atoning death, and resurrection. So Mark 1:1: "The beginning of the gospel of Jesus Christ, the Son of God." If Mark is a gospel, Matthew, Luke, and John are similarly. Here, the gospel is a detailed recital of the story of Jesus himself. It doesn't contain the level of theological reflection found in Romans, because that reflection presupposes the completion of Christ's atoning work. But according to Mark, the gospel is not only about the completed work of Christ; it is also about his earthly ministry. When Peter preaches the gospel in Acts 10, he, too, reflects on Jesus' earthly life,

> how God anointed Jesus of Nazareth with the Holy Spirit and with power. He went about doing good and healing all who were oppressed by the devil, for God was with him. (Acts 10:38)

Gospel in this sense includes Jesus' teaching about the life of believers in the kingdom, as in the Sermon on the Mount.

5. Still broader, perhaps, is the preaching of gospel by John the Baptist and Jesus himself. Mark writes:

> Now after John was arrested, Jesus came into Galilee, proclaiming the gospel of God, and saying, "The time is fulfilled, and the kingdom of God is at hand; repent and believe in the gospel." (Mark 1:14–15)

---

1. Since it includes ethics, it includes divine commands, or laws. This is true also of *gospel* in senses 4–6. It is therefore impossible to sharply separate law and gospel as in Lutheran theology. On this issue, see my "Law and Gospel," http://www.frame-poythress.org/frame _articles/2002Law.htm, and my *DCL*, chapter 14.

Here the gospel is the coming of the kingdom of God. See also in this regard the preaching of Philip in Acts 8:12. Acts 19:8; 20:25; 28:23, 31 also characterize the preaching of Paul in these terms. The idea of the kingdom as the content of the gospel goes back to the prophecy of Isaiah:

> Get you up to a high mountain,
>   O Zion, herald of good news;
> lift up your voice with strength,
>   O Jerusalem, herald of good news;
>   lift it up, fear not;
> say to the cities of Judah,
>   "Behold your God!" (Isa. 40:9)

> How beautiful upon the mountains
>   are the feet of him who brings good news,
> who publishes peace, who brings good news of happiness,
>   who publishes salvation,
>   who says to Zion, "Your God reigns." (Isa. 52:7)

Isaiah's prophecies look toward God himself coming to earth, establishing his rule against all who resist him and gently tending his flock like a shepherd (Isa. 40:11).

6. Broadest of all, the whole Bible is gospel.[2] The OT provides necessary background for understanding the gospel of the NT: the law that we have broken, God's requirement of sacrifice, the expectation of the coming Messiah, God's provision for believers through psalms and wisdom, positive and negative examples of godliness, the expectations of the OT people of God and their faith and failures. Both Peter (Acts 2) and Stephen (Acts 7) focus on this OT background in their preaching of the gospel. Then all of the NT sets forth the gospel, which includes, as we have seen, the quality of life that the gospel creates. And the Apocalypse, the book of Revelation, completes the picture. God will surely win the battle over all his enemies.

---

2. And of course, the whole Bible is also law, for on every page it presents God's authoritative Word, governing our beliefs and actions. This is another reason why law and gospel cannot be completely separate.

As God's covenant with his people,[3] Scripture as a whole spells out redemption as the basis of our fellowship with God, his demands on us, and the curses on those who disobey and the blessings on those who obey.

These formulations of *gospel* are somewhat different, but they are all consistent with one another, and together they set forth a single message: God has come and is coming, to vindicate himself against his enemies and to bring grace and blessing to his own faithful people. The final judgment is not yet, but it will surely come in God's own time. The grace and blessing come through Jesus Christ, God himself come in the flesh, who died for his people, rose again, and sent his people throughout the earth to bring this good news to every creature, looking to his coming in glory.

Now, given the breadth of the gospel, what does it mean for a church to have a "gospel-centered" ministry? Some seem to think that a gospel-centered ministry will focus on the gospel in the narrowest senses, 1 and 2, regarding the other senses as distractions from what is "really" gospel. Of course, that cannot be right. We cannot promote the gospel in the narrow senses by ignoring or disparaging it in its broader senses.

We need to be clear from the outset that *gospel* in senses 3–6 is really gospel. In those senses, too, it is the power of God to salvation (Rom. 1:16).

On the other hand, the Bible is not a flat screen, in which every verse is equally important, equally relevant to our salvation. As John Warwick Montgomery once said, when Christians evangelize on street corners, they often pass out copies of the gospel of John, rarely 2 Chronicles. John presents the gospel in a focused way so that its readers may "believe that Jesus is the Christ, the Son of God, and that by believing you may have life in his name" (John 20:31). Second Chronicles presents valuable background to the coming of Jesus, but the Chronicler could not have written a purpose statement like John 20:31.

3. See Meredith G. Kline, *The Structure of Biblical Authority* (Grand Rapids: Eerdmans, 1972).

So we are inclined to say that a gospel-centered church will emphasize parts of Scripture, such as the gospel of John, that put the basic truth of salvation clearly before their readers. Should such a church, then, ignore 2 Chronicles entirely? Certainly not. For one thing, a preacher may be able to effectively preach the gospel (senses 1–3) precisely by showing how a narrative from 2 Chronicles shows the need of the coming Messiah. For another thing, he may determine that his congregation may profit from learning something of the historical background of the gospel from 2 Chronicles.

In the end, it is a matter of emphasis, and emphasis is never a precise category. A *focus* is not a circle that precisely defines a territory and excludes all territory outside it. Rather, it is like a beam of light that illumines a particular area brightly, but also illumines other areas with lesser brightness. The gospel is not just the phrase "Jesus Christ and him crucified." It is also the defining, unpacking, applying of those words, a teaching process in which we receive considerable help from the broader senses of *gospel*. The gospel is Jesus Christ and him crucified. It is also the divine forgiveness that comes through Jesus' sacrifice. And it is also the new life that the Spirit gives to those who are in Christ. A gospel-centered church will focus on Christ and him crucified, presenting Jesus' sacrifice as the basis of all the blessings of the kingdom. But it will also present what those blessings are, and how the kingdom will change everything.

If a pastor preaches through 2 Chronicles as a mere listing of the facts of Israelite history, he cannot claim that his messages are gospel-centered. If, however, he preaches through 2 Chronicles specifically to show, in each sermon, how this history prepares the world for Christ and his gospel, then certainly he may claim to have a gospel focus.

It would be wrong for such a preacher to take verses and stories out of 2 Chronicles and manipulate them to make them sound equivalent to John 3:16. To do that sort of thing is to violate the meaning of the book and the function the book has in the Christian canon. That is not gospel-centeredness; it is false teaching.

Gospel-centeredness, therefore, is a quality of ministry and teaching that can be discerned, but it is not a precise quantity. It's a "centered set," not a "bounded set."[4] It does not exclude any part of God's Word, or any legitimate application of God's Word. It is a kind of general tone, in which people are caught up with enthusiasm for Jesus, a passion to show others Jesus' atoning love and to keep his commandments.

Redeemer Presbyterian Church (PCA) in New York is often cited as a good example of gospel-centeredness, and I agree with that characterization. Perhaps one illustration will show what I and others have in mind. The sermons of Pastor Tim Keller are often "apologetic," in that along with the other functions of sermons they address problems likely to be in the minds of skeptical visitors to the church.[5] But he typically addresses these in a gospel-centered way. When people ask why they should consider a church that is responsible for much injustice in the world, Keller points them to Christ:

> When people have done injustice in the name of Christ they are not being true to the spirit of the one who himself died as a victim of injustice and who called for the forgiveness of his enemies.[6]

For Keller, the difference between belief and unbelief is not simply a difference in people's worldview or epistemology. It is essentially the influence of the gospel on their thinking and living.

It would not be wrong, I think, for someone to argue the superiority of the Christian worldview or epistemology. But the goal of apologetics is always evangelism. A gospel-centered apologetic brings the conversation right away to its proper focal point.

It is in this sort of way that I think all churches should be gospel-centered. There should always be a sense that the work of Christ is the driving force of ministry, the passion of the congregation's heart.

But this passion, by its very intensity, reaches out to embrace every area of life and society. A gospel-centered church will show how the

4. For this distinction, compare http://www.nextreformation.com/wp-admin/general/centered.htm.

5. Examples of Keller's apologetic can be found in his book *The Reason for God* (New York: Dutton, 2008).

6. Ibid., 67.

gospel transforms everything. So some sermons may well seem to be about many things other than the gospel in sense 1 or 2. One may be about women's head-covering in 1 Corinthians 11. Another may deal with OT laws of cleanliness, or principles of Christian family life, or different ways of understanding the Apocalypse. The rule is not that every sermon push its text into a John 3:16 mold, but that every sermon show how its text is related to Christ.

4

The Main Thing

I HAVE HEARD the following slogan more than once in sermons: "The main thing is to keep the main thing the main thing." That slogan expresses our frustration that all too often the fundamental message of Christianity, the source of its vitality, is obscured by lesser things. We often feel the force of this admonition in daily life as we consider all the lesser things that clamor for our attention: money, entertainment, cars, gadgets, and so on. We can justify giving some attention to these matters, but they easily preoccupy us so that we have little time for or interest in the things of the Spirit. Even things clearly good in themselves, such as food, drink, family, and work, can overshadow the importance of Christ in our lives. Even matters involving Scripture itself can sometimes distract: Bible prophecy, controversies over evolution, detailed questions of biblical history (e.g., where did Cain get his wife?) and exegesis (e.g., "faith in Christ" or "faithfulness of Christ" in Phil. 3:9?). And distinctively theological questions can also disrupt our focus, as when sermons include long expositions of the order of divine decrees or the simplicity of God.

Sermons are often the main focus of admonitions to concentrate on the main thing. So we hear often that sermons should be "Christ-centered" or "redemptive-historical" or "covenantal." Certainly there is substance behind these concerns. I'm told that there were dark times in the history of preaching when clerics spent time in praise of strawberry jam, or the joys of bass fishing.

The problem is not the amount of time given to each subject. There is no biblical rule that we need to be thinking directly about Jesus for a certain percentage of our time. Making Jesus the main thing is not sitting around saying "Jesus, Jesus" to ourselves, however valuable that practice may occasionally be as a devotional exercise. Nor is it limiting thoughts about my car to forty-five seconds a day.[1]

Rather, the issue is contextual. If the great passion of my life is to seek the kingdom of God (Matt. 6:33), and I see my car as a means of seeking the kingdom, it doesn't much matter how long I think about it. (If it is stalled on the highway, certainly it is legitimate for me to think about it for as long as it takes to resolve the problem.) We do, of course, need to examine ourselves from time to time to make sure that our fundamental goal remains steadfast.

Christ and Him Crucified

But what is the fundamental goal? What is the main thing? It is easy to say "Christ" and to cite Paul:

> For I decided to know nothing among you except Jesus Christ and him crucified. (1 Cor. 2:2)

But as we saw above, this does not mean that Paul went around Corinth muttering "Jesus Christ and him crucified" over and over again. Paul uses this phrase as shorthand for a whole program of preaching, a program described in the book of Acts and set forth in Paul's letters. "Jesus Christ and him crucified" includes arguments from the OT that Jesus is the promised Messiah. It includes contrasts between the God of Scripture and the gods of the Gentiles (Acts 17). It includes the plan by which people can become right with God (esp. Rom. 1–5) and can become personally holy (Rom. 6–8). It includes a discussion of the role of the Jews (Rom. 9–11). And it contains a great many

---

1. Is this sort of time management what people sometimes refer to as *emphasis* or *focus?* I have heard scores of sermons on what we should "focus on," but what does that mean other than spending a certain amount of time in meditation? Same for books and articles that tell pastors what they should "emphasize."

exhortations about how to live a life appropriate to our redeemed status (Rom. 12–16; many other places).

So "Jesus Christ and him crucified" may sound like a formula that sharply narrows the apostle's concern. But it includes a broad range of teaching of many kinds. Of course, Paul was narrowing his concern in contrast with those who specialized in "lofty speech or wisdom" (1 Cor. 2:1). But within the limitations of his Christ-centered purpose, there was a great deal to say.

The Kingdom of God

In that respect, "Christ and him crucified" is not different from other biblical ways of stating "the main thing." For example, the main thing is also the kingdom of God. The hope of the OT was that God would come and install David's son upon the throne of Israel. The Jewish expectations tended to be worldly and political in a way that God did not intend. But the "kingdom of God" played a major role in the early preaching both of Jesus and of John the Baptist. Their message was: "Repent, for the kingdom of heaven is at hand" (Matt. 3:1; 4:17). The same message characterized the content of the apostolic preaching (Acts 8:12; 14:22; 19:8; 20:25; 28:23, 31).

As a summary of the biblical message, "kingdom of God" sounds more broad and general than "Christ and him crucified." But they both designate the whole message. To seek the kingdom of God is to seek God's righteousness (Matt. 6:33) and to receive everything that a child of God may need.

The Gospel

Gospel is another way to describe the content of the biblical message. Often writers will suggest that *gospel* is a narrow subset of what is in the Bible. So some churches will claim to have a "gospel-centered" ministry as opposed to other churches that presumably do not.

Now, it is sad that indeed many churches have lost the gospel, which is to say that they have lost the Christian message, the fundamental content of Scripture. Many have in one way or another exchanged the message of grace for a message of works-righteousness.

But among churches that believe the Bible and have not succumbed to humanism, I don't believe that *gospel* should be a kind of special emphasis distinguishing some churches from others.

Like "Christ and him crucified" and "kingdom of God," *gospel* is actually a broad category. It begins with the preaching of "good news" by the OT prophets:

> Comfort, comfort my people, says your God.
> Speak tenderly to Jerusalem,
>   and cry to her
> that her warfare is ended,
>   that her iniquity is pardoned,
> that she has received from the LORD's hand
>   double for all her sins. (Isa. 40:1–2)

> How beautiful upon the mountains
>   are the feet of him who brings good news,
> who publishes peace, who brings good news of happiness,
>   who publishes salvation,
>   who says to Zion, "Your God reigns." (Isa. 52:7)[2]

> The Spirit of the Lord GOD is upon me,
>   because the LORD has anointed me
> to bring good news to the poor;
>   he has sent me to bind up the brokenhearted,
> to proclaim liberty to the captives,
>   and the opening of the prison to those who are bound. (Isa. 61:1)[3]

This was the good news that the angel brought at Jesus' birth (Luke 2:10). It includes God's pardon of our sins, but also God's general kingdom

2. Note here the correlation between gospel ("good news") and kingdom ("Your God reigns"). Cf. the parallel passage in Nahum 1:15. Note also the phrase "gospel of the kingdom" in Matthew 24:14.

3. In his preaching in Nazareth, Jesus read this passage and said that he fulfilled it (Luke 4:18–21).

reign and the consequent healing of society (liberty to the captives; cf. Luke 7:22).

I do not believe that *gospel* in Scripture ever designates a content more narrow than the kingdom of God itself. Some have claimed that 1 Corinthians 15:1–8 is an exception:

> Now I would remind you, brothers, of the gospel I preached to you, which you received, in which you stand, and by which you are being saved, if you hold fast to the word I preached to you—unless you believed in vain.
>
> For I delivered to you as of first importance what I also received: that Christ died for our sins in accordance with the Scriptures, that he was buried, that he was raised on the third day in accordance with the Scriptures, and that he appeared to Cephas, then to the twelve. Then he appeared to more than five hundred brothers at one time, most of whom are still alive, though some have fallen asleep. Then he appeared to James, then to all the apostles. Last of all, as to one untimely born, he appeared also to me.

Certainly these great events—Jesus' death for our sins, his burial, and his resurrection—are indispensable to any preaching of the gospel. But it would not be right to say that the meaning of *gospel* is limited to these. Paul's purpose here is, of course, to rebut one kind of disbelief in the resurrection, so it is understandable that he focuses on this historical fact. But Paul goes on in the chapter to describe the consequences of Jesus' resurrection, beyond the resurrection itself. The resurrection is not an isolated event, but an event that is full of implications for the Christian life. So it displays the dominion of Christ over all things (vv. 27–28) and requires the Christian to accept tribulation for Jesus' sake (vv. 29–34). Ultimately, the resurrection promises victory to God's people and encourages us to be "steadfast, immovable, always abounding in the work of the Lord, knowing that in the Lord your labor is not in vain" (v. 58). All that is also part of the good news, the gospel.[4] By verse 58, *gospel* comes out sounding a lot like *kingdom*.

God's whole message to us is gospel. The gospel is the good news that the kingdom has come and is coming, and the whole Bible tells that story.[5]

The Main Heart Commitment

Christ, kingdom, gospel—all different ways of describing "the main thing." I could mention others, too: the glory of God (1 Cor. 10:31), the covenant (Gen. 17:1–8), the cultural mandate (Gen. 1:28), the Great Commission (Matt. 28:18–20), the image of God (Col. 3:10),[6] the fear of God (Ps. 111:10), fearing God and keeping his commandments (which in Eccl. 12:13 is called the "whole duty of man"), knowing God and Christ (John 17:3; Phil. 3:10).

But clearly, none of these is intended to surpass the others in importance. They are equal (and perspectival) ways to describe what is at the top of the believer's scale of values or priorities. Any of them, of course, may be contrasted with lesser priorities in a particular context:

> Therefore I tell you, do not be anxious about your life, what you will eat or what you will drink, nor about your body, what you will put on. Is not life more than food, and the body more than clothing? Look at the birds of the air: they neither sow nor reap nor gather into barns, and yet your heavenly Father feeds them. Are you not of more value than they? And which of you by being anxious can add a single hour to his span of life? And why are you anxious about clothing? Consider the lilies of the field, how they grow: they neither toil nor

4. I reject the common view that *gospel* is in every respect opposed to *law*. See my *DCL*, 182–92. That the gospel has ethical implications is evident in many passages, including this one. Of course, it is certainly true that the gospel warrants salvation by grace rather than as something we earn by our works.

5. The whole Bible is law, as well, because it is authoritative. Everything in Scripture tells me something to believe or do. But if the whole Bible is gospel and the whole Bible is law, then the two can never be separate.

6. The image of God is both a fact (Gen. 1:26–27) and a norm (Matt. 5:48). We *are* God's image, but (especially in the light of the degradation of that image by sin) we are also *commanded* to reflect him.

spin, yet I tell you, even Solomon in all his glory was not arrayed like one of these. But if God so clothes the grass of the field, which today is alive and tomorrow is thrown into the oven, will he not much more clothe you, O you of little faith? Therefore do not be anxious, saying, "What shall we eat?" or "What shall we drink?" or "What shall we wear?" For the Gentiles seek after all these things, and your heavenly Father knows that you need them all. But seek first the kingdom of God and his righteousness, and all these things will be added to you. (Matt. 6:25–33)

But I cannot recall (or imagine) a text saying that we should put the kingdom above the gospel or the glory of God above the covenant.

So to put the kingdom first is the same as putting the covenant first, the gospel first, and the like. Each of these, moreover, is an alternative way of seeing the whole content of Scripture. I said earlier that *gospel* includes the whole Bible. So do the others.

When people get their priorities skewed, or lack a proper "central focus," this may mean that they are not believers at all. Or it may mean that they have some other kind of problem, theological or practical. For example, when people abuse alcohol, we often say of them that they give alcohol a more central emphasis in their lives than it deserves—and at the expense of Christ, the gospel, and the kingdom. We might seek to deal with this problem by exhorting them about gaining a better "focus." Or we might counsel in the opposite direction: deal with the addiction, expecting the better focus to arise from that therapy. I am not a counselor, and experts in counseling can judge which direction is preferable. As a theologian, I am tempted to appeal first to the need of a proper focus, from the general to the particular. But it seems to me that Scripture is not biased in either direction. You can deal with a specific sin, which will lead to a healthier general emphasis, or you can do the reverse. And it is probably best in any specific case to do both at once.

"Keep the main thing the main thing" is an exhortation to emphasize the general (whether that is called *Christ*, *gospel*, *kingdom*, or something else). It is often good advice. But it is also good advice to focus on specifics, to ask God's grace to deal with individual areas of life that need to be more conformed to his image.

When we exhort preachers to focus on the main thing, typically the problem is not that they say too much about gospel and not enough about kingdom (though that may happen). Rather, the problem is either that they have lost confidence in the whole message of Scripture or that they are ineffective at communicating it. Problems of this sort are very serious indeed, and they are not well described as problems of "emphasis."

5

What the Bible Does *Not* Say: Contrast in Preaching, with Thoughts about Communication, Marketing, and Prosperity Theology

VERN S. POYTHRESS, following Kenneth Pike, identifies a triad, "contrast, variation, and distribution," as an important component of language theory.[1] Among other things, these categories are important for identifying the meanings of terms. Consider the meaning of *goat*. When we try to ascertain the meaning of this term (without a dictionary), we ask questions such as: "From what other terms is this word regularly distinguished?" We answer, "Sheep, cows, etc." That is the question of *contrast*. The question of *variation* deals with the range of the term, what different kinds of being can be designated by it. (Answer: mountain goats, domestic goats, doe goats, billy goats, kid goats, etc.) The question of *distribution* has to do with the contexts in which the term normally appears: agriculture, food, zoology, religious symbolism.

All members of this triad have implications for biblical exegesis and theology. In this essay, I want to consider only the concept of contrast. In interpreting Scripture, it is important to understand what the terms

1. Vern S. Poythress, *In the Beginning Was the Word* (Wheaton, IL: Crossway, 2009), 154–56.

and sentences "contrast with." When Scripture teaches A, it excludes non-A. When Genesis 1:1 says that God created the heavens and the earth, it logically also denies that God did *not* create the heavens and the earth. "God created the world" contrasts with his not creating it. It also contrasts with the idea that someone else created it, or the idea that something in the heavens or earth is not created at all.

But imagine someone saying, "God *created* the heavens and the earth. Note that it says he *created* the world, not that he predestined it." And then he goes on from here to deny divine predestination. Now, you don't need to be a Calvinist to see that this is a logical mistake. One way to describe this mistake is to point out that in Genesis 1:1, *created* is not "in contrast with" *predestined*. You cannot derive from "God created" that "God did not predestine." Creation is not inconsistent with predestination. And indeed, many biblical texts tell us that God predestines as well as creates (Rom. 8:29; Eph. 1:5, 11).

Possibly the example above is a mistake that nobody has actually ever made. In that sense it is a straw man. But it is a simple way of showing the nature of the difficulty. Still, I suspect that this is not merely a theoretical problem. Indeed, I wonder how many sermons make this mistake. I heard a preacher once say on 1 Corinthians 1:21 that God honors the "foolishness of preaching" (KJV), not videos, PowerPoint, praise bands, or other modern media. Now, when you hear that sort of thing, you should ask whether the preacher is making a contrast error. In this case: is it really likely that Paul is *contrasting* preaching with modern communications techniques?

Of course, in an obvious sense, the answer is no, because Paul was not acquainted with videos and the like. But the real question, of course, is whether Paul was contrasting preaching with other modes of communication (maybe scroll-reading or Greek drama). But in the context of the passage (the distribution element), Paul is not thinking of preaching as a method of communication. He refers to his preaching because of its *content*, namely, the gospel message. It is that gospel, not the medium of its expression, that contrasts with the wisdom of the wise. Paul is, after all, on this very occasion using the medium of writing, not preaching, to communicate his gospel to the Corinthians.

Paul's argument is that the gospel message of salvation rebukes the wisdom of the Greeks and creates a stumbling block for Jews because it is the wisdom of God, not because it is delivered by monologue.

Similarly, I have heard preachers say that Jesus commanded in Matthew 28:19 to "teach" or "disciple" the nations, not to "market the gospel." That example is a bit more difficult than the previous one. Marketing today has a terrible reputation, so much so that many Christians would buy that negation without question. Many think that marketing involves sleazy manipulation, exploitation, even fraud. But I have known marketers (particularly people who run actual markets) who are honest Christian believers and who market their products without deceit, simply to let people know that they have good products available for sale. Such honest marketing actually has much in common with the gospel proclamation of Matthew 28:19. So Matthew 28:19 may indeed stand in contrast with some kinds of marketing, but not with marketing in general. And people who are experts in marketing may actually have something useful to teach the church as it seeks the best ways of communicating the gospel.

Another example: I have heard preachers deal with the NT passages that promise persecution to believers (as Matt. 5:11; 2 Tim. 3:12), concluding that God does not promise us prosperity or happiness. In my view, that conclusion does not follow. The existence of persecution in the Christian life does not exclude the presence of happiness. Indeed, the beatitude of Matthew 5:11 says precisely that believers are "blessed" (sometimes translated "happy") when others persecute them. And of course, none of these passages say that the persecution of believers is uninterrupted. Believers will endure persecution, but there will also be times of rest and pleasure (Ps. 23). Keeping a balanced view is important, and Jesus provides that in Mark 10:29–30. The covenant between God and ourselves promises both suffering and blessing, and the blessing takes the form of earthly prosperity (Deut. 5:16).

In preaching we are often motivated to bring modern realities into our exposition of the ancient texts. In general, that is a good thing. Preaching is not just reading Scripture, nor is it a description of how the gospel would have sounded to ancient people. Rather, preaching presents the gospel to people today, applying it to their situation. So it is understandable that when Scripture condemns worldliness, preachers apply these admonitions to Internet pornography or social-media addiction. But application must be accurate. I think it is right to say that Internet pornography is an example of what Scripture calls worldliness. I don't think it's right to say the same of the use of guitars in worship.

So it is important when we read a Bible text to ask, "What does this include?" and "What does this exclude?" To the extent that we treat such questions in a slipshod way, our sermons will be unpersuasive. There are various exegetical techniques that help us answer such questions, but we may often have to rely on common sense. Pray that God will give to his teachers and preachers more of that in our time.

6

Contrast, Exegesis, and Preaching, with Reflections on Marketing, Prosperity, Human Responsibility, and Historical Disjunctions

WHEN LINGUISTS TRY TO understand a term in an unknown language, they often ask, "With what terms is this term typically contrasted?" So in English, we may explain the term *beautiful* by saying that it is typically contrasted with *ugly*. Vern Poythress says:

> Moreover, the meaning of most words is largely determined by the contrast of one word with other related words. The word "pig" functions to distinguish a certain group of animals within the class of domestic mammalian animals: it contrasts primarily with "dog," "horse," "cow," and "cat."[1]

Contrast is not the only determinant of linguistic meaning. As a principle it is part of the triad *contrast*, *variation*, and *distribution*:

---

1. Vern S. Poythress, *Symphonic Theology* (Grand Rapids: Zondervan, 1987), 57, also available at http://www.frame-poythress.org.

Description. The *Contrast* of an Item involves those features that identify it and contrast it with other Items. "Items which are independently, consistently different are in contrast."

Description. The *Variation* of an Item is the range of difference through which it may vary while still remaining recognizably the "same." (Obviously this depends on what kind of "sameness" we may be interested in.)

Description. The *Distribution* of an Item is comprised by the neighborhoods in which it may occur. This may be further analyzed into Distribution in class (Particle), in sequence of locations (Wave), and in system (Field).[2]

Thus, contrast is in contrast with other principles, though linked to them. It is also linked to other considerations of linguistics and interpretation, but this essay will treat only contrast.

In interpreting Scripture, particularly for purposes of teaching and preaching, it is important to understand what pieces of biblical language are "in contrast" with. For example, in 2 Timothy 4:2, Paul exhorts Timothy to "preach the word." I have heard people say, "See here? Paul says *preach*. He doesn't say to go on the radio, or to use pictures, or drama, or dance; he says *preach*. Therefore, preaching is the chief, or the only, medium for communicating the gospel." But the question here is: what is the word *preach* "in contrast with" in such a context? Is it likely that Paul is contrasting preaching with other media of communication? Or is Paul using preaching as a synecdoche for all gospel communication, mentioning it because at the time it is the most common means of such communication?

In 1 Corinthians 1:21, Paul says that "it pleased God through the folly of what we preach to save those who believe." The phrase "what we preach" in the ESV represents the Greek word *kerygma*. In the KJV, this is

2. Vern S. Poythress, *Philosophy, Science, and the Sovereignty of God* (Nutley, NJ: Presbyterian and Reformed, 1976), 123. In terms of the "three perspectives" that I have employed in other writings, contrast is normative, distribution situational, and variation existential. See my *DKG*, 236–37.

rendered "preaching," producing the phrase "foolishness of preaching." People who read it this way think Paul is intentionally offending Jews and Greeks by the *medium* of communication that he chooses to use. So this verse, too, has been used to say that we should present the gospel only through the medium of preaching, not through any other media.

Of course, that cannot be right. (1) Even if we accept the KJV rendering, it is not clear why the medium of preaching would be offensive to Jews and Greeks. Oral discourse was a common means of communication among both groups. (2) The context makes it plain that the issue bringing offense is not the medium, but the message: the content of the gospel. (3) The ESV reading is the most accurate interpretation of *kerygma*, one that certainly fits best into the context.

That is to say that *kerygma* in 1 Corinthians 1:21 is not in contrast with other media, but with other messages. The Christian *kerygma* is in opposition to the foolish worldly philosophies that Paul mentions in the same chapter. It would be fair to apply this contrast to other false teaching, such as Gnosticism, Docetism, Judaizing Christianity, and so forth. But it is not in contrast with literary publication, amplifiers, radio, TV, and the like.

Nor is preaching in contrast with *marketing* in anything like the modern sense of the term. It depends, of course, on how you define *marketing*. Most critics of marketing in the church don't define the term carefully. If it simply means to make something known, to advertise, using the most effective communication available, then certainly the church should market its gospel. Christianity is a missionary faith. It is charged in the Great Commission with bringing the gospel to everyone.

If one defines *marketing* in a narrower sense, as using various techniques unworthy of the gospel, then we need to discuss what those techniques are, and why they are unworthy. If they are, then they are excluded from *kerygma*. In this case, the means of communication contradict the content of the gospel, and certainly 1 Corinthians 1:21 rules out any presentation that obscures that content. Again, the focus is on content, not on media in themselves. But when the media obstruct the message, they must be changed. The church should have a dialogue on what means of communication obscure the gospel message. But simply to contrast *marketing* with *preaching* sheds no light on the issue.

As another example, look at John 10:10b, where Jesus says, "I came that they may have life and have it abundantly." I have heard Bible teachers say that *life* here is salvation from sin, not earthly prosperity, as though one could prove from this text that the gospel has nothing to do with earthly prosperity or happiness. Now, in the first place, Jesus does in fact promise earthly prosperity for his people, "with persecutions," in this life, and prosperity in the life to come:

> Jesus said, "Truly, I say to you, there is no one who has left house or brothers or sisters or mother or father or children or lands, for my sake and for the gospel, who will not receive a hundredfold now in this time, houses and brothers and sisters and mothers and children and lands, with persecutions, and in the age to come eternal life. But many who are first will be last, and the last first." (Mark 10:29–31)

This was God's promise to Israel in the OT (Ex. 3:8, 17; 13:5; etc.), and it appears that Jesus in Mark 10 announces at least a provisional fulfillment of it in the lives of his people. We should not doubt that such blessing is part of the "abundance" of life that Jesus offers in John 10:10.

In John's writing, life is in contrast with death, not with prosperity. I agree with the critics of the "prosperity gospel" that the true gospel always focuses on the forgiveness of sins. But I believe it is simplistic to say that the gospel is *limited* to such forgiveness. The prosperity preachers didn't get their idea out of thin air. The prosperity of God's people is a regular theme of Scripture. The prosperity movement misreads this promise, without the balancing teaching of Mark 10. But the prosperity gospel needs to be addressed by a more discerning exegesis than one finds in some of their critics.

Another issue: When Ephesians 1:11 says that God "works all things according to the counsel of his will," does that exclude all secondary causes? Does "God works A" stand in contrast with "Bill works A"? Certainly not. The Bible regularly ascribes events to human responsibility, sometimes speaking of God's causality and man's together in the same passage (Acts 2:23; 4:27–28; Phil. 2:12–13). The Bible's view is that God often brings about his comprehensive purposes by human means.

I have heard people say that one denies the sovereignty of God if one presses people to make "decisions for Christ." That is entirely illegitimate. Scripture itself, often, presses people to make godly decisions, as Joshua's command, "Choose this day whom you will serve" (Josh. 24:15). Paul commanded the Philippian jailer to "believe in the Lord Jesus, and you will be saved" (Acts 16:31). Here belief (faith) is a human choice, and Scripture represents faith as a necessary condition of salvation (as John 3:36). Divine sovereignty is not in contrast with human decisions as conditions of salvation. Both must be present, though of course God foreordains the human decision.

To summarize: it is never enough to say, "Scripture says A, therefore it excludes B." This argument works only with additional premises to show that A in fact excludes B.

The same issue also arises in historical studies. Note the comments of John Woodbridge in his critique of Jack Rogers and Donald McKim, *The Authority and Interpretation of the Bible:*[3]

> In logic, a disjunction is a proposition in which two (or more) alternatives are asserted, only one of which can be true. In their study Rogers and McKim work with a whole series of what we might coin "historical disjunctions." They assume that certain correct assertions about an individual's thought logically disallow other ones from being true. Their assumption is sometimes accurate, if the thoughts being compared directly contradict each other. However, in their historical disjunctions the authors create disjunctions between propositions that are not mutually exclusive. They engage in an empty form of deductive, historical speculation that assumes much without sufficient proof.
>
> A partial listing of the authors' more important "historical disjunctions" would include these: because a thinker believes the central purpose of Scripture is to reveal salvation history, it is assumed that he or she does not endorse complete biblical infallibility; because a thinker speaks of God accommodating himself to us in the words of

3. New York: Harper and Row, 1979.

Scripture, it is assumed that he or she does not believe in complete biblical infallibility.[4]

Woodbridge adds a number of other significant illustrations.

The moral is that whenever we interpret the Bible, or a human writer, it is important to understand what his words should be taken to exclude, as well as what they include. The answer to this question is not always obvious. I think that much theology and preaching is subject to the criticism that they have not been careful in dealing with this issue.

4. John D. Woodbridge, *Biblical Authority: A Critique of the Rogers-McKim Proposal* (Grand Rapids: Zondervan, 1982), 25–26.

7

Contexts

WHEN SOMEONE BEGINS to read his Bible seriously, often the first piece of hermeneutical advice he receives is to "read it in context." Usually the meaning of this advice is easy to discern. Say that a young Christian reads Joshua 1:3 and concludes that God is promising him ownership of every place he visits. A wise, older Christian may point out the context: that God is fulfilling a special promise made to the descendants of Abraham, Isaac, and Jacob, one that doesn't apply in a literal sense to believers today. But "read it in context" doesn't always lead to such obvious conclusions. In this essay, I would like to explore some of the difficulties that we often run into in trying to follow this simple advice.

The Multitude of Contexts

For one thing, there are many contexts, not just one. The word *context* combines *with* and *text*, referring to whatever a particular text is "with": its surroundings, its environment. But when you think of it, each text is "with" a great many things. Ultimately, each text holds a place in the whole universe, together with all the other things in the universe. So each text has a universal context.

We usually assume that the context of a Bible verse consists of a few verses preceding and a few verses following. But how many? There are larger contexts and narrower contexts. There is also the context of the chapter in which the verse is found. And there is the context of the whole book. Indeed, there is the context of the whole section of the

Bible in which the book is found (the Pentateuch, OT history, poetry, prophecy, gospels, epistles, apocalyptic). Overlapping this classification is the classification of genre ("this passage should be taken in the context of Hebrew poetry"). Further, there is the context of all the books with the same authorship ("we should take Romans 3:23 in the context of Pauline thought"). And there is the context provided by the eras of biblical history (e.g., "the context of postexilic writing") and by biblical covenants (Noachic, Abrahamic, Mosaic, etc.).

We might think the widest literary context is the entire Bible. But of course, scholars often say that the Bible itself should be seen in a wider context, such as "ancient Near Eastern literature." And beyond literary contexts there is the context of events: redemptive events, general historical developments, natural history.

Especially significant is the context of the contemporary hearer or reader. For the reader must ask, "How does this passage apply to me?" even though it was originally directed to people of a different time and place.

Usually the extent of *context* is not an issue. As in our example from Joshua 1:3, it is clear what someone means when he says, "Read it in context." But sometimes this advice raises perplexities that are not easily resolved.

The Use of Context

In Matthew 18:20, Jesus tells his disciples, "For where two or three are gathered in my name, there am I among them." This verse has often been used to give comfort to small churches: "Though our attendance is small, Jesus is here, and that's what is most important."

But some have argued that this attempt to comfort takes the verse out of context. The larger passage, verses 15–20, is about church discipline, dealing with sin within the church. According to verse 18, the judgments of the church are validated by God's heavenly judgment. Verse 19 extends this promise to the agreements reached in the church. And in verse 20, Jesus presents the basis of that promise: his personal presence in the church.

I have no quarrel with this understanding of the passage and the meaning of verse 20 within the passage. My only question is whether this is the *only* legitimate use of verse 20. Does this interpretation imply that we may never use verse 20 to comfort a congregation that is small in number?

The question is whether verse 20 is a principle that applies only in the case of church discipline, or whether it also has a broader reference. It is helpful here to keep in mind that other passages also speak of the presence of Christ in and with the church, without any specific reference to church discipline. Consider Matthew 28:20; John 14:16–18; Galatians 2:20; Colossians 1:27.[1] Someone might argue that if we wish to speak of Christ's presence in a small congregation, we should use one of these other passages instead of Matthew 18:20. But none of those passages mention specifically the smallness of the group in which Christ is present. So the use of Matthew 18:20 is certainly tempting, even if it is "wrong."

But is it wrong? I think not. Given that Matthew 18:20 is an exemplification of a widespread biblical principle, it seems to me that it serves as the application of that broad principle to the situation of church discipline. We often invoke broad principles so that we can apply them to specific cases. "Women and children first," for example, is most famously used to determine priorities in assigning lifeboats in a sinking ship. But that doesn't mean we should not use that principle to arrange a buffet line. Broad principles, by their very breadth, apply to a wide variety of situations.

That is often the case in Scripture. The lordship of God, for example, is a broad principle, but it applies to many specific situations. It describes God as Lawgiver (Ps. 1:2), as Ruler (Ps. 2), as Defender (Ps. 3), and so on.

So we should not use the "principle of context" to limit the application of a biblical principle to a very narrow subject matter. To the contrary: biblical principles tend to reflect the breadth of the Lord

---

1. The OT background of these passages is the "Immanuel" of Isaiah 7:14, "God with us," underscored in such passages as Genesis 21:22; Exodus 3:12; Deuteronomy 2:7; Joshua 1:5; Psalm 46:7, 11; and Isaiah 41:10. God's presence with his people is the essence of the covenant.

himself, so that they broaden out over all of human life, governing, comforting, and challenging that life.

Context and Theological Controversies

Let me discuss with you some theological discussions in which the term *context* sometimes plays a role.

Initial Faith and Subsequent Faith

A friend of mine complains that when Protestants read about *faith* in the NT, we too instinctively relate the term to a person's initial faith, the faith by which we are justified (Rom. 3:23–25). But, she says, a number of passages speak of faith not as initial, justifying faith, but as an ongoing trust in God that sustains all of life. For example, in Ephesians 3:12–17, Paul speaks of Christ,

> in whom we have boldness and access with confidence through our faith in him. So I ask you not to lose heart over what I am suffering for you, which is your glory.
>
> For this reason I bow my knees before the Father, from whom every family in heaven and on earth is named, that according to the riches of his glory he may grant you to be strengthened with power through his Spirit in your inner being, so that Christ may dwell in your hearts through faith—that you, being rooted and grounded in love . . . .

My friend says that people have taught her that *faith* in verses 12 and 17 is initial saving faith. But she thinks (with my agreement) that *faith* in these verses is our ongoing trust in Christ (as in 1:15, 19), our believing *now*. Paul's point in 3:12 is not that our initial commitment to Christ (with baptism, the very fact that we are Christians) gives us boldness and access, but the fact that we continue (by grace, of course) to trust in Christ through all of life. Of course, our initial faith is the beginning of our subsequent faith. But Paul is not saying that our boldness and access may be assumed because of something that happened at one time in the past. He is saying that our boldness and access to Christ are maintained through ongoing faith, our day-to-day experience of trusting the Lord.

I could be wrong about that. But we need to do the hard work of exegesis to determine which interpretation to accept and to preach. It will not be enough, whenever we see the word *faith*, to say, "Well, that has to be taken in the context of the Pauline doctrine of justification." Paul's doctrine of justification by faith is part of the context; in a way, every biblical teaching is part of the context. But the biblical doctrine of *progressive* sanctification, our ongoing faithfulness, is also part of the biblical context. To cite one context or the other settles nothing. We must engage in careful exegesis to determine how each context functions, and which is more specifically determinative.

Often tradition determines which context determines a theologian's conclusions. Lutherans tend to bring Paul's doctrine of justification by faith into as many theological discussions as possible. Christians of other traditions are more attracted to other contexts. In cases like this, the fact that justification by faith is a context is not determinative. For there are other contexts as well.

The Blessings of the Psalms

Christians of all ages have found in the Psalms descriptions of our walk with God—sometimes difficult, sometimes pleasant. Psalm 23 speaks of God's leading his people beside still waters, restoring our soul, leading us in the paths of righteousness, but also watching over us in the valley of the shadow of death.

But does the psalm-writer (David) intend to describe every believer's walk with God? Or is he speaking only about his own walk as the shepherd-king of Israel? Or is he speaking of the experience of Israel under the old covenant, not to be applied to new covenant believers? Sometimes "read it in context" applies to one of these limitations of the Psalms.

To make a long story short: in my view, David is speaking of himself and, implicitly, of the nation of Israel represented in him. But the

NT presents the church as the fulfillment of ancient Israel. Followers of Christ are the seed of Abraham (Rom. 4:16; Gal. 3:7–9), the branches grafted onto the vine of Israel (Rom. 11:17–24), indeed the "Israel of God" (Gal. 6:16). God's covenant with David is fulfilled in Jesus Christ. So (making some adjustments for the passage of time) the Psalms do describe the Christian's walk with God, and hence the church has always used the Psalms in its liturgy. Given all the differences between old and new covenants, there is an analogy between the two, focused on the fact that God is Lord of both covenants.

So this sort of question requires some theological care. Nothing can be resolved by saying, "Read it in context," for there are too many contexts: the context of biblical kingship, of God's covenants with Abraham, Moses, and David, and the context of the analogy (and disanalogy) between Old and New Testaments.

Traditional Differences

As I mentioned, when theologians and exegetes say, "Read it in context," they often have in mind a context based on their particular tradition. When an exegetical or theological problem comes up, Lutherans typically turn to the context of Paul's (Luther's!) doctrine of justification. Calvinists typically think about the context of God's overall sovereignty. Baptists focus on the context of evangelism and missions. Anglicans focus on the church. Pentecostals want to relate everything to the Spirit. Others focus on various understandings of eschatology, or dispensational distinctions. Some are drawn to relate everything to the law of God, others to relate everything to grace and gospel.

In more sophisticated academic theology (G. C. Berkouwer is a good example), we often hear that doctrine A "should not be abstracted from" doctrine B. So sanctification should not be abstracted from justification, or law from grace, or judgment from love. Karl Barth warned over and over that nothing could be "separated from" Jesus Christ, that we should never separate Jesus' person from his work, that we should not abstract the atonement from faith. This polemic against "abstraction" is the same as the more popular admonitions about context.[2] But academic theologians prefer to deal with more sophisticated contexts.

This same issue can be put in other terms as well: we should never "separate" A from B; we should always see A "in the light of" B, and so on. But there are many different ways of separating something from something else, or of bringing them together. In itself, "don't separate A from B" means almost nothing. *Separation* is a metaphor of place that doesn't easily relate to theological concepts. Separating a tire from a car is very different from separating justification from sanctification. There are many ways of separating a tire from a car (which lug nut do you start with?); there are many more ways of separating justification from sanctification. A typical theologian will say, "We must distinguish, but not separate," as if every reader understood how the two are different. But that means nothing either.

"Read it in context," then, is a shorthand way of telling a Bible student or scholar to focus on something outside the text itself, to see how that could illumine the text. That advice is sometimes self-explanatory, as in the first example I cited. But more often, it tells the Bible student to embark on a program of relating the text to any amount of explanatory data (the "contexts"). Ideally, of course, everything should be illuminated by everything else.[3] But "read it in context," if it is to be helpful advice, should be followed by a specific reference to material that the adviser thinks will be especially illuminating. Beyond the common-sense level, someone who advises you to "read it in context" should be willing to show you *what* context you should focus on, and how you should go about seeking help from it. And he should tell you why you should focus on that particular context, rather than another one.

2. This was the point I tried to make (albeit unclearly) in my discussion of "anti-abstractionism" in *DKG*, 169–91.

3. Philosophers such as Hegel in the idealist tradition thought you really couldn't understand a single thing until you had understood everything. That was a contextual argument *par excellence*.

8

The Picture Theory of Theology

IN THE EARLY PART of the twentieth century, Bertrand Russell and Ludwig Wittgenstein developed a philosophical theory of meaning that was called "the picture theory of language."[1] Essentially it was that language ought to be a picture of reality. Wittgenstein argued that in a logically perfect language every sentence would correspond to a fact in the world, and every word in every sentence would correspond to an element of a fact, that is, to a thing, property, or relation.

Of course, even this perfect language fell short of picturing in the usual sense: the sentence "This is a chair" does not, even in the perfect language, actually look like a chair. What Wittgenstein meant to argue is the more sophisticated thesis that in a perfect language every sentence does a perfect job of stating a fact. But he later came to see that language has many functions other than stating facts.[2] It contains questions, commands, promises, thanks, jokes, symbolism, and on and on. In his later philosophy, he determined that meaning is not picturing the world. Rather, in general, the meaning of language is its *use*. Language is a tool that we use for many human purposes: carrying out tasks, playing games, solemnizing marriages, and asking questions, as well as conveying information.

I do not agree with all of Wittgenstein's ideas, but I think his discovery about meaning ought to be helpful to all who use language, including theologians.

1. See especially Wittgenstein's *Tractatus Logico-Philosophicus* (London: Kegan Paul, 1922). Many editions since.
2. See Ludwig Wittgenstein, *Philosophical Investigations* (London: Wiley-Blackwell, 2009), and other editions.

I have the impression that some theologians and preachers are "bewitched" (as Wittgenstein would say) by the idea that theology ought to *resemble* the Bible, that it should somehow conjure up a *picture* of the Bible. I get that impression, for example, when people tell me that since the Bible is narrative, sermons should be narratives as well.

I do think the present renewal of interest in the narrative of Scripture is generally to the good. Scripture does convey a "story" of creation, fall, and redemption, though of course there are many parts of Scripture that are not narrative in form: the Psalms, wisdom literature, Prophets, Epistles, Apocalypse. That story is tremendously important to Scripture, and none of the non-narrative parts of Scripture can be understood without it.

I agree also that the narrative form tends to interest people more than, say, listings of dogmatic propositions. But I don't believe that non-narrative forms should be excluded from sermons, for there are non-narrative forms in Scripture, too, and we need to do justice to those as well.

At least some of the pressure toward narratival theology and preaching, however, comes in my view from the supposition that theology and preaching need to *resemble* Scripture. The thought is that it is not enough to agree with Scripture, or to communicate biblical content. One must, somehow, also communicate that content "as the Bible does it."

But where does the Bible tell us to seek a resemblance in form between Scripture and theology? I have argued that our theology should *agree* with Scripture, indeed to treat it as infallible. But I see no reason to assume that our teaching and preaching ought to mimic the *form* of Scripture.

Another example: I have heard the suggestion that our theology and preaching ought to have the same *emphasis* as the Bible. That is, if the Bible places a strong emphasis on the kingdom of God, let's say, our sermons ought to contain the same emphasis. But how do we calculate the percentage of Bible passages on the kingdom and establish that our sermons contain the same percentage of references? And again, where does Scripture admonish us to do anything like that?

At the extremes, this suggestion makes some sense. For example, if a pastor presents a series of sermons on the Christian life and never mentions union with Christ, clearly something is wrong. Such an omission would lead to fundamental misunderstandings. But this is not to say that if, say, 6.7 percent of the Bible contains references to union with Christ, our sermons must include exactly that percentage. Preaching ought to be *true* to Scripture, but it doesn't need to be a picture of Scripture.

Some years ago, a theologian wrote that he can evaluate any systematic theology just by looking at the table of contents. If the Trinity comes at the end, it is a poor work; if it comes at the beginning, it has a chance of being great. Similarly, other theologians have gotten into major conversations over the normative order of topics in a systematic theology. I presume that the point of this is that they want each topic to be given a proper emphasis. But it never seems to occur to them that the Bible itself does not present any commands concerning the order of topics in a systematic theology. Systematic theologies certainly need to be true to Scripture, but they may employ different orders out of pedagogical considerations. Again, they need to be true to Scripture, but they don't need to be pictures of Scripture.

Preaching and teaching are not picturing. Rather, to pick up Wittgenstein's other suggestion, their function is to *use* Scripture, to the edification of God's people. Or, as I have often put it, their job is to *apply* Scripture to all aspects of human life.

To apply Scripture, it is not only legitimate but mandatory to use different language and forms from those in the Bible itself. The main reason why God has given preachers to the church is that believers don't always make proper use of the Bible in the forms in which it was written. The job of the preacher is not simply to read the Bible to his people, but to *apply* it, which is to put it in new forms that engage the mind, heart, and feet.

The first new form, of course, is a translation. Nobody advocates the preaching of sermons in Hebrew and Greek. But if preaching is picturing, why not? As we have seen, however, preaching is not picturing, but edifying. Therefore (as the Reformers emphasized), it must be presented in the languages of the people.

But of course, translation is not the only new form that the Bible takes in the preaching and teaching of the Word. There should be explanations, illustrations. There should be analogies. There should be hymns and poetry. These will drive the Word into the heart. But they will not picture it very well.

If we can free ourselves from the concept of picturing the Bible, it seems to me, the way is open for many different approaches in Bible teaching. We will be free from the fruitless debates about supposedly normative forms of theological instruction. And we can look closely at our readers and hearers and develop forms that effectively communicate the truth to different audiences.

9

Narrative and the Picture
Theory of Theology

NARRATIVE, OR STORY, has been a major subject of interest for the last fifty years in the literature on exegesis and theological method.[1] Today, much enthusiasm remains for the concept, not only in discussions of theological method, but also in preaching and evangelism. The thrust is that the Bible is not a collection of theological propositions or moral maxims. It is a story, a narrative, about creation, fall, redemption, and the consummation of history. The story tells of the coming of God's kingdom, its anticipation, establishment, and growth throughout the earth.

We ourselves are part of the story, living between Jesus' ascension and his return. To listen to Scripture is not primarily to construct a theology, or even to obey commands (though such activities are legitimate), but to hear the story and place yourself into it.

This emphasis has brought excitement to theology and preaching for many students of Scripture. For that we may be thankful to God.

---

1. Hans Frei, *The Eclipse of Biblical Narrative* (New Haven, CT: Yale University Press, 1974), was perhaps the most influential single volume in this recent development. But in conservative Reformed circles, the "biblical theology" movement spearheaded in the United States by Geerhardus Vos has long emphasized the nature of Scripture as narrative, as "history of redemption." See, e.g., Geerhardus Vos, *Biblical Theology* (Grand Rapids: Eerdmans, 1948). More broadly, the idea that theology should focus on "history" in some way or other has been a commonplace of mainstream liberal theology since Albrecht Ritschl. Of course, many who have urged such a focus have differed greatly with Ritschl and with one another about how that history should be construed. Consider Harnack, Barth, Bultmann, Cullmann, Käsemann, Moltmann, Pannenberg.

It has also helped to make more central to believers those great events that accomplish our salvation from sin, for the center of the narrative is Jesus' incarnation, atoning death, resurrection, and ascension. It makes clear that the gospel declares the coming of the kingdom under the lordship of Christ. So it focuses on what is truly central. That, too, is commendable.

Many, however, have jumped on the narrative bandwagon in order to promote other kinds of theological agendas. (1) Some seem to think that if we accept Scripture as redemptive narrative, we no longer need to worry about whether Scripture is truthful, reliable, or inerrant. After all, we can profit from "stories" that are fictional, as the parables of Jesus attest.[2] (2) Some maintain that preaching should be simply a narration of redemptive history, without any moral "application." They think it is especially wrong to appeal to Bible characters as moral or spiritual examples. The role of these characters is merely to advance the narrative and nothing more. (3) Others, whatever they may think about the historicity of the story, insist that a narrative approach can serve as a replacement for traditional theology and ethics: don't pontificate, just narrate.

I address the first issue in my *DWG*. The narrative of Scripture is a story about human beings responding, obediently or disobediently, to the word of God, a word that speaks with absolute authority and that God has committed to writing in Scripture. So the narrative itself compels us to trust Scripture as the very Word of God. And trusting it as God's Word is incompatible with negative criticism.

The second issue I have discussed in a number of places. Scripture itself commends the characters of the narrative for our imitation, as positive or negative examples.[3]

2. N. T. Wright, in *LW* (see my review at http://www.frame-poythress.org), does not go this far. He insists against many that it is important to know "what really happened." But he does think the narrative character of Scripture renders it unsuitable for use as "a list of rules" or a "compendium of true doctrines," and he urges us to get beyond the "Bible wars." He seems to believe that if we understand Scripture in its narrative-kingdom context, we can ascend above the battles concerning biblical inerrancy. In the above-cited review, I take issue.

3. I have replied to the exclusion of "moral examples" (which these writers call *moralism*) in my *DCL*, 137–38, 290–97, and elsewhere.

In this essay, I would like to address the third issue. First, however, I will mention some background matters. In *DKG*,[4] I discussed the question whether a theology should have a particular "emphasis." Many theologies have emphasized a particular concept in Scripture: hope, faith, covenant, kingdom, community, grace, lordship, righteousness, crisis, Word of God, personal relationship, history, liberation, justice, glory, and so on. It is perfectly legitimate, often useful, to study such concepts in Scripture and to show how they are significantly related to others. It is problematic, however, when a theologian argues that his concept is *the* center of Scripture, and that it should be the governing principle for all other books of theology.[5]

The late Stanley Grenz, for example, wrote a one-volume theology stressing "community." The title was *Theology for the Community of God*.[6] He takes note of the fact that Scripture places great emphasis on community, from the relationships of the divine Trinity, to the families of the OT, to the body of Christ in the NT. Everything that happens is "in community," and all of the church's reflections on God are "in community." So Grenz develops his theology in a fairly standard way, but always inserting observations about "community." This is fine, often insightful. But I demur at Grenz's insistence that theology should always have the same emphasis that his own theology has. He says:

> The contemporary interest in "narrative" offers one helpful insight
> that points toward a more adequate understanding of theology. Nar-

4. *DKG*, 182–83.

5. More can be said about the very tendency to form theology around biblical *concepts* rather than biblical *teachings*. This tendency came about, I think, because of theological resistance to the idea of "propositional" revelation. It was thought that even if we doubt many of the assertions of Scripture, we can still gain theological content by appealing to biblical concepts. James Barr, in *The Semantics of Biblical Language* (London: Oxford University Press, 1961), debunked this notion, but theologians continue to appeal to biblical concepts of this and that, as though these concepts could be an alternative basis for theology. I reject the substitution of concepts for propositions. Still, I think it is often edifying to look at what the whole Bible says about hope, faith, kingdom, and so on, and that's what I would mean by a study of biblical concepts—a summary of biblical *teachings* on various subjects.

6. Nashville: Broadman and Holman, 1994.

rative thinkers remind us that we must view theology in terms of its relationship to the story of God's action in history. This seminal assertion carries important implications.

One ramification is that we can pursue the theological task only "from within"—only from the vantage point of the faith community in which we stand.[7]

He goes on to make some observations about how our very identity is formed within community, observations that I largely agree with. But note the argument: The narrative takes place within community; therefore, theology must make community its central concept, or one of its central concepts. In Grenz's volume, this requires that every subject refer to "community" in some way. In my judgment, these references in the book to "community" often seem labored and arbitrary. I am not, however, criticizing these specific references so much as the claim that this is *the* right way to do theology.

When you think about it, there are many, many concepts in the Bible that have at least equal claim to be "central." God himself, for one. His lordship. The Trinity. Jesus. Incarnation, atonement, resurrection. Any of those concepts that I placed in the earlier list (hope, faith, covenant, kingdom, and so on) can also provide the structural framework for theology. The issue regarding community is not whether it is central, or even whether building a theology from the perspective of community is legitimate. The question is why of all these central concepts we should choose "community" as our *pou sto*.

In fact, (1) all these concepts and many more can be found in Scripture and are legitimate areas of theological reflection. Scripture itself does not tell us that our reflection should focus on any one as opposed to the others. (2) Many of them can be taken as perspectives—vantage points by which to view the entire content of Scripture.[8] But using one as a perspective does not permit the theologian to deny the validity of

7. Ibid., 8.
8. See Vern S. Poythress, *Symphonic Theology* (Grand Rapids: Zondervan, 1987), also available at http://www.frame-poythress.org.

other perspectives. (3) Scripture itself is not the exposition of a single concept, but a complex set of writings that presents now one, now others, in the context of the history of redemption. So no theological exposition of a particular concept can claim to be following the example of Scripture itself. (4) Indeed, theology, because it is not Scripture, can in the nature of the case never have exactly the same emphasis of Scripture, nor should it try.

The same should be said about the frequent theological mantra[9] that concept A should never be discussed "in abstraction from" concept B. "In abstraction from" here is roughly synonymous with "in isolation from" or "without relationship to." Ironically, such language is itself very abstract. I take it, however, that "don't take A in abstraction from B" means, more or less, "when you talk about A, make sure that you emphasize B in the same context."

I call such arguments "anti-abstractionist" or "emphasis" arguments. In *DKG* I tried to show that such arguments rarely accomplish anything, for reasons noted above. Basically, Scripture does not require of us any particular emphasis as we expound it. Nobody would claim, for example, that the head-covering of women in 1 Corinthians 11 is a "central doctrine" or a "fundamental emphasis" of Scripture. But there can be no biblical objection to studying these head-coverings and trying to come to a better theological understanding of them. In this case, and in many others, the emphasis of the theologian *must* be very different from that of Scripture.

When you put it that way, the conclusion is obvious. Theology is not the Bible, and therefore it will inevitably have *different* emphases from Scripture. Indeed, to maintain precisely the same emphasis of Scripture, one would have to simply recite Scripture, from Genesis to Revelation, in the original languages! But such recitation is not theology. The very nature of theology opens to it the freedom to emphasize

9. For examples, see *DKG*, 169–78. I find this kind of language often in Barth, Van Til, Buber, Brunner, Ebeling, and many other modern theologians. In G. C. Berkouwer's doctrinal studies, it is a constant refrain. Berkouwer over and over again criticizes other theologians for seeing A "in abstraction from" B. Note references to Berkouwer in my "The Spirit and the Scriptures," in *Hermeneutics, Authority and Canon*, ed. Donald Carson and John Woodbridge (Grand Rapids: Zondervan, 1986), 217–35.

what Scripture does not emphasize and, indeed, not to emphasize (at times, at least) what Scripture does emphasize.

We are so accustomed to emphasizing that theology should conform to Scripture that we have virtually ignored the ways in which theology is different from Scripture. But both the similarities and differences are important. Indeed, I think it is unlikely that we will have a very clear idea of what it means for theology to be scriptural until we come to see how theology is different from the Bible.

How, then, is theology different from the Bible? It is, as I have argued elsewhere,[10] *application* of the Bible. Scripture is God's Word; theology is the application of that Word, by human beings, to all areas of human life. Theology is the *teaching* of the Bible, the *didache* or *didaskalia* commended in Paul's Pastoral Letters.

This consideration, then, brings us back to the third issue I listed concerning narrative: can narrative serve as a substitute for traditional theology or ethics? Or, to put it differently, should theology and ethics necessarily be done in the form of narrative, to imitate the structure of Scripture? Or at least, should theology always focus on the narrative as its central concern?

I do think it is possible to exaggerate, especially in such discussions, the extent to which Scripture itself is narratival in form. It is certainly not pure narrative, any more than it is theological propositions or ethical maxims. There is a narrative arc to Scripture, but there are also prophecy, psalms, wisdom literature, epistles, and apocalyptic, none of which is narrative in form, though they all reflect on the narrative in various ways.

But even if we grant that the main structure of Scripture is narrative, does this imply that theology must take narrative form or emphasize narrative, that it must "tell a story"?

I think not. Again, theology is not Scripture. It is a reflection upon Scripture, an application of Scripture to human questions, problems, and needs.

There is a parallel here to a development in the history of philosophy in the early twentieth century. Bertrand Russell and his pupil

10. *DKG*, 76–88. I revisit this argument in *DWG*'s chapter on "Theology."

Ludwig Wittgenstein developed a philosophy called *logical atomism*, which claimed that a perfect language would be a "picture" of the world.[11] This view was known as the "picture theory of meaning." But after Wittgenstein went through mighty labors trying to purify language so that it would "picture" the world, he determined that the task was impossible.[12]

Wittgenstein's later philosophy developed in a very different direction. In his *Philosophical Investigations*,[13] he argued that language has a great many purposes: not only stating facts (the closest thing to picturing the world), but also issuing commands, asking questions, promising, joking, cursing, and so forth. Language, even perfect language, whatever that might be, is not a picture of the world, but it is a way for human beings to get along in the world: to communicate with one another, to get things done.

I think some theologians (although they would never say this) imagine that theology at its best should be a picture of the Bible (or in some communions, the Bible plus tradition). That notion stands behind the idea that theology should have the same emphasis as Scripture, employ the same structure, be arranged around the same central doctrines. Nobody, of course, would admit to holding a "picture theory of theology." But I suspect that notion lies behind the claims about narrative, emphasis, and abstraction that I have been discussing.

And if we grant that theology is not Scripture, but the application of Scripture, the plausibility of such claims vanishes. We can emphasize anything that raises a genuine question or need. We can discuss biblical concepts, both "in relation to" one another and "in abstraction from" one another, as the need arises. We can put our theology into narrative form or not, as the need indicates. We can "focus on" the narrative or

11. The major document of this position is Ludwig Wittgenstein, *Tractatus Logico-Philosophicus* (London: Routledge and Kegan Paul, 1961–63). For a philosophical account, see J. O. Urmson, *Philosophical Analysis* (London: Oxford University Press, 1956).

12. Wittgenstein noted later that in one sense the task is easy, for anything can be a picture of anything given the right method of projection. But he insisted that when we move beyond this trivial sense, we can see that it is not the task of language to picture the world.

13. New York: Macmillan, 1953.

not, as the situation requires. And we can discuss these concepts in an order different from the Bible's own order.

The narratival understanding of Scripture itself, far from eliminating theology as I have described it, requires it. Theology shows us how to understand those aspects of narrative that perplex us. It asks why this event led to that event, how we should evaluate the actions of this or that character, whether there is regularity in the actions of God, and of what kind. Theology helps us precisely to understand and apply the narrative, to understand how the narrative applies to ourselves.

10

Focus

I WISH I HAD A NICKEL for every sermon I've heard in which the preacher told me to *focus* on something. Usually it is Jesus, but often other things, such as hope, love, joy, the Word of God, the atonement, the resurrection, the return of Christ, the things that are true, honorable, just, pure, lovely, commendable, and excellent (Phil. 4:8). The thought is that if I focus on these things, I will focus less on this world's goods, and on my worries, discouragements, and doubts.

My problem is that I don't quite understand what it means to *focus*. When I hear such an exhortation, I usually conjure up a mental picture of whatever my focus is supposed to be upon: often Jesus. But apart from the fact that my Reformed tradition is somewhat negative to mental pictures of Jesus, I'm never sure what the mental picture is supposed to do for me. It just stands there in my mind, and otherwise my life (including my attitudes and motivations) stays the same. In any case, I cannot sit there and gaze all day. I must use my mind for other things.

Maybe *focus* means to keep reminding myself of Jesus, the cross, the resurrection, and the like. That is sometimes a good devotional exercise. But there are so many different things to focus on. I honestly need to stop focusing on one in order to focus on the others. When I take my mind off one of them to think about another one, am I committing sin? What balance must I strike between remembering Jesus and remembering, say, the substitutionary character of the atonement? Don't tell me that that's a bad question because these are "involved in one another." That's a theologians' game. Yes, they are involved in one another, but we are now talking about a concrete practice, the practice of reminding ourselves of something. And even though all truths of the Bible are involved in one another, that doesn't help. In fact, that makes the exercise all the more difficult.

Maybe the exhortation to focus is an exhortation to *emphasize* one thing or another in our lives. The preacher is not telling us to keep imaging, or even to keep reminding ourselves, but to put more emphasis on living according to a certain truth. "Focus on God's generosity" means that we ought to be more generous ourselves, to think more often about our need to improve in that respect and Jesus' provision to make us more generous. That seems more to the point. But we run into the same problem: we cannot emphasize everything. There just isn't time and energy for us to devote ourselves to self-examination and repentance in every area that Scripture sets before us. Further, this emphasis isn't scriptural. Scripture itself doesn't emphasize everything everywhere. Its own emphasis changes from section to section, book to book, chapter to chapter, paragraph to paragraph.

I think that in the end, *focusing* just means, or should mean, to live your life consistently with your faith—in Jesus, in the hope of the gospel, in God's righteousness, in the atonement, and so on. Sometimes, of course, we need to be reminded of one thing more than others. That's why we preach sermons on different texts from week to week and apply them to different areas of life from time to time.

But if so, why confuse us with talk of focusing? Just tell us how to live. Tell us and show us how to live in accord with the truths of Scripture, how to bring our decisions into accord with the gospel.

Focus can sometimes be a convenient metaphor for such exhortations. It is close to the language of Hebrews 12:2, which tells us to "look unto Jesus." But the writer is aware of how much and how little he conveys by that expression. It is not an exhortation that could be followed apart from the practical context. To look to Jesus is to endure suffering, like the saints in Hebrews 11, looking forward to the kingdom that is to come. It is to patiently endure the Father's discipline, as the writer exhorts us to do in 12:3–11, and to live as he urges us in verses 12–17. *Focus* is a way of talking about motivations. People who "look to Jesus" may do the same things (e.g., philanthropy) as those who do not, but they will do them for different reasons. But looking to Jesus, then, is not an occasional or frequent devotional practice. It is a motivation of everything we do. And with that meaning, focusing on Jesus is no different from focusing on grace, joy, patience, love, and so on. For they are meaningless without him, and he motivates all of them.

PART 2

Theological Topics

11

Introduction to the Reformed Faith

WHEN I FIRST came to Westminster Theological Seminary[1] as a student (1961), the student body was largely Reformed in background. Many of the students had been trained in Calvinistic[2] schools and colleges; even more had studied the Reformed catechisms and confessions. Today, that is rarely the case. More and more, students have come to Westminster from non-Reformed backgrounds, or even from recent conversion experiences. And those from Reformed backgrounds don't always know their catechism very well.

Many Westminster students, when they first arrive, don't even understand clearly what Westminster's doctrinal position is. They know that Westminster maintains a strong view of biblical authority and inerrancy; they know that we hold to the fundamental doctrines of evangelical Christianity. And they know that we explain and defend these doctrines with superior scholarship. But they are sometimes not at all aware of the fact that Westminster is a *confessional* institution, that it adheres to a definite historic doctrinal tradition—the Reformed faith.

I am very happy to have all these students here! I am very pleased that Westminster is attracting students from far beyond our normal

---

1. When I wrote this essay, I was a professor at Westminster Theological Seminary. I now teach at Reformed Theological Seminary, Orlando, Florida. But I decided for this volume to leave the place references as they were.

2. In this essay, I will be using *Calvinistic* and *Reformed* synonymously.

confessional circles. But their presence necessitates some teaching at a fairly elementary level concerning the seminary's doctrinal position. It is essential that students be introduced to the Reformed faith early in their seminary career. That Reformed faith energizes and directs all the teaching here. Students must be ready for that. Hence this essay.

I also have another reason for providing this introduction: When you have begun your seminary study, you will come to see that there are a number of variations within the general Reformed tradition. You will learn about *hyper-Calvinism*, *theonomy*, *antinomianism*, *presup-positionalism*, *evidentialism*, *perspectivalism*, *traditionalism*, and so on—the various names we call ourselves and call each other. It will not always be easy to determine who is "truly Reformed" and who is not—or, more important, who is "truly biblical." In this essay, I would like to show you, at least, where I stand within the Reformed tradition, and to give you a bit of guidance, helping you to find your way through this maze.

This is, of course, only an "introduction" to the Reformed faith, rather than an in-depth analysis. The in-depth analysis is to be found in the entire Westminster curriculum. Particularly, the doctrinal points expounded here will be expounded at much greater length in your later courses in systematic theology and apologetics. Still, there are obvious advantages in your having a general overview at an early point in your studies. Together with this document, I suggest that you read the Westminster Confession of Faith and Larger and Shorter Catechisms, as well as the "Three Forms of Unity" of the continental European Reformed churches: the Belgic Confession, the Heidelberg Catechism, and the Canons of Dordt. These are wonderful summaries of the Reformed doctrinal position—thorough, concise, and precise. The Heidelberg is one of the great devotional works of all time. I also believe there is much to be gained from the opening summary of Reformed theology in Cornelius Van Til's *The Defense of the Faith*.[3]

3. Cornelius Van Til, *The Defense of the Faith*, abr. ed. (Nutley, NJ: Presbyterian and Reformed, 1975), 7–22.

Before I get to substantive doctrinal matters, allow me to address this question: "Why should we subscribe to any confession at all, besides the Bible?" This is a good question. In my heart, I wish there were no need for creeds or for the denominations that subscribe to them. Denominations are always to some extent the result of sin, of party spirit.[4] I wish that when someone asked me my religious affiliation, I could simply say "Christian," and that when someone asked me my religious beliefs, I could simply say, "The Bible."

Unfortunately, such simple answers are no longer sufficient. All sorts of people today claim to be Christians, and even Bible-believers, who are actually far from the kingdom of Christ. Liberals, cultists, and New Age syncretists abound. When you visit a neighbor, inviting him to church, he has a right to know what you believe. If you tell him that you are a Christian and believe the Bible, he has a right to ask the further question, "What do you (and your church) think the Bible teaches?" This is the question that creeds and confessions are designed to answer. A creed is simply a summary of an individual's or church's beliefs as to the teachings of Scripture. And there can be no objection, surely, to placing such a summary in writing for the convenience of members and inquirers.

Confessions are not Scripture, and they should not be treated as infallible or as ultimately normative. Indeed, I believe it is important that in a church fellowship it be possible to revise the creeds, and for that purpose, it must also be possible for members and officers to dissent from a creed within some limits. Otherwise, the creed will, practically speaking, be elevated to a position of authority equivalent to Scripture. A "strict" view of subscription in which ministers are never permitted to teach contrary to any detail of the creed might be seen as a way to protect the orthodoxy of the church. In my opinion, however, such a view is actually subversive of orthodoxy, because it is subversive of biblical authority and sufficiency. Under such a form of subscription, Scripture is not given the freedom to reform the church according to God's will.

---

4. See the condemnation of parties in 1 Corinthians 1–4. I expound this issue in my *Evangelical Reunion* (Grand Rapids: Baker, 1991).

But creeds themselves are perfectly legitimate—not only for churches and individuals, but even for seminaries such as Westminster. For seminaries, too, need to be able to tell supporters, students, and prospective students what kind of doctrine is taught in the curriculum.

The Reformed faith is a wonderful discovery for many Christians. I have heard many people testify that when they began to study Reformed theology, they saw for the first time that the Bible really made sense. In other forms of theology, there is a lot of artificial exegesis: implausible divisions of verses, rationalizing "hard passages," imposing extrascriptural schemes on the text. Reformed theology takes Scripture very naturally, as the authors (human and divine) evidently intended it to be taken. There are, of course, difficulties within the Reformed system as in others. But many people, when they begin to read the Bible under Reformed teaching, experience an enormous increase in comprehension and in confidence. The Word of God speaks to them in greater power and gives them a greater motivation toward holiness.

To be sure, many oppose the Reformed approach. Westminster does not require its students to have Reformed convictions, either when they enroll or when they graduate. Thus, you will have to make up your own mind. But my experience is that when Westminster students from non-Reformed backgrounds give the Reformed approach a fair shake, they generally find themselves embracing it. In my thirty-five-year association with Westminster, I can count on one hand the number of students who have, to my knowledge, graduated holding an Arminian position. That is not because the school pressures students to conform to its doctrinal position. Most of us professors will go out of our way to avoid doing that. It is rather that we will provide you the fullest possible opportunity to expose yourself to Reformed theology, and to compare it to non-Reformed theologies. When you complete that study, I believe that you will rejoice as we do in the Reformed faith.

What, then, is the Reformed faith? In what follows, I will argue that (1) the Reformed faith is evangelical, (2) the Reformed faith is predestinarian, and (3) the Reformed faith teaches the comprehensive covenant lordship of Jesus Christ.

The Reformed Faith Is Evangelical

It is often difficult for Bible-believing Protestant Christians to know what to call themselves. *Christian* itself, even *Bible-believing Christian*, can be too vague, even misleading (see discussion above). *Orthodox* suggests priests with beards. *Conservative* sounds like a political position or a temperamental stodginess rather than a religious conviction. *Fundamentalist* today is a reproach, suggesting anti-intellectualism, though it has in the past been applied to some very great Christian scholars.

I think the best term to describe all Bible-believing Protestant Christians is the term *evangelical*, though that term has also become somewhat ambiguous through history. It was used by the Lutheran Reformers to indicate the character of their movement, and to this day in continental Europe the word *evangelical* is more or less a synonym for *Lutheran*. In the English-speaking world, however, the predominant use of *evangelical* stems from the revivals of the "evangelical awakening" in the eighteenth century under the preaching of John Wesley, George Whitefield, and others. Wesley's theology was Arminian, Whitefield's Calvinist; so the evangelical movement itself had both Arminian and Calvinistic elements. Many denominations in the English-speaking world were profoundly influenced by this movement.

In the nineteenth century, many denominations that had earlier been influenced by the evangelical movement became liberal. It was not unusual to hear people such as the liberal Charles Briggs described as *evangelical*; *liberal evangelical* was not at that time considered an oxymoron. One still hears that phrase in reference to the English theological scene, though the usage is not consistent on that point. But in America, the term has since World War II been generally limited to theologically conservative positions. After that war, a number of conservative Christians came to the conclusion that *fundamentalism* was a discredited concept, and they adopted the term *evangelical* as a self-description, reverting to something like the eighteenth-century usage. Many of these, such as Carl F. H. Henry, Harold John Ockenga, and J. Howard Pew, were Calvinistic in theology; others were not. Thus, *evangelical* became an umbrella term, covering both Reformed and non-Reformed

Christians who held high views of Scripture and adhered to the "fundamentals of the faith."

Not all Reformed people have been willing to accept the label *evangelical*. For one thing, Reformed people have sometimes opposed revivalism, although some great revival preachers, such as Whitefield, have been Reformed. Thus, some Reformed people have been reluctant to accept a label that arose out of a revivalist context. For another thing, many Reformed people do not want to be joined to Arminians under a common label, believing that the differences between the two types of theology are too great. Thus, for some Calvinists, including Cornelius Van Til,[5] *evangelical* means "non-Reformed Protestant."

I reject this usage, despite the example of my mentor Van Til. That usage is unhistorical, because the word has, historically, included Calvinists. More important, it seems to me that we do need some term that unites Bible-believing Protestants, and the only label suitable for that purpose is *evangelical*.[6]

And in my view, the Reformed and the evangelicals are united on many significant doctrinal points, arguably on the most important ones. Thus, I maintain, the Reformed faith is evangelical.

What are the main beliefs of evangelical theology? An evangelical, in my definition, is one who professes historic Protestant theology. That includes the following beliefs:

1. God is one being in three distinct persons, infinitely wise, just, good, true, and powerful, the ultimate reality, exclusively deserving religious worship and unquestioning obedience, who made the world out of nothing.

2. Man, made in the image of God, willfully disobeyed God's command, and thereby became worthy of death. From that time

5. *A Christian Theory of Knowledge* (Nutley, NJ: Presbyterian and Reformed, 1969), 194 and elsewhere.

6. It is true that even in the United States, the lines dividing evangelicals from others have become blurred. Some have denied the total inerrancy of Scripture, while claiming to be evangelicals. In my view, this is inappropriate. Still, it seems to me that the term *evangelical* has not entirely outlived its usefulness, and I know of nothing better for my present purpose.

on, all human beings except Jesus Christ have been guilty of sin before God.

3. Jesus Christ, the eternal Son of God, became man. He was (literally, really) born of a virgin. He worked miracles. He fulfilled prophecy. He suffered and died for our sin, bearing its guilt and penalty. He was physically raised from the dead. He will come again (literally, physically) to gather his people and to judge the world.

4. Salvation from sin comes to us not by our good works, but by receiving the free gift of God by faith. Saving faith receives the sacrifice of Christ as *our* sacrifice, as our only basis for fellowship with God. And such saving faith inevitably motivates us to obedience.

5. Scripture is the Word of God, which makes us wise unto salvation.

6. Prayer is not mere meditation or self-improvement, but a genuine conversation with our Creator and Redeemer. In prayer we praise God, give thanks, ask forgiveness, and make requests that bring concrete changes in the world.

These statements might be called "the fundamentals of the faith." They represent the central biblical gospel, and on that gospel Reformed people are united with all other evangelicals. It hurts me when I hear Reformed people saying that "we have nothing in common with Arminians." In fact, we have the biblical gospel in common with them, and that is a great deal. I would certainly argue that Arminian theology is not consistent with that gospel. But I cannot doubt that most Arminians believe that gospel from the heart.

In this respect, Reformed people not only stand with their Arminian brothers and sisters in confessing biblical truth, but also stand with them against common corruptions of the faith. We stand with all evangelicals against secular humanism, the cults, the New Age movements, and the liberal traditions in theology. By *liberal* I mean any kind of theology that denies any of these "fundamentals." In this sense, I include as liberal not only the modernists of J. Gresham Machen's day,[7] but also the neoorthodox tradition (Barth and Brunner, the "new modernists" according to Van Til) and the more recent movements such as liberation theology, process theology, and pluralist theology. The more recent movements are often contrasted with liberalism, but just as I believe we need a term to describe all Bible-believing Protestants, so I believe we need a term to describe professing Christians who deny one or more of the fundamentals; and *liberalism* is the best term for that purpose.

Let me summarize some formulations typical of the liberal tradition in categories corresponding to statements 1–6 above:

1. God is "beyond personality," "beyond good and evil," and does not demand obedience or punish sin or answer prayer.

2. Sin is not disobedience to a law external to man, but alienation from others and from one's own true humanity.

3. Jesus was a man who was in various ways aligned with God. Literal miracles and resurrection are impossible, but they are symbolic of some higher reality.

4. Salvation comes not through the substitutionary sacrifice of Christ, or through faith in Christ as the exclusive way of salvation. Either all are saved or the "saved" are those who adhere to various ethical and political programs.

5. Scripture is a human writing, fallible and prone to error, that somehow communicates a divine message.

6. Prayer is essentially self-referential.

As we see the evangelical gospel in stark contrast to the liberal denial of that gospel, it is important that we take a clear stand. I would especially urge students who are starting their course of theological study to take these issues personally. This is the time when you must

---

7. See Machen's *Christianity and Liberalism* (Grand Rapids: Eerdmans, 1923), still the best account of the fundamental differences between the two ways of thinking.

be clear as to your own relation to God. Do you believe that the God of Scripture really exists? that he is the majestic Lord of heaven and earth? Do you believe that you are personally guilty of sin and deserve only his fierce anger and eternal punishment? Are you trusting in your own works (which may include church attendance, Christian service, intellectual correctness) to save you, or only in the perfect righteousness of Christ?

If you have never answered these sorts of questions, I implore you for Christ's sake to answer them now! Not everyone who comes to seminary is a believer in this sense. It is easy to deceive yourself when you have been going through the motions of the Christian life. As you study at seminary, it will become more and more difficult to go back to basics in this way. As you yourself become a theological expert, you may become proud of your achievement, and therefore impatient with anybody who suggests that you need to become as a little child and put your whole trust in the wisdom of another. "For by grace you have been saved through faith. And this is not your own doing; it is the gift of God, not a result of works, so that no one may boast" (Eph. 2:8–9).

The Reformed Faith Is Predestinarian

The term *Reformed*, for some reason, early became attached to the Swiss branch of the Reformation (Zwingli, Bucer, Bullinger, Calvin), and eventually became synonymous with *Calvinist*. The most controversial teaching of these men was their doctrine of predestination, and that is often seen as the chief distinctive of Reformed teaching over against other forms of evangelicalism. In 1618–19, an international Reformed synod meeting at Dordrecht (or Dordt) in the Netherlands was presented with five points summarizing the teachings of Jacob Arminius (*Arminianism*). In opposition to those, the synod adopted what have been called the *five points of Calvinism*, summarizing its doctrine of predestination. These points are popularly summarized by the initials of that fine Dutch flower, the TULIP: total depravity, unconditional election, limited atonement, irresistible grace, perseverance of the saints.

We should not look at the five points as a summary of the Reformed system of doctrine. At Dordt, the five topics were in effect selected by the Arminians, not the Calvinists. The five points are actually a summary of "what Arminians don't like about Calvinism," rather than a summary of Calvinism itself. They summarize not Calvinism as such, but the controversial aspects of Calvinism. I suspect that had the synod been asked for an actual summary of the Reformed faith, they would have structured it rather differently—more like the Belgic and Westminster confessions.

Controversial points are not necessarily the most fundamental concerns of a system. In the case of the Reformed faith, the doctrinal system is far more than five points; it is a comprehensive understanding of Scripture, and thus a comprehensive world and life view. I will try to summarize this system in the next section.

Here, however, I would like us to look briefly at the "five points." Although their centrality can be exaggerated, they are nevertheless certainly important, and often misunderstood. My treatment here will not begin to anticipate the detailed analyses of your later courses in systematic theology, but I trust that it will start you in the right direction. Let us look at each of the five in turn:

1. *Total depravity*: Although fallen persons are capable of externally good acts (acts that are good for society), they cannot do anything *really* good, that is, pleasing to God (Rom. 8:8). God, however, looks on the heart. And from his ultimate standpoint, fallen man has *no* goodness, in thought, word, or deed. Man is therefore incapable of contributing anything to his salvation.

2. *Unconditional election*: When God elects (chooses) people for salvation, therefore, he does not choose them because of anything in them. He doesn't choose them because of their own goodness, or even because he foresees they will believe, but simply out of his totally unmerited favor—out of grace (Eph. 2:8–9).

3. *Limited atonement*: This is the most controversial of the five, because of Bible passages *apparently* teaching that Christ died

for every individual. See, e.g., 2 Cor. 5:15; 1 Tim. 4:10; 1 John 2:2. There are "universal" dimensions of the atonement: (a) it is for all nations, (b) it is a re-creation of the entire human race, (c) it is universally offered, (d) it is the only means for *anyone* to be saved and thus the only salvation *for* all people, (e) its value is sufficient for all. Nevertheless, Christ was not the substitute for the sins of every person; if he were, everybody would be saved. For the atonement is powerful, efficacious. It does not merely make salvation possible; rather, it actually saves. When Christ "dies for" somebody, that person is saved. One of the apparently "universal atonement texts," 2 Corinthians 5:15, makes that point very clearly. Thus, Christ died only for those who are actually saved. The biblical concern here is more with the *efficacy* of the atonement than with its *limitation*; perhaps we should call it *efficacious atonement* rather than *limited atonement*, and, having then lost the TULIP, develop through genetic engineering a flower we could call the TUEIP. But of course, efficacy does imply limitation, so limitation is an important aspect of this doctrine.

4. *Irresistible grace*: Grace is not like a box of candy that you can send back if you don't want it. Grace is divine *favor*, an attitude of God's own heart. We cannot stop him from loving us, if he chooses to do so. Nor can we stop him from giving us blessings of salvation: regeneration, justification, adoption, sanctification, glorification. His purpose in us will certainly be fulfilled (Eph. 1:11; Phil. 1:6).

5. *Perseverance of the saints*: If you are born again by the Spirit of God, justified, adopted into God's family, you cannot lose your salvation. God will keep you (John 10:27–30; Rom. 8:28–29). *Perseverance* does not mean that once you profess Christ, you may sin all you please and still be saved. Many people have professed Christ hypocritically and have later renounced the Christian life. Those who apostatize, and do not return to embrace Christ from the heart, die in their sins. But if you have confessed Christ

from the heart, you will certainly persevere, for you will not
be dominated by sin (Rom. 6:14).

The Reformed Faith Teaches the Comprehensive Covenant Lordship of God

Let me now proceed to a more comprehensive summary of the
Reformed system of doctrine. What I will argue is this: the biblical
God is the "covenant Lord," and all his work in creation and salvation
is a working out of his covenant lordship. "God is covenant Lord,"
therefore, summarizes the biblical message. The Reformed faith can also
be summarized in this way: all the essential elements of the Reformed
faith can be seen as outworkings of God's covenant lordship. The fact
that covenant lordship is central to Scripture and also to Reformed
theology is a major argument in favor of Reformed theology as the best
formulation of scriptural teaching.

You will discover that *covenant* has been defined differently by
different theologians, even within the Reformed camp. But the following seems to me to capture the essential elements of the biblical
covenants between God and man. A covenant is a relationship between
a "Lord" and a people[8] whom he has sovereignly called to be his. The
people may be called the Lord's vassals or servants. He rules over them
by his power and law and brings upon them a unique blessing (or, in
some cases, a unique curse). To better understand covenant, therefore,
we must better understand lordship.

The Meaning of *Lordship*

Lord represents, first of all, the mysterious Hebrew term *YHWH*
(generally pronounced "Yahweh," sometimes found as *Jehovah* or Lᴏʀᴅ
in English translations). It is somehow related to the verb *to be*, as in
the *I ᴀᴍ* of Exodus 3:14 (note the presence of *YHWH* in v. 15). Besides
Exodus 3:12–15, several other passages in Scripture seem in some measure

8. Contrary to dispensationalism, Reformed theology teaches (following Scripture, in my
opinion) that there is only one people of God, embracing all of God's elect, receiving the same
blessings in Christ, the blessings promised to Abraham and his seed.

to be expounding the meaning of that mysterious name. See Ex. 6:1–8; chaps. 20, 33, 34; Lev. 18–19; Deut. 6:4ff.; Isa. 41:4; 43:10–13; 44:6; 48:12f. In the NT, Jesus takes the name *kurios*, a Greek term used to translate *YHWH* in the Greek OT. As he takes that name, he takes the *role* that Yahweh had in the OT as the Lord, the head of the covenant. In my mind, that is one of the most powerful Scripture proofs of the deity of Christ. Therefore, certain passages in the NT are also important to our understanding of the biblical concept of lordship, such as John 8:31–59; Romans 10:9; 1 Corinthians 12:3; Philippians 2:11.

In my lectures on the doctrine of God, I will examine these passages in some detail to show you how they combine to teach a certain concept of divine lordship. In this essay, however, I will merely present the conclusions of my study. But you will find it edifying to examine these passages, to see how the following concepts are interwoven through them.

My conclusion is that lordship in Scripture involves three aspects: control, authority, and presence.

(1) *Control*: The Lord is the One who is in total control of the world. When God redeems Israel from Egypt, he does it with a strong arm and mighty hand. He controls all the forces of nature to bring curses upon Egypt and to defeat the forces of the greatest totalitarian ruler of the time. See Ex. 3:8, 14, 20; 20:2; 33:19; 34:6; Isa. 41:4; 43:10–13; 44:6; 48:12f.

I have already expounded this biblical theme in connection with the doctrine of predestination. It should also be mentioned that not only salvation but also the entire course of nature and history is fully in God's control. Ephesians 1:11 and Romans 11:36 state this truth specifically, and many other passages of Scripture attribute various happenings to God's direction. That includes such details as the falling of the sparrows and the number of the hairs of our heads.

Sin and evil are also part of God's plan. This is very mysterious, and we must be cautious in our statements. Nevertheless, Scripture does ascribe human sins to God's purposes. See, e.g., Gen. 45:7; 50:20; 2 Sam. 24:1, 10 (cf. 1 Chron. 21:1); 1 Kings 22:19–23; Acts 2:23; 4:27–28; Rom. 1:24, 26, 28; 9:11–23.

How can we reconcile these facts with God's righteousness and
goodness? I have discussed this "problem of evil" in some detail in my
AGG, 149–90. I do not believe that we can fully understand God's reasons
for incorporating evil into his plan. Clearly, he does so for a purpose that
in the total context of history is a good purpose (Gen. 50:20). Beyond
that, it is best to emulate the silence of Job in the face of the mystery
of evil (Job 40:4–5; 42:1–6). Certainly we may not compromise God's
sovereignty by appealing to such ideas as the Arminian concept of *free
will*, that is, human acts that are not foreordained by God.[9]

Divine control does not, of course, imply that secondary causes,
human choices, and so forth are unimportant. God generally achieves his
great purposes by using finite agents. Thus, it is his purpose to spread
the gospel throughout the world not by miraculous revelation, but by
human preaching and teaching (Matt. 28:19ff.). And there is no salvation (at least among adults) without human faith and repentance (John
3:16; Acts 2:38). Those who argue on the basis of divine sovereignty
that evangelists should never call for "decisions" do not understand the
biblical balance. God's sovereignty does not negate secondary causes;
rather, it empowers them, gives them significance.

The God of Scripture is not a kind of abstract opposite to the
world, so that everything ascribed to him must be denied to creatures
and vice versa. Rather, God is a person, and he has created the world
according to his plan. Some divine prerogatives are denied to creatures,
such as God's right to exclusive religious worship and his right to do
as he pleases with human life. But most events in the world have both
divine and creaturely causes; the one does not annul the other. Both
Arminians and hyper-Calvinists err at this point.

(2) *Authority*: Authority is the right to be obeyed. The Lord
supremely has that right. When he speaks, his word must be followed.
Covenants always involve words, as we will see in our study of the
doctrine of the Word of God. The covenant Lord speaks to his covenant people concerning his holy name, his past blessings to them, his
requirements for their behavior, his promises and threats. The words are

9. There are, however, other concepts of free will that are fully biblical; see my *AGG*.

written in a document; and to violate the Lord's words in the written document is to violate the terms of the covenant itself.

When God comes to Moses in Egypt, he comes with an authoritative word for Israel and for Pharaoh—a word that they disobey at their peril. See Ex. 3:13–18; 20:2ff.; Lev. 18:2–5, 30; 19:37; Deut. 6:4–9; Luke 6:46ff. His authority is *absolute* in three senses: (a) He cannot be questioned (Job 40:1f.; Rom. 4:14–20; 9:20; Heb. 11). (b) His covenant transcends all other loyalties (Ex. 20:3; Deut. 6:4f.; Matt. 8:19–22; 10:34–38; Phil. 3:8). (c) His covenant authority covers all areas of human life (Exodus–Deuteronomy; Rom. 14:23; 1 Cor. 10:31; 2 Cor. 10:5; Col. 3:17, 23).

(3) *Presence*: The Lord is the One who takes a people to be his. He becomes their God, and they become his people. Thus, he is "with [them]" (Ex. 3:12). This presence of the Lord with his people is a wonderful theme that pervades the Scriptures (see Gen. 26:3; 28:15; 31:3; 46:4; Ex. 3:12; 33:14; Deut. 31:6, 8, 23; Judg. 6:16; Isa. 7:14; Jer. 31:33; Matt. 28:20; John 17:25; 1 Cor. 3:16ff.; Rev. 21:22).

Thus, Yahweh is *near* his people, unlike the gods of any other nation (Lev. 10:3; Deut. 4:7; 30:11–14 [Rom. 10:6–8]; Ps. 148:14; Jer. 31:33; Jonah 2:7; Eph. 2:17; Col. 1:27). He is literally "near" to Israel in the tabernacle and temple. Later he draws near in Jesus Christ, and in the Spirit. And in his omnipotence and omniscience, he is never far from anybody (Acts 17:27–28). For in one sense, the whole creation is bound to him by covenant.[10]

God's presence is a means of blessing, but it can also be a means of curse, when the people break the covenant. See Ex. 3:7–14; 6:1–8; 20:5, 7, 12; Ps. 135:13f.; Isa. 26:4–8; Hos. 12:4–9; 13:4ff.; Mal. 3:6; John 8:31–59.

I will refer to these three categories as the *lordship attributes*. They are not separable; each involves the other two. The Lord's control is exercised through his authoritative speech to the creation (Gen. 1); therefore, *control* involves *authority*. That control is comprehensive and thus amounts to a divine presence throughout creation. Similarly,

10. See Meredith G. Kline, *Images of the Spirit* (Grand Rapids: Baker, 1980).

each lordship attribute includes the other two. Each therefore presents not a "part" of God's lordship, but the whole of it, from one particular "perspective."[11]

The Centrality of Lordship in Scripture

Lᴏʀᴅ is the basic covenant name of God (Ex. 3:13–15; 6:1–8; John 8:58; Rom. 14:9). There are other names of God, but this is the name he bears as head of the covenant with his people. This is the name by which he wishes to be known by his covenant people.

It is found in the basic confessions of faith of God's people within Scripture. See Deut. 6:4ff.; Rom. 10:9; 1 Cor. 12:3; Phil. 2:11. The basic confession of the old covenant is "The Lord our God is one Lord." The basic confession of the new covenant is "Jesus Christ is Lord."[12]

All of God's mighty acts in creation and history are performed so that people may "know that I am the Lᴏʀᴅ" (Ex. 14:18; see also 1 Kings 8:43; Ps. 9:10; etc.). Again and again in Isaiah, the Lord announces that "I am the Lᴏʀᴅ; I am he" (e.g., Isa. 41:4; 43:10–13). The *I am*s recall Exodus 3:14.

The Centrality of Covenant Lordship in the Reformed Faith

The Reformed faith also emphasizes God's covenant lordship over his people. The concept of covenant was not used systematically by Calvin, though the idea, in particular the constituent ideas of control, authority, and presence, are quite prominent in his thought. It was natural that among Calvin's successors there was a very thorough development and application of the covenant idea, and that concept has been a major concern of Reformed theologians down to the present day.

(1) *Control*: Obviously, Reformed theology has emphasized God's control, which "works all things according to the counsel of his will"

---

11. Such "perspectival" relationships are common in Scripture, and I will introduce you to many others in your courses with me.

12. It should be obvious, then, that the Bible teaches "lordship salvation," as does the Reformed faith. Those are saved who confess Christ's lordship from the heart. This does not, of course, mean that those who confess Christ's lordship must be perfect from the start in their devotion to him. The *application* of Jesus' lordship to the Christian life is a process that is not complete until we get to heaven.

(Eph. 1:11). We have already expounded this emphasis in our discussion of predestination, and Reformed theology also emphasizes the sovereignty of God in creation and providence. With Scripture, it also maintains the importance of secondary causes. Hyper-Calvinists,[13] verging toward fatalism,[14] have sometimes denied the importance of creaturely decisions and activity; but this does not represent the main Reformed tradition.

(2) *Authority*: The Reformed have always stressed, more than most other branches of Christianity, that human beings are subject to God's law. Some professing Christians have said that law and grace, or law and love, are always opposed, so that Christians have nothing to do with the law. The Reformed recall, however, that if we love Jesus, we will keep his commandments (John 14:15, 21; 15:10; 1 John 2:3f.; 3:22f.; 5:2f.; 2 John 6; Rev. 12:17; 14:12). Of course, keeping the law does not bring us salvation. It does not justify us before God. Only the righteousness of Christ can do that. But those who are saved will keep God's commandments.

The Reformed have also stressed the continuing normativity of the OT law, specifically, over the NT believer (Matt. 5:17–20). There is a controversy in Reformed circles over *theonomy*, which is essentially a controversy over how the OT law is to be used in the Christian life.[15] Both theonomists and Reformed critics of theonomy agree that the OT law has an important, edifying, governing role in the Christian life; both parties also agree that some OT commandments are no longer literally binding because we now live in a different situation from that to which these commands were addressed. The argument is over which

13. It is hard to define hyper-Calvinism. Often I am inclined to say that a hyper-Calvinist is somebody who thinks I am not Calvinistic enough! But it is probably best to associate hyper-Calvinism with the historical tradition represented in the twentieth century especially by the teaching of Herman Hoeksema and the Protestant Reformed Church.

14. Fatalism is the view that "what will be will be" no matter what we do. Biblical Christianity is not fatalistic, because it teaches an orderly relation between first causes, second causes, and eventual results. God's plans will certainly be successful, but they will be successful because God will provide the finite means necessary. It is not the case, for example, that the elect will be saved apart from the preaching of the gospel.

15. See the Westminster Theological Seminary symposium *Theonomy: A Reformed Critique*, ed. William S. Barker and W. Robert Godfrey (Grand Rapids: Zondervan, 1990), especially my essay in that volume.

commands belong in which category. All Calvinists believe that the OT laws are the Word of God and profitable for "teaching, for reproof, for correction, and for training in righteousness, that the man of God may be competent, equipped for every good work" (2 Tim. 3:16–17).

Particularly in the area of worship, the Reformed have stressed the authority and sufficiency of God's Word. While Lutherans and Roman Catholics have argued that anything is permitted in worship that Scripture does not condemn, the Reformed maintain that nothing is permitted in worship that Scripture does not authorize. That is known as the *regulative principle of worship*. There have been some debates within Reformed circles as to the concrete implications of this principle. Some have argued that it requires the exclusive use of Psalms in worship and prohibits the use of musical instruments, soloists, and choirs. Others have argued that it requires a worship service modeled after the worship services used among the seventeenth-century Puritans. My own analysis is different.[16] I am not persuaded by the hermeneutics that has been used to reach these restrictive conclusions. And in line with the principles of the Reformation, I see the regulative principle essentially as a principle that grants to us *freedom* from human tradition, binding us only to the Word of God.

That raises an important point of a more general nature. Reformed theology is not only a theology of God's lordship, but also a theology of human freedom. Reformed theology rejects, of course, the Arminian concept of free will, discussed earlier. But it recognizes the importance of creaturely decisions, as we have already seen. And it also sets us free from bondage to human tyrannies, so that we may be slaves only of God himself. To be sure, God does ordain legitimate authorities among human beings, and he calls us to honor and obey those authorities. But when those authorities command something contrary to God's Word, or when they place their own ideas on the same level as Scripture, we may and must dishonor their claims. We must obey God rather than man. Hence, you can see that the covenant authority of God is not a burdensome doctrine. It is the most sublime liberation.

16. See my *Worship in Spirit and Truth* (Phillipsburg, NJ: P&R Publishing, 1996).

The Reformed faith, therefore, is not in essence "traditional-ist," although some Reformed people have had, in my estimation, an unhealthy reverence for tradition. There is a Reformed slogan *semper reformanda*, "always reforming." Hence, *fides reformata semper reformanda est*, "the Reformed faith is always reforming." There is some division in Reformed circles between some who emphasize *reformata* (Reformed) and others who emphasize *reformanda* (reforming). Both are important, and both should be kept in balance. Our faith should be *Reformed*, that is, in agreement with the fundamental principles of the Scriptures, as summarized in the Reformed confessions. But it should also be *reforming*, seeking to bring our thought and practice *more* in line with Scripture, even if that process requires the elimination of some traditions. The Reformers were both: conservative in their adherence to biblical doc-trine, radical in their critique of church tradition. We ought to do the same. Beware, therefore, of people who tell you that you must worship, or think, or behave, in accord with some historical tradition. Prove all things by God's Word (1 Thess. 5:21). Search the Scriptures daily to see if what you hear is really true (Acts 17:11).

Because the Reformed faith has, at its best, been critical of human traditions even within its own circles, the Reformed faith has the resources for effective *contextualization*. Contextualization is the attempt to present scriptural truth in terms understandable to cultures different from our own and different from the culture in which the Scriptures were written. Reformed preaching has been remarkably suc-cessful through history in the work of contextualization. Calvinism has profoundly affected cultures very different from the Swiss culture in which it began: Dutch, German, British, Hungarian, Korean. Calvinism had large followings in France and Italy until it was largely snuffed out there by force.

It is, therefore, entirely Reformed to say as I do in *DKG* that theol-ogy is the application of scriptural truth to human situations. Progress in theology is the continual *application* of Scripture to new situations and contexts as they arise. It is not the mere repetition of doctrinal for-mulations worked out in past generations, as some traditionalists might suppose. Rather, the work of theology engages our creativity, without compromising the authority and sufficiency of Scripture.

Calvinism has been a very "progressive" kind of theology. Reformed theology, typically, has not simply reiterated the statements of Calvin and the confessions. It has gone on to develop new applications of Scripture and Reformed doctrine. In the seventeenth century, there was a significant development in Reformed thinking about God's covenants. In the eighteenth-century thinker Jonathan Edwards, there is new teaching on the subjective dimensions of the Christian life. In the nineteenth and early twentieth centuries, there was the remarkable development, under Geerhardus Vos and others, of *biblical theology*, the analysis of Scripture as a history of redemption. In the twentieth century there was Van Til's apologetics and Meredith Kline's *Structure of Biblical Authority*.[17]

The work of *reforming* under God's authority is not limited, either, to theology and the church. Calvinists have often emphasized the "cultural mandate" of Genesis 1:28–30, that God commands the human race to take dominion of all the earth in his name. This means that all spheres of human life must be reformed by the Word of God. Abraham Kuyper, the great Dutch genius who made enormous contributions to theology, philosophy, journalism, education, and politics, argued that there should be distinctively Christian politics, art, and literature, as well as theology.[18] God's Word governs all areas of life (Rom. 14:23; 1 Cor. 10:31; 2 Cor. 10:5; Col. 3:17, 23). Thus, Reformed people have stressed the need for distinctively Christian schools, labor movements, businesses, universities, philosophy, science, political movements, economic systems.

Understandably, then, Reformed theology is concerned not only about individual salvation and piety (see below), but also about the structures of society. *Covenant*, after all, has to do with corporate relations to God more than merely individual ones.[19] In covenant, God chooses a *people*. And Scripture makes it clear that God chooses households,

17. Grand Rapids: Eerdmans, 1972.

18. See his *Lectures on Calvinism* (Grand Rapids: Eerdmans, 1931), a wonderfully moving, challenging, life-transforming book, which every Christian should read.

19. Although there are certainly individual aspects to salvation and the Christian life: God calls on individuals to repent and believe.

families. Therefore, Calvinists have typically believed in infant baptism. Infant baptism says that when God claims a parent, he claims the whole household to be his (Acts 11:14; 16:15, 31–34; 18:8; 1 Cor. 1:16).

Considering the doctrine of divine authority helps us to see from another direction[20] the relationship between divine sovereignty and human responsibility. Human beings are responsible because they are subject to God's commands. Therefore, Reformed teachers do not present human responsibility as some grudging concession to Arminianism. Rather, they *emphasize* human responsibility and *rejoice* in it. Human responsibility is a *Calvinistic* doctrine. It presupposes the meaningful structure of God's sovereign plan and the normative authority of God's sovereign law.[21]

Historically, people have sometimes wondered why Calvinists, believing as they do in the sovereignty of God, do not take a passive attitude toward life. In fact, Calvinists have been hard workers, zealous missionaries, eager to transform themselves and society into God's image. This remarkable energy is not a contradiction of their belief in divine sovereignty, but an implication of it. Calvinists serve a Lord who calls us to the utmost effort in his service. The results are in his hands, but we have the privilege of serving him in the greatest of tasks, that of bringing all of life captive to Christ.

(3) *Presence*: Reformed theology at its best has been profoundly devotional, aware of the intimate closeness of God to us at every moment of life. Of course, some Reformed thinkers have been, by their own profession, "intellectualist," and have disparaged any Christian concern with human subjectivity or inwardness. But that intellectualism does not, in my opinion, represent the best or the most typical Reformed mentality. Calvin began his *Institutes of the Christian Religion* by saying that the knowledge of God and the knowledge of self are interrelated,

---

20. We have already mentioned the *importance* of human decisions and actions within God's overall plan.

21. Arminian *responsibility* amounts to the power of the human will to perform uncaused events. But uncaused events are accidental, possibly bizarre, events without any connection to a preordained rational structure. Performing actions that are sheer accidents is hardly "responsible." Further, responsibility in Scripture is always responsibility to God, not oneself. Therefore, it presupposes God's law.

and "I know not which comes first." He was aware that since we are made in God's image, we cannot rightly know ourselves without knowing God at the same time. God is, in other words, found in every corner of human life, including the subjective. Calvin also insisted that the truths of God's Word be written deeply on the heart, rather than merely "flitting about in the head."[22] His emblem shows a heart in a hand, extended to God, with the inscription, "My heart I give you, promptly and sincerely."

Thus, Reformed people have spoken of living all of life *coram Deo*, in the presence of God. This intense sense of God's reality encourages a rich piety, as well as energetic obedience in all areas of life.[23]

Conclusion

You can see that the Reformed faith is exceedingly rich! Understandably, there have been controversies among Reformed people, some of which I have mentioned here. There have also been many different emphases among Reformed theologians and churches. Some have put more focus on the "five points," the "doctrines of grace." This emphasis is especially prominent among Reformed Baptists, but is found in other circles as well. Others (theonomists) have focused on the authority of God's law. Still others (Kuyperians, Dooyeweerdians) have emphasized the application of God's truth to social structures.

Nicholas Wolterstorff and others have suggested a way of distinguishing various theological mentalities within the Reformed churches (especially those of Dutch background). They speak of *piets*, *Kuyps*,

22. Calvin, therefore, is the source of the *head/heart* contrast that is so often belittled by Reformed "intellectualists." Calvin does not, nor would I, advocate an *anti*-intellectualism. The "heart" in Scripture is a heart that thinks. But there is a kind of intellectual knowledge that is accepted superficially, a knowledge that doesn't actually *rule* one's life. That is not the knowledge that Calvin and Scripture would urge upon us.

23. The Reformed attitude toward revivalism is somewhat divided. W. Andrew Hoffecker in his *Piety and the Princeton Theologians* (Grand Rapids: Baker, 1981) argues that the professors at Old Princeton were much influenced by revival and were, along with their intellectual emphasis, aware of the need for a deep subjective relation between the believer and God. See also Jonathan Edwards, *Religious Affections* (New Haven, CT: Yale University Press, 1959). Some Reformed thinkers, especially in more recent years, have been opposed to talk of "emotions" and "subjectivity" in the Christian life. But as I said earlier, I think this pattern of thought does not represent Reformed theology at its best.

and *docts*. The piets, somewhat influenced by pietism, seek above all a deeper personal relation to Christ. The docts are concerned above all with maintaining theological orthodoxy. The Kuyps are concerned to bring great changes in society.[24]

It seems to me that there is room in the Reformed movement for all these different emphases. None of us can maintain a perfect balance of emphasis. And different situations require of us different emphases, as we "contextualize" our theology to bring God's Word to bear on the situations we are in. Also, God gives different gifts to different people. Not all are gifted in the area of political action, or in the formulation of doctrines with precision, or in personal evangelism. We all do what we can do, and we do what seems most to need doing in a situation. Within the boundaries of the Reformed faith sketched here, we should be thankful for the different emphases, not critical of them. The different emphases supplement one another and complete one another.

---

24. In my terminology, these three movements are *existential*, *normative*, and *situational*, respectively.

12

Reformed and Evangelicals Together

THIS ESSAY IS SOMEWHAT "in house," contrary to my usual custom. I speak here as a Reformed theologian, mainly to people in Reformed churches, though I certainly do not forbid people from outside those churches to listen in. There are some in my circles, to be sure, who do not believe I am "truly Reformed." My paper trail is long enough for readers to make their own judgment about that. Otherwise, I will not interact with that group of detractors in this piece. My self-image is that indeed I am Reformed. I treasure the doctrines of God's sovereign grace. I don't believe in the inerrancy of Reformed confessions, theologians, or churches. But I believe that in its theological formulations, the Reformed tradition has, better than any other, accurately set forth the teaching of Scripture.

I am also an evangelical. How *evangelical* and *Reformed* relate to each other is one of the concerns of this essay. But first, a bit more about myself.

Some Autobiography

I first trusted Christ as my Lord and Savior at around thirteen years of age. The church I attended, Beverly Heights in Pittsburgh, was Presbyterian by denomination and tradition, evangelical in its respect for the Bible and in its desire to bring people to trust in Christ. But its ministry was not theologically intensive. As I grew up, it did not seem to me that there was much difference between the theology of my church and that of other churches in the area: Lutheran, Methodist, Episcopal.[1] When I left home for college, I had the impression from the church's teaching that almost any Protestant church would proclaim the same gospel I had heard as a teenager.

That impression was mistaken. The churches around Princeton University, where I studied, even the Presbyterian ones, were in various ways and degrees "liberal," denying the authority of Scripture, the supernatural events of redemption, and the necessity of faith in Jesus' blood sacrifice. Of the churches I visited initially, none of them preached the gospel that I remembered from Beverly Heights. And, not coincidentally, none of them encouraged the kind of vital love for Christ and the Christ-centered fellowship that I had known in my home church.

Through that experience, I first became doctrinally aware. Eventually God led me to a campus group, the Princeton Evangelical Fellowship, and a church in Princeton, the Westerly Road Church, that rejected emphatically the liberalism of the other Princeton churches and embraced the biblical gospel of Jesus Christ. The people at PEF and WRC were not Presbyterians for the most part, but they preserved what I believed was most important in the Christianity of Beverly Heights. So at that point in my life I happily adopted the label preferred by those believers, *evangelical*.

My years at Princeton were a time of great spiritual growth. My knowledge of Scripture grew by leaps and bounds. My Christian friends and I often prayed daily in dorm rooms and tried to bring the gospel to fellow students. We corresponded with missionaries and tried to grow in personal holiness.

But I wanted to learn more than just the basics of theology. Although Beverly Heights was not theologically focused, I had the impression from them (and especially through the teaching of Prof. John Gerstner of Pittsburgh Theological Seminary) that the Reformed system of doctrine was the closest to the Scriptures. And I learned that of all the

---

1. Later I learned that I was wrong. There were indeed significant differences between my church and the other churches. But my church did not stress those differences in its teaching ministry, at least so that a thirteen-year-old could understand them.

seminaries available, Westminster in Philadelphia offered the most thorough, rigorous, and scholarly training in Reformed theology. So I studied at Westminster from 1961–64, an evangelical seeking to learn the ways of the Reformed community. My teachers were, on the whole, first-rate in their scholarship, in the clarity and thoroughness of their teaching, and in their personal piety.

I came also to admire many of my fellow students at Westminster. But the community was somewhat divided. The two main parties were the "fundamentalists" (or "fundies") and the "truly Reformed" (or "TRs"). The fundies liked to gather for prayer and to do evangelism in the community. They talked of missions and wanting to see people come to know Jesus. The TRs wanted mainly to see people embrace Calvinism. Of course, there was no exclusivity here. Both parties acknowledged the truth of Calvinist doctrine, and both parties acknowledged the Great Commission. But the differences in emphasis were rather stark. The fundies emphasized knowledge of the Bible, the TRs knowledge of the Reformed tradition.

History carried a lot of weight. TRs despised the altar call. Fundies did not see anything wrong with it. When asked the reason for their disapproval, TRs would typically say that the altar call had been invented by Charles Finney, who was strongly Arminian or worse, and that to invite people to "come forward" was to appeal to their will apart from divine sovereignty. But we fundies never understood why Finney, or opposition to Finney, should govern our evangelistic practice, and we couldn't understand where Scripture forbade inviting people to confess faith or to inquire further about the gospel. And we couldn't understand the apparent premise of the TR argument, that divine sovereignty excludes the necessity or importance of human decision.

I was early classified as a fundie, but perhaps most of my close friends were TRs. They appreciated my scholarly-philosophical bent, and they spent much time with me discussing the fine points of Reformed theology and history. That I didn't care too much about Reformed history didn't seem to bother them, though it may have perplexed them. They seemed to believe that the Bible was not a sufficient intellectual challenge, and that one should move on to levels of expertise in Calvin,

Turretin, Ursinus, Voetius, Owen, and the like. Certainly one with scholarly inclinations should have the same motivation. But I did not. And they seemed to think that if one is to embrace the doctrines of divine sovereignty associated with Calvinism, he should also be enthusiastic about the history of the movement. But I was not. I was thankful for the providence of God in the history of the Reformed churches, but I saw that same providence in other theological and denominational traditions. And although I certainly believed that the Reformed tradition had the best theology, I was not convinced that overall it had the best churches.

The TRs thought it important to adopt the Reformed faith not as a few doctrines, but as a whole historical tradition. In time I was convinced of the doctrines distinctive to the Reformed faith, but only as an accurate way of expounding the gospel of grace from the Bible.

Some History

The division in the student body was illumined as we studied the historical relationships between Calvinism and evangelicalism. The term *evangelical*, though used in the medieval period, was during the Reformation period associated with Luther and his followers. From the etymology of the words, there is no good reason why *evangelical* was associated with Lutherans and *Reformed* with Calvinists; it could as easily have been the other way around. But to this day in Europe, *Evangelical* is found in the names of Lutheran churches.

The history of *evangelical* in America and Britain, however, is somewhat different from its history on the continent of Europe. In the English-speaking world, *evangelical* refers to the eighteenth-century revivals under the preaching of John Wesley and George Whitefield. In these movements, Lutheranism did play some role. Wesley in particular was moved by writings of Luther as well as by Moravian piety. But in time British and American evangelicalism became a movement unto itself. It represented Christian orthodoxy as over against liberalism, but also a concern with individual conversion and a personal experience of God.

In the fundamentalist/modernist controversy in the early twentieth century, the fundamentalists preferred to be called *evangelicals*.

So *evangelical vs. liberal* became the fundamental division within Protestantism. This is not to say that the old divisions between Reformed,
Lutheran, Methodist, Baptist, and Anglican were now irrelevant, but
that there was a more fundamental division, between evangelicals in
all these traditions and liberals in all these traditions.

Within evangelical ranks there were, for example, both Calvinists
and Arminians. That subdivision, indeed, goes back to the evangelical
revivals of the eighteenth century. Wesley was Arminian, Whitefield
Calvinist.

For both these parties to labor together under the *evangelical* label
hasn't always been easy. One hears at times of evangelical organizations (Calvary Chapel is one example) expelling strong Calvinists from
their membership. On the other hand, some Calvinists have argued that
Reformed Christians should be separate from evangelicals. Cornelius
Van Til, my revered mentor in matters of apologetics and philosophy,
wrote this:

> On these questions [i.e., about the sovereignty of God—JF] there
> are two answers given among Protestants. The first answer is that
> of evangelicalism. By this term we would indicate those who hold to
> either the Lutheran or the Arminian view of the human will. The
> evangelical view of the human will is that it does have some measure
> of ultimate power of its own over against the overtures of the gospel
> as presented in Scripture.[2]

Van Til here presents evangelicalism as completely distinct from Calvinism, in effect not recognizing any Whitefieldian influence in the movement, and as if it were united in holding to Wesley's view of free will. So
Van Til often said that the Reformed faith was "isolated" in the modern
theological discussion. My TR friends in the Westminster student body
agreed with Van Til. I agreed with Van Til that one must choose between
Whitefield's and Wesley's views of the will, but I couldn't appreciate the
implication that Reformed and evangelical have nothing in common.

2. Cornelius Van Til, *A Christian Theory of Knowledge* (Nutley, NJ: Presbyterian and
Reformed, 1969), 194. "Some measure of ultimate power" is a rather curious phrase, but I digress.

In the PEF at Princeton, Calvinists and Arminians prayed together, evangelized together, worshiped together, fellowshiped together. If we disagreed on some teachings of Scripture, we accepted that disagreement as a symptom of our finitude and sin. Sometimes we joked about our differences—such familiar gags as: "Oh, of course you Arminians are wrong; you were predestined to be." Nobody tried to break fellowship with anyone else over these differences. We agreed that Jesus is Lord, and that everyone needs to trust Jesus as Lord and Savior. That was the profoundest level of agreement, and it was certainly sufficient for us as a test of fellowship. And I've often wondered since why Calvinists and Arminians cannot get along to the same degree in a seminary student body—or in a church.

But at Westminster very few students, if any, were serious Arminians. Those who argued Arminian positions generally did it in a devil's-advocate mode. Nobody there seriously argued that Reformed churches should welcome Arminians as officers or pastors. Rather, the argument was over whether the Calvinistic, Whitefieldian branch of evangelicalism should be considered truly Reformed.

Often the debates concerned the cultural trappings of Arminianism: the altar call, the popular choruses, the tent meetings, TV evangelism. That is, the argument was about *traditions*. The TRs thought Reformed Christians should be radically separate from any of the cultural trappings of Arminian evangelicalism. We fundies (whom I will henceforth call *evangelicals*) thought otherwise.

It sometimes seemed as if the TRs governed their thought and behavior on the principle that they should be as unlike the evangelicals as possible. A kind of *via negativa*. If the evangelicals favored mass evangelism, the TRs opposed it—and one of their main arguments was that the evangelicals favored it.[3] If evangelicals held a prayer meeting, many TRs would stay away, claiming that this was a "pietistic"[4] practice.

D. James Kennedy worked very hard to develop a method of evangelism that would be compatible with Reformed theology. The result

3. A genetic fallacy, of course.
4. Another genetic fallacy. Of course, "pietism" was a major charge against the evangelicals.

was known as "Evangelism Explosion" and was very successful after 1970. But a number of TRs criticized EE because it called on inquirers to make "decisions." That was bad, they thought, because Finney had done the same, as did Billy Graham.[5] My own view is that the TR view was a misunderstanding of Reformed theology. Scripture does call us to make a definite commitment to Christ, and nothing in that requirement is contrary to the sovereignty of God. And Scripture does not forbid—rather, it encourages—visible expressions of that commitment.

It sometimes seemed that anytime evangelicals seemed to be successful at something, the TRs were there to detract. When thousands of people came forward at a Billy Graham meeting to make what were first called *decisions* and later *inquiries*, TRs complained that mass evangelism of this sort was somehow wrong.

When Bruce Wilkinson's *Prayer of Jabez* became a best seller, a number of TRs produced books and articles to tell us why we should never ever pray the prayer of Jabez. I did not find their arguments biblical or cogent.

When Rick Warren's *The Purpose Driven Life* sold over 30 million copies, presenting the arguably Reformed thesis that "there are no accidents—God planned everything and everyone,"[6] the TRs were there to show how Warren's book did not teach the true gospel.

When a number of churches adopted new songs and instruments to use in worship, the TRs disapproved. They presented some arguments dealing with the broad values they thought should be incorporated into worship, but I confess that I could not discern any biblical warrant for their objections.[7]

Sometimes in retrospect the ironies are amusing. In the 1960s and early 1970s at Westminster, TRs criticized evangelicals because evangelicals were interested only in saving souls. Supposedly, evangelicals cared nothing about society; the gospel was only "fire insurance."

---

5. Still another genetic fallacy. The genetic fallacy became the theological method of choice for many of the TRs.

6. From the summary at http://www.amazon.com.

7. See my *Contemporary Worship Music: A Biblical Defense* (Phillipsburg, NJ: P&R Publishing, 1997).

The reason was that they were not truly Reformed and therefore did not have a "full orbed[8] world and life view." The evangelicals, said the TRs, lacked the vision of Abraham Kuyper and Herman Bavinck. But in the late 1970s and '80s, Jerry Falwell, Pat Robertson, and others (possibly under the influence of Francis Schaeffer and other Reformed thinkers) decided that evangelicals ought to have a greater concern for government, the arts and culture, abortion, poverty, and other pressing issues. One might have hoped that the TRs would have congratulated the evangelicals on gaining this insight that they had had all along. But instead, thinkers such as Meredith Kline, Michael Horton, and Darryl Hart emerged, saying that all this interest in politics was precisely contrary to the Reformed faith. The true Reformed faith, they argued, was entirely concerned with law and gospel, not with culture, society, or government.[9] So when the evangelicals turned in one direction, the TRs (who prided themselves on their historical consistency) turned in the other. One imagines that if there were a movement among evangelicals to wear blue socks, the Reformed would argue the necessity of wearing any color other than blue.

But all of this shows the extent to which tradition played a leading role in the discussion. Whatever the opposite tradition preferred had to be wrong, simply because they preferred it. The Reformed and the evangelicals followed a pattern we know well from politics (the Republicans and the Democrats) and other fields (the Yankees and the Red Sox). And we need to remind ourselves that tradition is not the final rule of Protestantism. The Reformers taught *sola Scriptura*, the doctrine that Scripture alone has final authority. This means that every tradition must submit to the critical scrutiny of the Word of God.[10]

The Case for Reformed Evangelicalism

In my view, the Reformed and the evangelical traditions need each other. From the Reformed, evangelicals can and should gain more

8. I don't know if I've ever heard the term *full orbed* except in discussions of this issue.

9. See my book *The Escondido Theology* (Lakeland, FL: Whitefield Publishers, 2011).

10. See my essay "Traditionalism," Appendix P of my *DWG*, also available at http://www.frame-poythress.org/frame_articles/1999Traditionalism.htm.

theological acuity. I do not believe that the movement is committed to
Arminianism to the extent that the quote from Van Til above suggests.
From my experience, I would not be surprised if a majority of evangelical pastors were biblical Calvinists. But certainly those who primarily
designate themselves evangelicals do not usually have the theological
sophistication of those who designate themselves Reformed. They can
learn a more comprehensive and precise theology from Reformed men-
tors, if there can be less pride on both sides.

But the Reformed can also learn from evangelicals. In 1998 I had an
online debate with Darryl Hart, a historian and prolific author within
what I have been calling the TR camp. The debate was originally over
worship, but it spilled into other areas. As the debate progressed, Hart
consistently defended the Reformed tradition, even suggesting that all
truth of religious value could be found within the Reformed tradition.
I indicated to the contrary, that there were a number of things that the
Reformed could learn from other traditions. At the end of the debate, the
moderator, Andy Webb, asked me if I would enumerate some of those.
Here is how that exchange went. I have updated a few of the references.[11]

> WEBB: Dr. Frame, you wrote "Shouldn't our bias include the proposi-
> tion that God has, most likely, not given all the truth to one tradition
> or perfectly preserved any tradition from error? Shouldn't we assume
> that if there are gifts of the Spirit in non-Reformed Christians, these
> brothers might have important things to teach us?"
>
> I'm wondering if you can cite a few examples of the important things
> (specifically doctrinal things, seeing that you used the words "impor-
> tant" and "gifts of the Spirit") that our brothers in non-Reformed
> traditions like Pentecostalism or Wesleyan Methodism might have
> to teach us?
>
> FRAME: As I said to Hart, I somewhat share his bias in favor of
> the Reformed tradition. So I don't expect to learn a whole LOT of
> things from non-Reformed people, but I do think it's important to
> keep open and to be teachable.

11. The whole original debate can be found at http://www.frame-poythress.org/frame_
articles/1998HartDebate.htm.

By the way, I do not draw the equation implicit in your question between "important" and "doctrinal." That is itself a kind of Reformed prejudice that I think should be challenged. Beliefs are not more important than actions from God's perspective. Nor should we see the "gifts of the Spirit" as having primarily a doctrinal rather than a practical function. The teaching office teaches actions as well as beliefs.

But I will mention some issues that involve both beliefs and actions in varying mixes:

1. I do think that American conservative Reformed churches in recent years have not been very strong in evangelism. There has been all too little practice of it, and the theological reflection about it has been mainly negative: "don't do what the Arminians do, especially Finney." Jack Miller, Presbyterian Evangelistic Fellowship, and Evangelism Explosion represent a few encouraging signs in this respect.

2. Reformed churches, in my experience, have done a very poor job of discipling adults who are new converts or who come from non-Reformed backgrounds. People like this typically have huge problems in their past, and often they haven't a clue about how to study the Scriptures, raise their kids, develop godly habits. Often the big evangelical churches are better than we are at discipling, in my view.

3. I would also say that Reformed Christianity is rather narrow in its appeal today. We seem only to be able to reach people of the white middle-to-upper class, people with some college education. We have not reached minorities, the poor, the uneducated. That should be a special concern, because in Scripture the church is ethnically and socially universal, and it has a special concern for the poor. Again, there are a few exceptions to this general rule: Center for Urban Theological Studies in Philadelphia, books of George Grant and others. But I still don't see us on the whole making much of an impact. Groups like the Salvation Army and Victory Outreach have much thinner messages than we, but they have done far more good in poor communities. We can learn from them.[12]

4. For all our Kuyperian talk about bringing the Word to bear on all areas of human life, we have not addressed issues in our society

12. Later I wrote an essay called "Minorities and the Reformed Churches," http://www.frame-poythress.org/frame_articles/2003Minorities.htm, which I revised somewhat for inclusion in my *DCL*.

very often or very effectively. The strongest Christian movements influencing public discussions in politics, ethics, etc. are Charismatic (Christian Coalition, Robertson), Fundamentalist (Falwell, Dobson, Bauer, et al), Roman Catholic, Lutherans (Wurmbrand et al) and Anabaptist (Sider and others). These leaders are sometimes dependent on Reformed scholarship, but the Reformed haven't followed up on their insights. One bright spot: *World Magazine*. We need to learn from Christians outside our tradition in the practical work of communicating our ideas to the public.

5. Part of the problem in all these areas is that Reformed Christianity has been too intellectual in its emphasis. Zwingli actually eliminated music from the worship service and turned the service exclusively into a teaching meeting. Other Reformers did not follow Zwingli's lead in this connection, but they were all very scholarly people, and they put a great emphasis on learning as a necessity for pastors. So many Reformed people have taught the "primacy of the intellect," the notion that God's truth always enters (and should enter) us by the intellect, before it affects the will and the emotions. Van Til differed with Gordon Clark on this, and I follow Van Til's lead. Not only does the intellect affect the will, but the reverse is also true: the will often directs the intellect, as when the unbeliever suppresses the truth. Among intellect, emotions and will, none is higher than the others. All of these fell together in Adam's transgression; all are redeemed together in Christ. That is to say that our sin, salvation, decisions and knowledge pertain to the whole person, not to isolated faculties.

So I think we need to put much more emphasis on will and emotion in our preaching and worship. In these respects, we need to be much more like Scripture itself. In my view, the charismatics err on the other side, but we can learn from them. And we should be less shy about appealing to the will. Scripture calls on people to make commitments, decisions if you will. In Scripture, God pleads with sinners. We, however, tend to just state the truth and wait to see how people respond. Here I think the Arminians are actually closer to the truth than we are.

I think Reformed people greatly err when they criticize Evangelism Explosion for emphasizing decisions. That criticism is hyper-Calvinistic, rather than Calvinistic. Man does have an important responsibility to respond to the gospel. Demanding that response is part of the gospel. Such human responsibility is not at all antithetical to divine sovereignty. Man cannot respond apart from grace, certainly. But scriptural preaching of the gospel does not tell people to wait passively for God to do something. Rather, it tells them to repent, believe, and be baptized.

Reformed intellectualism can be countered as we open ourselves to listen to preachers like Billy Graham. Graham sometimes says Arminian things and worse; he also says Calvinistic things, sometimes. But he has a wonderful ability to speak with crystal clarity to people of all backgrounds. And yes, I believe that he preaches the gospel. I would not hesitate to take an inquirer to hear him. Graham might say some things I would disagree with, but I think he will usually communicate more truth to my unbelieving friend than would be communicated by the average Reformed preacher. Why can't we teach ministerial students to preach like that?

Another remedy for hyper-intellectualism: coming to realize that at bottom it is a form of pride. The hyper-intellectualist looks down his nose at younger or less educated people and senses no obligation to minister to them.

6. And as you might guess from the earlier debate I fault traditional Reformed worship (as practiced today) because it has an inadequate vocabulary (musical and otherwise) for expressing joy and for edifying people of all sorts.

7. I think we do a fairly poor job at evaluating ministerial candidates and preparing them for the ministry. Our seminaries give them a good academic preparation: the intellectual area, again, is the Reformed strength. But most of Paul's qualifications of elders are qualities of character, and the responsibilities of pastors require interpersonal and counseling skills of a high degree. We don't have very good ways of evaluating men in the non-academic areas, assessing their strengths and weaknesses, helping them to grow. I'm inclined to think (1) we should not ordain any elders under thirty (maybe 35), (2) that everyone seeking ordination undergo assessment, such as PCA missions agencies (MTW and MNA) require of missionaries and church planters, (3) there should be a multi-year internship before ordination and supervised ministry for those newly ordained. Here we can learn

from Episcopal churches, black churches, Reformed Baptist ministerial academies, Latin American "street seminaries," etc.

8. I also think that the demand for doctrinal precision in conservative Reformed circles has become rather unbalanced, so that the matter of church unity gets short shrift. Earlier in this debate, when I spoke of unity, Hart berated me for advocating "unity at the expense of truth." Of course I wasn't advocating that. But that's what tends to happen in our circles when the subject of unity comes up. Unity always gets trumped by a concern for doctrinal purity, with the implication that we shouldn't ever seek unity.

And often our concern for doctrinal purity is distorted. Think of all the controversies among us in recent years that have divided congregations and presbyteries and created parties within the church, pitting us against one another: the incomprehensibility of God, apologetics, the millennium, preterism, Christian liberty, counseling, subscription, Psalmody, contemporary worship, redemptive-historical preaching, theonomy, Shepherd's view of justification, six-day creation, cessationism, common grace and now (God help us!) the alleged necessity of subscribing to the Scottish national covenants. Only a few of these issues involve differences over the confession, but in all these areas there have been parties contending with one another, sometimes very ferociously, sometimes dividing churches and presbyteries, with people even trying to hinder ministries that hold the contrary view. We seem to have no conscience about calling one another terrible names, if they are on the other side from us of one of these ideological divides.[13]

Some elders of the Orthodox Presbyterian Church voted against union with the Presbyterian Church in America because the two groups had different home missions practices, or because the PCA operates a denominational college.

I don't object to people presenting their views in these areas and seeking to persuade others in the church. I do object, in most of the above issues, to making them tests of orthodoxy, reviling those on the other side, and denying encouragement to ministries on the other side. This constant battling embitters fellowship and weakens

13. I later expanded this discussion into a paper, "Machen's Warrior Children," which reflected on the recent history of controversies within American conservative Presbyterianism. See http://www.frame-poythress.org/frame_articles/2003Machen.htm.

ministry in all areas of the church's life. In the immortal words of Rodney King, "Can't we all just get along?" We need to remind ourselves that love (not only the traditional three marks) is a mark of the church (John 13:35).

9. In our circles, pastors have almost no pastoral care. That can lead to shipwreck in the ministry. The idea of presbytery as the pastor's local church becomes quite meaningless when presbytery meetings consist entirely of business, or, even worse, consist largely of partisan battles. We can learn from Baptist, charismatics, and others with association-type polities, where much time at ministers' meetings is spent in prayer and edification, and where people do not look down their noses at touchy-feely emotional support.[14]

10. I think that dispensational fundamentalists do a better job at teaching Scripture to their kids than Reformed churches do. In my view the teaching of Scripture should take precedence over the teaching of catechism.

I could say some more things, but I think I've given you a "few examples," probably too many. I do love Reformed theology, but I don't believe that Reformed churches have always been the best churches. We need to do a lot of growing, in many areas. That's why I think the idea of making Reformed *tradition* normative (in addition to the confessions) is entirely wrongheaded.

Thanks for the soap box! My thanks to Darryl Hart, Andy Webb, and all the list participants. It's been an interesting exchange.

So I am a Reformed evangelical. My theology is Reformed: Calvinistic, Whitefieldian, even Van Tillian. But I have learned much from evangelicals, even from non-Whitefieldian evangelicals. I emerge from this discussion quite unsympathetic with Van Til's call for the "isolation" of the Reformed from evangelicals, and convinced that an alliance between these movements is important for the work of the church in our time.

I have for many years been critical of all denominational division within Christianity.[15] But my ecumenism has not been successful. Even

---

14. In the time since our debate, I believe that some presbyteries in my denomination, the Presbyterian Church in America, have greatly improved in this respect.

15. See especially my *Evangelical Reunion* (Grand Rapids: Baker, 1991), also available at http://www.frame-poythress.org/frame_books.htm. I have also discussed this matter under

within the Reformed community, it is difficult to get Dutch Calvinists and American Presbyterians to worship together, let alone Presbyterians and broad evangelicals. Humanly, the prospects for bringing Christians together do not look good. But I persevere. In the meantime, I try to encourage Reformed and evangelicals to become more and more like one another (generally, Reformed in theology, evangelical in outreach). Reformed evangelicalism so conceived will have a strength that neither movement has on its own. That is up to God, of course. But I believe that a deeper respect, love, and accommodation between these two movements is the will of God, and that God will therefore bless the effort.

---

the first commandment in my *DCL*. I'm happy that my friend John Armstrong has developed this biblical theme and others in his *Your Church Is Too Small: Why Unity in Christ's Mission Is Vital to the Future of the Church* (Grand Rapids: Zondervan, 2010).

13

Is Justification by Faith Alone the Article on Which the Church Stands or Falls?

THE TITULAR QUESTION is derived from a saying attributed to Martin Luther,[1] indicating the importance that the Reformer ascribed to the doctrine of justification by faith alone. I gladly subscribe to that doctrine, but I have some questions about what it means to regard it as Luther did in this saying, and whether we should so regard it.

First, what would it mean for the church to "fall" for lack of this article? This might mean that the church would not exist if it were not for God's willingness to justify us by faith in Christ apart from works. Scripture teaches that justification by faith alone is the only means of salvation. Without it, we are eternally lost. So if this article were untrue, we would have no hope, and there would be no point in having a church. In that sense, then, we should all affirm Luther's judgment about the importance of this article. In this sense, of course, the issue is a very solemn one, an issue of eternal, vast importance.

But in discussions of this article, what people usually understand by *fall* is something different: not the falsity of the article, but the failure of the church to affirm it. My guess is that this second meaning is the

---

1. This terminology does not explicitly appear in Luther's writings, but some have ascribed it to his oral conversation, and his disciples used it often. See http://thegospelcoalition.org /blogs/justintaylor/2011/08/31/luthers-saying/.

one Luther chiefly had in mind. Whether or not the church affirms this article is also an important matter, but it is not as important as whether the article is objectively true.

But we need still more clarification. What would it mean for the church to fail to affirm justification by faith alone? Various possibilities present themselves: (1) The church authorities contradict this doctrine. (2) The church authorities contradict this doctrine, and the church members follow them in denying it. (3) The church authorities do not contradict the doctrine, but they fail to affirm it vigorously and emphatically. (4) Same as (3), but to such an extent that knowledge of the doctrine becomes very rare within the church and church members are very confused about the nature of justification.

Did the Roman Church Fall?

Let us apply these distinctions to the situation of Luther's own time. In their response to Luther, and in the later Canons of Trent, it could be argued that the Roman Catholic Church contradicted the doctrine (point 1 above). The case can also be made that the church misunderstood Luther's doctrine, in which case the doctrine it denied was not the biblical doctrine of justification by faith alone. I will not try to resolve this historical issue here. My judgment, for what it's worth, is that the truth is somewhere in between these two theses. But let's assume the worst case, that the church authorities in fact denied the biblical doctrine of justification by faith alone. Did the church, then, "fall" at this point?

If the word *fall* is taken seriously, it must mean that the church became apostate, that it was no longer a church. Some Protestants have taken the position that the Roman Catholic rejection of Luther's doctrine amounts to apostasy, so that we should no longer regard the Roman Catholic Church as a true church of Christ, or as a part of the true church. Others, such as Charles Hodge, have taken a different view: that the Roman church, for all its failings, and despite Trent, remains a Trinitarian church, worshiping Christ as Lord.[2] Clearly, Hodge's criteria

2. See Charles Hodge, "Is the Church of Rome a Part of the Visible Church?" available at http://www.hornes.org/theologia/charles-hodge/is-the-church-of-rome-a-part-of-the-visible-church.

for a true church differ from those of other Protestants. But as his essay proves, the definition of a true church is not perfectly easy to formulate.

One of Hodge's points is that even if the authorities of the Roman church have denied important doctrines, that does not settle the question whether the church members believe them. So the falling of sense 1 above does not necessarily entail falling in sense 2, though certainly the first can lend momentum to the second.

Was the Church of 100–1520 a Fallen Church?

When I read Luther's statement, I have to ask what it means for the church between Paul and Luther, say, from A.D. 100 to 1520. Historians regularly refer to Luther's theology as a "discovery" or "rediscovery" of Paul's doctrine of justification by faith alone. If this is the case, then this doctrine was not widely taught after Paul and before Luther. Should we read Luther's statement as implying that during this period the church was apostate and that there was therefore no church?

The affirmative would, of course, be a very extreme position, one that Luther himself never held. But what should be said about that period? Certainly it was a time in which clear, explicit, emphatic statements of justification by faith alone were rare. Even in the writings of the earliest church fathers following the apostles, such as the first-century 1 Clement, there are suggestions of what Luther would have called a works-righteousness theology. Subsequent generations of Christian writers, of course, affirmed Paul's statements about justification in their commentaries on the NT Epistles. But none of them described Paul's doctrine with the clarity, urgency, and emphasis of Luther's writings. Augustine was certainly a great teacher of divine grace, but even in his voluminous writings one must search to find clear, emphatic, uncontroversial affirmations of justification by faith alone.

The situation in the church between the time of Paul and that of Luther would therefore have to be described in terms of positions 3 and 4 above. The church authorities did not deny the doctrine of justification, but the teaching of the church on the subject was very weak, often nearly extinguished.

Should we then say that the church of that time "fell" in some sense because of its failure to observe Luther's article? Certainly the relative lack of teaching on justification during this period was a major weakness of the church, and the Reformation, or something like it, was necessary in order to remedy it. But the church was not apostate. The gates of hell had not prevailed against it. The church was still proclaiming Christ as Lord and Savior, and God as Father, Son, and Holy Spirit.

What of the Church of Today?

This discussion would be only academic if it weren't for the fact that some are using Luther's statement to rebuke the churches of our own times. Can it be said, for example, that American evangelical churches have "fallen" for lack of adequate teaching of justification by faith alone? But if it is difficult to answer that question even for the Roman Catholic Church of Luther's day, and for the church from 100 to 1520, surely it is difficult to answer the question when it is directed at churches of our own time.

I know of no instance in which the authorities of any evangelical church have denied the doctrine of justification by faith alone. One might argue in many cases that the teaching of this doctrine is weak. But weakness and strength are matters of degree. They have to do with such qualities as clarity and emphasis, which are also matters of degree. So I cannot agree with writers who state in general terms that American evangelicalism or some other church tradition has "lost" the doctrine of justification and is therefore fallen.

Conclusions

1. Although the lack of emphatic, clear preaching of justification by faith alone greatly weakens the church, it does not destroy the church.

2. The rejection of Luther's doctrine by the Roman Catholic Church was a great error, but it did not clearly render that church apostate. Its status as a church is still a matter of discussion.

3. The same restraint is warranted in discussions of present-day churches that are said to "neglect" the doctrine of justification, either in their official documents or in their practice of teaching. We should ask (a) to what extent a lack of emphasis constitutes neglect, and (b) how this lack of emphasis compares with the church's affirmation of other elements of the church's creed.

14

The Regulative Principle: Levels of Specificity

WE ARE FAMILIAR WITH the different levels of specificity within everyday language. When I say, "There is a dog," I am speaking fairly generally, and someone might well ask, "What dog?" But when I say, "There is Bam Bam," I am speaking more specifically.

In biblical commands we should also distinguish levels of specificity. "Honor your father and your mother" (Ex. 20:12) is a general command, but 1 Timothy 5:8 is more specific:

> But if anyone does not provide for his relatives, and especially for members of his household, he has denied the faith and is worse than an unbeliever.

But "Pay to all what is owed to them: . . . honor to whom honor is owed" (Rom. 13:7) is even more general than Exodus 20:12. Even more general yet is "abhor what is evil; hold fast to what is good" (Rom. 12:9). And perhaps Deuteronomy 7:11 is the most general of all:

> You shall therefore be careful to do the commandment and the statutes and the rules that I command you today.

So we may make a list of Bible commands that move from the most general to the most specific:

- Deuteronomy 7:11
- Romans 12:9
- Romans 13:7
- Exodus 20:12
- 1 Timothy 5:8

This is a bit like the "abstraction ladder" that we learned in school: *being, organism, animal, mammal, dog, Fido. Being* is more abstract than *organism, organism* more concrete.

Now, Reformed theology has been much concerned with "God's commands for worship." The regulative principle of Reformed worship is that our worship should consist entirely of obedience to divine commands:

> But the acceptable way of worshipping the true God is instituted by Himself, and so limited by His own revealed will, that He may not be worshipped according to the imaginations and devices of men, or the suggestions of Satan, under any visible representation, or any other way not prescribed in the holy Scripture. (WCF 21.1)[1]

Scripture contains many prescriptions, commands, concerning worship. Some are more general, some more specific. Here are some of them, listed in order from more general to more particular:

> You shall worship the Lord your God and him only shall you serve. (Matt. 4:10)

> You shall not make for yourself a carved image, or any likeness of anything that is in heaven above, or that is in the earth beneath, or that is in the water under the earth. You shall not bow down to them or serve them . . . . (Ex. 20:4–5)

---

1. I have dealt with the regulative principle extensively in *Worship in Spirit and Truth* (Phillipsburg, NJ: P&R Publishing, 1996); *Contemporary Worship Music* (Phillipsburg, NJ: P&R Publishing, 1997); "The Regulative Principle: Scripture, Tradition and Culture" (a debate with Darryl Hart), http://www.frame-poythress.org/frame_articles/1998HartDebate.htm; and *DCL*, chapters 25–26.

> Sing to him; sing praises to him; tell of all his wondrous works!
> (1 Chron. 16:9)

> Let the word of Christ dwell in you richly, teaching and admonishing
> one another in all wisdom, singing psalms and hymns and spiritual
> songs, with thankfulness in your hearts to God. (Col. 3:16)

The first passage says that we should worship only the true God. The
second, more specific, says that we should not worship him by means
of idols. The third mandates one specific aspect of worship, namely,
song. (Of course, there are other passages that mandate other worship
activities, such as prayer, teaching, and sacrament.) The fourth gives us
some specific direction about what and how we should sing.

But even Colossians 3:16 is not perfectly specific. We know that
we should sing psalms and hymns and spiritual songs (setting aside
the questions of what songs are included in these categories). But
we are not told specifically *what* psalms, hymns, and spiritual songs
we should sing, or what songs we should choose to sing this coming
Sunday. Nor are we told how these songs should be accompanied, or
arranged. We are not told what, if any, instruments should be used.
We are not told how fast or slowly we should sing, how loud or soft,
though Psalm 33:3 and other verses tell us that loudness is sometimes
appropriate. We are not told whether the whole congregation must
sing every part of every song or whether some of it may be sung by
a soloist or choir.

And there are even more specific questions: Should the people
stand or sit while they are singing? Should I sit toward the front or
toward the back? Should the church be heated or air-conditioned? If
so, to what temperature?

So it is literally impossible to arrange *all* worship actions by biblical prescriptions. The Bible gives us some prescriptions, some relatively
general, some relatively specific. But none of the biblical prescriptions
are so specific as to dictate everything we do during worship.

The Westminster Confession understands that in some matters
there is scope for human wisdom:

And that there are some circumstances concerning the worship of God, and government of the Church, common to human actions and societies, which are to be ordered by the light of nature, and Christian prudence, according to the general rules of the Word, which are always to be observed. (WCF 1.6)

But note that these circumstances pertain only to matters that are "common to human actions and societies." An example would be the time of worship. Scripture does not prescribe the time of day at which we must worship God. But we must agree on a time, if we are to have a public meeting. So we use the light of nature and Christian prudence to determine when to meet, trying not to violate the general rules of the Word.[2] Our lack of a biblical command here might seem to violate the regulative principle. But since this is a matter "common to human actions and societies," it is legitimate. The Elks Club, the Oviedo City Council, the Orlando Magic basketball team—all these human societies do the same thing. They choose meeting times. And so the church must do the same.

But what justification is there for this? Is it legitimate to choose a meeting time by our own wisdom just because everybody else does it? That doesn't seem to be an adequate rationale for the church of Jesus Christ to employ. We aren't like everybody else. They make no pretense of following Scripture. Why should we imitate their procedures?

The writers of the confession seem to believe that we may follow the procedures of the Elks Club because the matter of a start time is *secular*, not religious. I have argued against this distinction in other contexts, but here I will take it for granted, for the sake of argument.[3] Nevertheless, there are other cases in which we do not have specific prescriptions of Scripture, even on matters that are clearly religious. For example, the specific words of a sermon or a hymn. Or the specific passage of Scripture to be read on a particular Sunday. Or the words to be used in the pastoral prayer. On these religious matters, we do not

2. In this case, I take it that we should not agree to meet at 3 A.M., since that would violate the biblical command to love one another.
3. See my *DCL* and *The Escondido Theology* (Lakeland, FL: Whitefield Publications, 2011).

have specific prescriptions from Scripture. So we must use our human wisdom, "according to the general rules of the Word."

How shall we describe this procedure? We might enlarge the concept of *circumstances* from WCF 1.6 to include some aspects of worship that are not "common to human actions and societies." Or we may limit the term *circumstances* as in WCF 1.6 and use another term for the worship actions mentioned in the previous paragraph. Reformed writers have sometimes used terms such as *expressions* and *forms* to refer to those. That gives us a threefold classification: elements (e.g., prayer, teaching, praise, sacrament), expressions (e.g., the specific words of sermons), and circumstances (e.g., the meeting time).

But this discussion narrows the differences that are supposed to exist between the Reformed, on the one hand, and the Lutherans and Anglicans, on the other. Often Reformed writers will claim that Reformed worship is limited to the commands, the prescriptions of the Word, while Lutherans and Anglicans see the Word only as a negative constraint. Popularly: the Reformed say that whatever is not commanded is forbidden. The Anglicans and Lutherans say that whatever is not forbidden is permitted. That makes it sound as though Anglicans and Lutherans might include anything in worship—three-legged races, hamburger-eating contests, talent shows—because these activities are not specifically forbidden in Scripture. But of course, we know that is a foolish criticism of Anglicans and Lutherans. In fact, these Christians are quite conscientious about what is to be included in worship, and they are generally eager to conform their worship to Scripture.

Though they do not use terms such as *elements*, *forms*, and *circumstances*, Anglicans and Lutherans are as eager as Reformed to limit their worship to actions with biblical warrant. They use their human wisdom, judgment, prudence, aesthetic sensitivity, and the like to make judgments about the *application* of those biblical principles. But the Reformed do, too, under the labels of *forms* and *circumstances*.

Indeed, the Reformed slogan "Whatever Scripture does not command it forbids" is misleading. In the area of forms, Scripture does not command me to read Psalm 36 in church this coming Sunday. But neither does it forbid me to do so. In that sense, we do not do "everything according to divine commands." In another sense we do, of course. When I read Psalm 36, I am following the general biblical command to read God's Word. The general command warrants all specific actions that are legitimate applications of it. But we need to be clear on the logic of this issue.

It would be less confusing to formulate our regulative principle this way: whatever we do in worship must be a legitimate *application* of a biblical command.

As for the supposed Lutheran principle, "Whatever Scripture does not forbid is permitted," we have seen that in a sense that phrasing is misleading, too. But there are phases of worship planning in which it is important to talk about what Scripture forbids, not only about what it commands. For example: As we have seen, Scripture commands us to sing. As an application of that command, I may choose hymn 122. But I may not just choose any hymn. I need to ask whether any hymn I choose, no. 122 in this case, is acceptable to Scripture in detail. In other words, I use my human wisdom, but I use it "according to the general rules of the Word," as WCF 1.6 requires.

As I examine hymn 122, I will likely be frequently asking the "Lutheran" question: is there anything here that Scripture forbids? I have already answered the question of what Scripture commands. Now it is important to ask what Scripture forbids.

So people who plan Reformed worship services will typically ask both "what does Scripture command?" and "what does Scripture forbid?" And I think my Lutheran and Anglican brothers will typically do the same. So although Reformed formulations are typically weighted toward *command*-language, and Lutheran toward *forbid*-language, both parties must be concerned with both command and prohibition.

I think this discussion of levels of specificity clarifies the discussion of the regulation of worship. When someone says that "everything in worship must follow biblical commands," we should reply, "Yes, but at what level of specificity?" For example, the question whether we should sing psalms exclusively in worship is not a question whether we should or should not be restricted to biblical commands, but rather how specifically Scripture directs our singing. Does it simply tell us to sing to God's glory and the edification of his people (Col. 3:16–17), or does it also direct us to use certain words and no others?

The difference between Reformed and Anglicans is this: Reformed typically think that God has regulated worship in very specific ways, while Anglicans see that regulation in more general terms.

I conclude, therefore, that when we get a clear idea of the relation between general and specific biblical commands, we will have a more balanced and biblical view of the regulation of worship, and we will abandon some of our traditional polemics against our brothers and sisters in the Lutheran and Anglican communions.

15

Dualities within
Divine Covenants

I AM BEST KNOWN FOR making threefold distinctions, but there are times when twofold distinctions are also useful. I wish here to briefly indicate some twofold distinctions that I consider important for understanding the nature of biblical covenants between God and man. To some extent, this essay will belabor the obvious, but I do think there will be some value in having these distinctions in front of us, before we try to tackle the more controversial and contentious points.

The chief covenants in Scripture[1] are as follows:

1. The **eternal covenant of redemption**, sometimes called the *pactum salutis*, a covenant made in eternity between God and those people whom he has eternally chosen to bless (Eph. 1:4). Scripture represents this covenant as God the Father's bestowing on his Son an elect people, to be allowed to fall and be redeemed by the atoning work of the Son and the power of the Spirit.

2. The **universal covenant**, the kingship of God over all that he has made (Pss. 74:12–21; 95:3–5; Isa. 66:1). God's ordering of the world is called *covenant* (*berith*) in Jeremiah 31:35–37 and 33:20, 25, and his care for the natural world is called *hesed*, covenant faithfulness (Pss. 33:5; 36:5, 10; 119:64).

1. In my *ST*, especially chapter 4, I explain my choice of terminology and develop in more detail the nature of each covenant.

3. The **Edenic covenant**, made between God and the human family in Eden before the fall (Gen. 1:28; 2:16–17).

4. The **covenant of grace**, made between God and the human family after their fall into sin (Gen. 3:14–19).

5. The **covenant with Noah** (Gen. 6:18; 8:20–22; 9:1, 7, 15–17).

6. The **covenant with Abraham** (Gen. 12:1–3; 15:13–16; 17:4–8).

7. The **covenant with Moses** (Ex. 19:4–8; 20:1–17).

8. The **covenant with David** (2 Sam. 7:8–16).

9. The **new covenant** (Jer. 31:31–34).

In my judgment, each of these covenants contains some features that can be described as dualities.[2]

All Covenants Are Eternal and Progressive

All of these covenants originate in God's eternal plan, but God achieves their goals by a historical process. Of course, Scripture teaches this explicitly with regard to the eternal covenant of redemption (Eph. 1:4). We do sometimes speak of it as eternal in contrast with the other covenants, which are announced and ratified in history. But they, too, are part of God's eternal plan, for Ephesians 1:11 tells us that God "works all things according to the counsel of his will." At the same time, all the covenants are oriented toward a historical process. They have results in history, and they promise further results as history progresses, the blessings and curses of the covenant relation.

All Covenants Are Gracious, but They Require Human Works

Like everything else in the historical process, covenants originate in the mind of God. Making a covenant is God's free choice, unconstrained by anything outside himself. So the very fact that God makes a covenant with a human being is grace, unmerited, unearned. Scripture

---

2. *Dualities*, of course. Never, never *dualisms*.

stresses the graciousness of covenants in many places (Deut. 7:7–8; 9:4–6; Eph. 2:8–10).

But in all covenants God requires his covenant people to respond with obedience. That is plain in the three texts just mentioned. There are even "warning passages" in both Testaments to the effect that people should not expect the blessings of the covenant if they are living in disobedience (Deut. 5:9–10; 7:9–11; Heb. 3:7–4:13; 6:1–8; 10:26–31).

All Covenants Are Unconditional and Conditional

It is common to hear people say that some covenants are unconditional (particularly God's covenant with Abraham) and others conditional (particularly God's covenant with Israel under Moses). But that distinction is oversimplified. All of God's covenants are unconditional, for the same reason that they are all gracious. God makes covenants with us out of his sovereign grace. But as we have seen, the covenants have conditions attached, which we must fulfill if we are to receive the blessings. Those who are eternally elect fulfill these conditions because God enables them to fulfill them.

This is as true of the Abrahamic covenant as it is of the rest. God makes the covenant by his gracious choice of Abraham and his family. But the covenant relation begins with a command: in Genesis 12:1, God commands Abraham to go to the Promised Land. If Abraham had not done that, the blessings would not have been his. See also Genesis 17:1–2, where the very making of the covenant depends on Abraham's obedience. So Genesis 26:5 says that God would fulfill the covenant "because Abraham obeyed my voice and kept my charge, my commandments, my statutes, and my laws."

All Covenants Are Individual and Universal

The eternal covenant of redemption indicates God's purpose of bringing a specific group of people into eternal fellowship with him. In that sense, Scripture is not universalist. But Scripture does teach what is called *ethnic universalism*, namely, that the full body of God's elect will include people from all nations. So when Adam and Eve violated the Edenic covenant, all their descendants, the whole human race, also fell into sin, and those who believe are all redeemed in Christ by the covenant of grace (1 Cor. 15:22).

In the Abrahamic covenant, the focus of biblical history shifts from the human race as a whole to one family. But the blessing on that one family in turn blesses all nations (Gen. 12:3). And the universal reach of God's salvation is a common theme of Scripture from this point (Gen. 18:18; 22:18; 26:4; 28:14; Matt. 28:18–20; Acts 3:25; Rev. 5:9; 7:9; 12:5; 14:6; 15:4; 21:24–26; 22:2). In general, Christ is the individual, whose kingdom has a universal extent.

All Covenant Communities Are Invisible and Visible, Internal and External

In each covenant, God establishes a community of persons. Since he has chosen to redeem in history, those communities are established with external events and symbols. Sometimes the covenant is instituted by ceremonial events, as with the Mosaic covenant in Exodus 19–20. Sacrifice is often an important feature of covenant institution, foreshadowing the perfect sacrifice of Christ, which establishes the new covenant in his blood.

In the Abrahamic covenant, circumcision is the outward sign of covenant membership. In the new covenant, that sign is baptism. Continuing membership is reaffirmed in institutions such as the Passover and the Lord's Supper.

Still, there is not a perfect congruence between those who have received these signs and the actual membership of the covenant community. The thief crucified with Jesus is an example of one who has not received baptism, but will enjoy fellowship with Jesus in heaven (Luke 23:43). And the reverse is also true. Some Jews who have received the outward sign of circumcision are not truly Jews, according to Paul (Rom. 2:25–29). True circumcision is of the heart. So he says later that "not all who are descended from Israel belong to Israel" (Rom. 9:6). He also says that "it is those of faith who are the sons of Abraham" (Gal. 3:7).

All Covenants Bring Both Heavenly and Earthly Blessings

All of these covenants create fellowship between God and the people of the covenant community. Their goal is the goal of the eternal covenant of redemption: eternal fellowship with God. These are sometimes called "spiritual" blessings or "heavenly" blessings. But we should be clear on the fact that the ultimate hope of believers is the "new heavens and the new earth," a realm not only of spirit, but of the resurrection body of believers. Our hope is not an ethereal existence, but a tangible, physical existence, without suffering or sadness.

Clearly in the Noachic, Abrahamic, and Mosaic covenants many of the blessings, even before the new heavens and new earth, are earthly, the promise of prosperity within the land that God has given. It is sometimes thought that in the new covenant the blessings have nothing to do with physical prosperity. But in fact the promise of the new covenant is nothing less than the new heavens and the new earth. God also promises the NT Christian the blessing of the fifth commandment, "that it may go well with you and that you may live long in the land" (Eph. 6:3). And as God sent Joshua on a mission of conquest in the land of Canaan, so Jesus sends his people (without the sword) to disciple all the nations by his power (Matt. 28:18–20). When nations are discipled, they are transformed in all areas of their culture as they seek to do all things to the glory of God (1 Cor. 10:31). So through the spiritual warfare of missions, Christ and his people take dominion of the whole earth. His return in glory seals that transaction, but the transformation is taking place here and now.

In the life of the present-day Christian, there is also suffering and persecution. But it is important to maintain a balanced picture, as Jesus sets it forth in Mark 10:29–30:

> Jesus said, "Truly, I say to you, there is no one who has left house or brothers or sisters or mother or father or children or lands, for my sake and for the gospel, who will not receive a hundredfold now in this time, houses and brothers and sisters and mothers and children and lands, with persecutions, and in the age to come eternal life."

16

N. T. Wright and the
Authority of Scripture

I'VE BEEN ASKED TO PRESENT some thoughts on N. T. Wright's view of Scripture. N. T. Wright is one of the best known among NT scholars today. He has been a prolific author, of both scholarly and popular works. Many of his popular writings are published under the less formal name Tom Wright. Perhaps you didn't know that N. T. Wright and Tom Wright were the same person. Now that you do, you may be quite astounded at the size of his published output. I stopped counting at fifty books, and of course he has also produced a huge number of articles, published sermons, audio lectures, multimedia presentations, and so on. He was also Bishop of Durham in the Church of England for a number of years, but he is currently a research professor at the University of St. Andrews in Scotland.

Wright is best known for his development of the so-called New Perspective on Paul, advocated originally by E. P. Sanders and James D. G. Dunn. His view of Paul has led him into controversy, especially concerning the doctrine of justification. But beyond this controversy, Wright is considered conservative. He believes that the story recorded in Scripture is substantially historical, and he has no bias against the supernatural as such. Indeed, he has published a significant defense of the resurrection of Jesus, setting forth its historicity, centrality, and saving power. He has little regard for the skeptical trends in modern biblical scholarship, such as the famous Jesus Seminar.

I'm especially enthusiastic about Wright's understanding of the broad narrative structure of Scripture. For Wright, the Bible is the story of the coming of God's kingdom in power, a political event that from its beginning challenged the Roman Empire. He is therefore an opponent of privatized religion, an advocate of a Christian faith that seeks with God's help to bring all things subject to Christ. He recognizes the centrality of the *lordship* of Christ.

Wright, then, has excellent insight into the content of Scripture and has effectively defended the truth of Scripture. But what does he say about the nature of Scripture? What is his *doctrine* of the Bible?

Wright does not put much emphasis on the doctrinal question. He wants to avoid emphasizing general questions about the Bible's nature— its authority, infallibility, and inerrancy—so that he can focus on the content of Scripture. We'll see why a bit later. But in fact, he does address the theological doctrine of Scripture, chiefly in three places. First, in a 1989 lecture called "How Can the Bible Be Authoritative?" published in *Vox Evangelica* in 1991.[1] Second, in a 2005 book called *The Last Word: Scripture and the Authority of God*.[2] Beside the title and the subtitle, there is a significant sub-subtitle: *Beyond the Bible Wars to a New Understanding of the Authority of Scripture*. I reviewed this book, and you can find the review as an appendix to my book *DWG*. Third, Wright's apologetic work *Simply Christian: Why Christianity Makes Sense*[3] discusses the nature of Scripture in a number of places. As is implicit in the title, intentionally reminiscent of C. S. Lewis's *Mere Christianity*, this book is a popular rather than academic text. *LW* is a bit more technical, directed, I believe, to church leaders, but not to the academy as such.

These writings will be disappointing if the reader is looking for a traditional systematic account of the doctrine of the Word of God, revelation, and Scripture.[4] But there are a number of ideas that Wright

---

1. 21, 7–32. Available online at http://www.ntwrightpage.com/Wright_Bible_Authoritative .htm. I will refer to it in this essay as *VE*, for *Vox Evangelica*.

2. San Francisco: HarperSanFrancisco, 2005. Published in the United Kingdom as *Scripture and the Authority of God*. I will refer to it as *LW*.

3. San Francisco: HarperSanFrancisco, 2006. I will refer to it as *SC*.

4. In *VE*, he says, "One might even say, in one (admittedly limited) sense, that there is no biblical doctrine of the authority of the Bible." But later in the article he says, "But, according

does want to convey. I think the best way to proceed is for me to list
these ideas one by one with some of my own comments.

The Authority of Scripture Is the Authority of God Expressed through Scripture

In *LW*, Wright says that the "central claim of this book" is

> that the phrase "authority of scripture" can make Christian sense only
> if it is a shorthand for "the authority of the triune God, exercised
> somehow *through* Scripture."[5]

I think most theologians of all traditions would agree with this statement. To conservative evangelicals, the most important thing about the
Bible is indeed its relation to God, in the sense that it is God's Word and
therefore speaks with God's own authority. That evangelical conviction
can be formulated by means of Wright's statement.

On the other hand, Wright's statement seems intended to make
a *distinction* between God's authority and Scripture as its instrument.
The little word *somehow* enlarges the distance between God and Scripture. Certainly there are distinctions between God and Scripture,
even for conservative evangelicals, but some kinds of distinctions are
controversial.

Karl Barth, for example, has used this kind of formulation to suggest
that only God speaks literal words of God, and that the Bible, though a
derivative of God's authority, does not itself speak with divine authority. It is a witness or instrument of divine revelation, but it is not itself
divine revelation. So Barth would agree with Wright that the authority of Scripture is the authority of God expressed through Scripture,
but his view is very different from that of evangelical theologians. So
it becomes important to understand what kind of differences between
Scripture and God Wright has in mind.

---

to Paul in Romans 15 and elsewhere, the Bible is itself a key part of God's plan. It is not merely
a divinely given commentary on the way salvation works (or whatever); the Bible is part of the
means by which he puts his purposes of judgement and salvation to work."

5. *LW*, 23; cf. 116; *SC*, 185; *VE*.

As we will see, Wright's view is not Barthian, but he does not assert the equation between God's words and the Bible's that is typical of evangelical accounts. He wants to indicate, I think, that the relationship between Scripture and God is more complicated, more problematic, than evangelicals, especially American evangelicals, have thought it to be. It is a "somehow" relationship. We can hope to gain some clarity on this issue as we look at his further assertions.

Scripture Is Narrative

Wright gives us some insight into the sorts of problems he wrestles with in regard to biblical authority when he asks what kind of book Scripture is. In *LW*, he says:

> The Bible itself, as a whole and in most of its parts, is not the sort of thing that many people envisage today when they hear the word "authority."
>
> It is not, for a start, a list of rules, though it contains many commandments of various sorts and in various contexts. Nor is it a compendium of true doctrines, though of course many parts of the Bible declare great truths about God, Jesus, the world and ourselves in no uncertain terms.[6] Most of its constituent parts, and all of it when put together . . . , can best be described as a *story*.
>
> The question is, How can a story be authoritative? If the commanding officer walks into the barrack-room and begins "Once upon a time," the soldiers are likely to be puzzled. . . . At first sight, what we think of as "authority" and what we know as "story" do not readily fit together.[7]

Now, many theologians today identify Scripture as a story or narrative. But I think that identification oversimplifies the nature of Scripture, even as a literary description. Certainly there is a great deal of historical narrative in Scripture, what we call redemptive history, the story of

6. Nor, he says later, should Scripture be described primarily as revelation, or as a devotional manual (*LW*, 30–34). He opposes the idea that Scripture is a *lectio divina* in *LW*, 64, though in *SC*, 188, he does endorse that use of Scripture.

7. *LW*, 25–26.

creation, fall, and redemption. But much of Scripture is not narrative, but law, poetry, wisdom, letters, apocalyptic. It can be argued that these other literary forms depend on the narrative, but they should not be reduced to narrative.

I have found more persuasive Meredith Kline's contention[8] that the *combination* of these literary forms in Scripture suggests that the best way to characterize Scripture as a whole is not *narrative*, but *covenant*. *Covenant* in this sense refers to a complex literary form represented in ancient Near Eastern suzerainty treaties. The biblical term *covenant* often describes this sort of treaty, particularly treaties between God and people such as Noah, Abraham, Moses, and David.[9] These treaties included historical narrative, but also law, sanctions, and administrative matters. In the ancient world, the great king would command the lesser king to reverence the treaty document, the covenant, between the two parties, to put it in a holy place, and to hear it over and over again. In Israel, God ordered the people to put the Decalogue and the various additions to it in the holiest place of the tabernacle and later the temple. The covenant document was their supreme constitution. It is narrative, but not only narrative. It is, like the U.S. Constitution, the highest law of the land for God's people. This model, far better than Wright's, shows how Scripture functions as authority for God's people.

To some extent, the search for a general literary description of Scripture is futile. Since Scripture is God's Word, it is unique, *sui generis*. But if we need a general term for the literary nature of Scripture, we should describe it as *covenant*, God's treaty with us, the constitution of the people of God. To say this is not to disparage the narrative. Certainly, in a sense, all the content of the Bible depends on that narrative. But Scripture is not *only* narrative.

8. Meredith G. Kline, *The Structure of Biblical Authority* (Grand Rapids: Eerdmans, 1972). My own understanding of the content of Scripture follows his to an extent. See my *DWG*, 145–62.

9. These treaties were documents that a greater king would impose on a lesser king, including the name of the great king, the "historical prologue" indicating the past relationships of the two parties, laws of various kinds, then sanctions (benefits for obeying and curses for disobeying), and finally administrative matters. Kline argued that the elements of these treaties correspond to the elements of biblical covenants such as the Decalogue and that the elements of the biblical canon reflect this structure. If Kline is right, the narrative of Scripture is historical prologue, a prelude to the laws, the sanctions, and the administration of God's kingdom.

Whether Kline is right or not about the general content of Scripture, his proposal should open us to see that Scripture contains a rich variety of literary genres, each of which conveys to us a form of authority. Narratives are to be believed, commandments to be obeyed, psalms to be taken to heart, wisdom to be cultivated in our hearts, apocalyptic to arouse our amazement, letters to play the many functions that letters play in our experience.

The Authority of Scripture Is the Application of Its Story

Wright acknowledges this complexity in the material I quoted above. But when he formulates the question of the nature of biblical authority, as we have seen above, he thinks it reduces entirely to the question of how a narrative or story can have authority. To answer this question, he thinks, is like answering the question of how a commanding officer can give orders that begin "once upon a time."

He answers that question as follows:

> For a start, the commanding officer might well need to brief the soldiers about what has been going on over the past few weeks, so that they will understand the sensitivities and internal dynamics of the peace-keeping task they are now to undertake. The narrative will bring them up to date; now it will be their task to act out the next chapter in the ongoing saga.[10]

Other examples:

> A familiar story told with a new twist in the tale jolts people into thinking differently about themselves and the world. A story told with pathos, humor or drama opens the imagination and invites readers and hearers to imagine themselves in similar situations, offering new insights about God and human beings which enable them then to order their own lives more wisely.[11]

10. *LW*, 26.
11. Ibid., 27.

In the first example, the narrative informs the soldiers of events relevant to their military task. In the second, it motivates imaginations and gives insight. Now, as we saw, Wright earlier said that even though Scripture is not "a compendium of true doctrines," it does "declare great truths about God." It certainly seems to me, and I think Wright would agree, that these great truths could be among the "new insights about God and human beings which enable them then to order their own lives more wisely." So it is certainly possible for the traditional concerns of systematic theology to be integrated into Wright's narrative theology. The same certainly can be said for the traditional concerns of Christian morality. So Wright's model, though I prefer a different one as I have said, is flexible enough to incorporate most, if not all, of our traditional uses of the Bible. It does not require a radical change as might be expected from Wright's sub-subtitle, *A New Understanding of the Authority of Scripture*.

Traditional theology and ethics have always understood, to a greater or lesser degree, that narrative is important in Scripture. The narrative is the good news that God has saved his people through his actions in history. There is no such gospel in Hinduism, or Buddhism, or Islam. Traditional Christian theology explains these events and, I should add, the worldview they presuppose. Christian ethics tells us not only what the God of the narrative expects of us, but also the new motivation for obedience that comes through the narrative. Wright's narrative emphasis may give a fresh impetus to these themes, but he has not told us anything here that we haven't known already. If he had denied that there were any "great truths about God" in Scripture, or that there are no ethical norms and motivations in Scripture, that Scripture is *only* narrative and nothing else, then he would have said something very original, radical, and peculiar. But he is, in the final analysis, a rather traditional Christian in his conception of the content of Scripture. My earlier suggestion that he broaden his concept of the content of Scripture beyond narrative to covenant would constitute tweaking of his concept, not fundamentally changing it.

Scripture Is Power, Not Only Word

But Wright, seeking to establish the newness of his supposedly new understanding of biblical authority, often resorts to the idea that Scripture is not merely a text, but also a vehicle of the power of God. It not only says things; it does things as well. That is to say that the functions of Scripture are not only verbal, but something more.

Wright speaks of God's authority as

> his sovereign power accomplishing the renewal of all creation. Specific authority over human beings, notably the church, must be seen as part of that larger whole.[12]

What role does Scripture play in this divine project?

> It is enormously important that we see the role of scripture not simply as being to provide *true information about*, or even an accurate running commentary upon, the work of God in salvation and new creation, but as taking an active part *within* that ongoing purpose.... Scripture is there to be a means of God's action in and through us—which will include, but go far beyond, the mere conveying of information.[13]

Here, Wright touches on the question of "propositional revelation" that in the 1940s and '50s was central in the debate between evangelicals and neoorthodox thinkers. The neoorthodox, such as Karl Barth and Emil Brunner, thought that it was unworthy of God for us to imagine him conveying propositions, or items of information, to human beings. Evangelicals, on the other hand, insisted that much of Scripture, including its historical narrative, was informative, and so propositional revelation was an obvious feature of Scripture. They conceded, in their best formulations, that Scripture contained not only items of information, but also commands, questions, poetic expressions, parables, wisdom sayings, and so on. But that was not enough for the neoorthodox, who thought that by renouncing propositional revelation entirely they could

12. Ibid., 29.
13. Ibid., 30.

escape the whole idea of revelation as words in favor of some kind of nonverbal revelation that we may be inclined to call mystical.

Wright, too, wants to get beyond the idea of propositional revelation, though unlike the neoorthodox he does not want to deny verbal revelation altogether. Still, he agrees with the neoorthodox that biblical revelation is not only more than propositional revelation; it is more even than verbal revelation. Beyond words, it is a power. The Word of God, he says, is

> not . . . a synonym for the written scriptures, but . . . a strange personal presence, creating, judging, healing, recreating.[14]

> The early Christians discovered that telling this story [the gospel] carried a power which they regularly associated with the Spirit, but which they often referred to simply as "the word."[15]

In *SC*, he uses the metaphor that Scripture is a kind of holy ground, a place where heaven and earth meet. This is a frequent theme of the book. He presents three worldview options: In his Option One, there are writers (pantheists, in effect) who identify heaven and earth so that they are indistinguishable. But there are others, he says (deists), who make heaven and earth far apart so that God cannot get involved in earthly history. This is Option Two. Scripture, he says, presents still a third option: heaven and earth are distinct, but they often come together so that we experience heaven, God's presence, in history.[16]

So when he considers the nature of inspiration, he opposes the "dictation" view, which he thinks comes out of an alternative version of Option Two: heaven and earth are generally separated, but God sometimes breaks through the division, "'zapping' the (biblical) writers

14. Ibid., 38.

15. *SC*, 134. He refers also to the advance and growth of the "word" in Psalm 33:6; Acts 4:31; 6:7; 12:24; 19:20; Romans 10:8–9; Colossians 1:5–6; 1 Thessalonians 2:13. In *LW* he speaks of the word as "not . . . a synonym for the written scriptures, but . . . a strange personal presence, creating, judging, healing, recreating" (38).

16. I have made a very similar point in my own books, speaking of various views of transcendence and immanence, rather than of heaven and earth.

with some kind of long-range linguistic thunderbolt."[17] That is not a plausible view, he thinks, of the relationship between God and the biblical writers. But, he says,

> once again Option Three comes to the rescue. Supposing scripture, like the sacraments, is one of the points where heaven and earth overlap and interlock? Like all other such places, this is mysterious. It doesn't mean that we can see at once what's going on. Indeed, it guarantees that we can't. But it does enable us to say some things that need to be said and that are otherwise difficult.
>
> In particular, it enables us to say that the writers, compilers, editors, and even collectors of scripture were people who, with different personalities, styles, methods, and intentions, were nonetheless caught up in the strange purposes of the covenant God—purposes which included the communication, by writing, of his word.[18]

So Scripture is a sacred place, where heaven and earth meet, not just a book. It is a book, but more, something mysterious, something powerful, as we have seen.

Wright says that this is strange, and indeed it is. This is evidently what he means when he says that "somehow" God exerts his authority through Scripture. But like his emphasis on narrative, it is not unprecedented in Protestant theology. The idea of the "power" of the Word has been part of Protestant thought since the Reformation, and the classical Reformers have referred to the same collection of biblical texts that Wright does here. The Word is "living and powerful," as Hebrews 4:12 (NKJV) says. It is "the power of God for salvation" (Rom. 1:16). Indeed (wouldn't you know it?), there has been a debate between Reformed and Lutherans as to *how* we should understand the relationship between the power of the Word and the power of the Spirit; but I digress. The idea of Scripture as a sacramental location of God's presence sounds more Catholic than Protestant, but Protestants, too, have drawn many parallels between the Word and the sacraments. The sacraments are

17. *SC*, 181.
18. Ibid.

visible words, and the sense in which God is present in the sacraments, for Protestants, is easily applicable to the Word.

So even Wright's mysterious talk about the Word as a power and as a sacramental location of God does not justify the notion that he is proposing a "new understanding of the authority of Scripture." Rather, Wright has reformulated, and perhaps rediscovered, ways of thinking about Scripture that are common in Protestant theological tradition. If he were to deny that revelation is also a written text, he would be departing from that tradition and joining the neoorthodox. But as we have seen, he does not do that.[19]

But God Does Speak to Us by Word

To underscore the previous sentence, I should point out that most of Wright's references to God's speech are in conventional linguistic terms, though as we have seen he sometimes describes divine communication as something more than language. We recall that for him the authority of Scripture is the authority of narrative; but narrative is a verbal form and propositional to boot. Although Wright stresses in context that the function of Scripture is to "energize" us for God's task, he rejects the notion that revelation is nonverbal. Of course, it is the *words* of Scripture, as we read, hear, and understand them, that energize us for God's task. Option Three, he says,

> enables us to speak about God the creator (the one we know supremely through the living Word, Jesus) being himself (so to speak) a wordsmith. Option Three enables us to insist that, though words are not the only thing God specializes in, they are a central part of his repertoire ... [;] he wants to communicate with and through [his people] verbally—in addition to, but also as a central point within, his many other ways of getting things said and done.

The Bible is far more, in other words, than what some people used to say a generation or so ago: that it was simply the (or a) "record

19. Some readers may find it interesting or amusing that Wright has here uncovered what I have elsewhere referred to as a *covenantal triad*: The authority of the Bible is by word (normative), by power (situational), and by its sacramental nature as a dwelling place of God (existential).

of the revelation," as if God revealed himself by some quite other means and the Bible was simply what people wrote down to remind themselves of what had happened. The Bible offers itself, and has normally been treated in the church, as part of God's revelation, not simply a witness or echo of it.[20]

In *LW*, he says that the existence of the Bible

> reminds us that the God Christians worship is characterized not least as a God who *speaks*, who communicates with his human creatures in words. . . . It means that the idea of reading a book to hear and know God is not far-fetched, but cognate with the nature of God himself.[21]

The bottom line, then, is that God speaks to his people, in a very ordinary sense of "speaking," but that Scripture is more than that. Again, we find a clear correspondence between Wright's view and the traditional Protestant view of Scripture. So far we have seen nothing that looks like a "new understanding of the authority of Scripture."

We Should Not Ask Whether the Whole Text of Scripture Is True

So far I have not differed very much with Wright, save some quibbles about his overemphasis on the narrative character of Scripture. But there are some other matters about which I have more serious reservations with his formulation, particularly his statements about biblical inspiration, infallibility, and inerrancy.

In my review of *LW*, I criticized Wright's understanding of biblical inspiration. He says that it is

> a shorthand way of talking about the belief that by his Spirit God guided the very different writers and editors, so that the books they produced were the books God intended his people to have.[22]

20. *SC*, 181–82.
21. *LW*, 34.
22. Ibid., 37.

I replied:

> But the same can be said about the books in my library: that God
> moved writers, editors, publishers, et al., so that the books in my
> library are the ones God wants me to have. Nevertheless, there are
> some horrible books in my library (which I keep for various good
> reasons). So it is important to ask whether inspiration is simply divine
> providence, or whether it carries God's endorsement. Is God, in any
> sense, the *author* of inspired books?

I was hoping that in his later book, *SC*, he would have responded to
this sort of question. But I cannot find there any improved definition or
understanding of biblical inspiration. In that book there is a chapter (13)
called "The Book God Breathed" and a subsection of that chapter titled
"God's Inspired Word."[23] But in that subsection he denies the dictation theory, as we have seen, propounds his metaphor of Scripture as
a sacramental presence of God, and reiterates his view of the *purposes*
for which God gave Scripture to us. He does not address the question
whether divine inspiration confers truth upon the biblical text.

He does mention the question, only to express his irritation with it:

> Though I'm not unhappy with what people are trying to affirm when
> they use words like "infallible" (the idea that the Bible won't deceive
> us) and "inerrant" (the stronger idea, that the Bible can't get things
> wrong), I normally resist using those words myself. Ironically, in
> my experience, debates about words like these have often led people
> away from the Bible itself and into all kinds of theories which do no
> justice to scripture as a whole—its great story, its larger purposes, its
> sustained climax, its haunting sense of an unfinished novel beckoning
> us to become, in our own right, characters in its closing episodes.[24]

Yes, I, too, have seen and read about people who became so preoccupied
with infallibility and so on that they missed out on other important
biblical themes. Wright would say "more important biblical themes,"

23. *SC*, 180–84.
24. Ibid., 183.

2

4

but I'm not sure. The biblical writers say over and over again that God's Word is true and is the truth (that's all that *inerrancy* means[25]). That must have been important to them. If as on my suggested model Scripture was the Constitution of Israel, its highest authority, the very Word of God, then of course to deny its infallibility would have been a great insult to God.

In *LW*, Wright asks:

> Which is the bottom line: "proving the Bible to be true" (often with the effect of saying, "so we can go on thinking what we've always thought"), or taking it so seriously that we allow it to tell us things we'd never heard before and didn't particularly want to hear?[26]

Again, he pits the issue of truth against the issue of practical seriousness about Scripture. But are these really opposed? Indeed, why should we take the Bible with such seriousness if we don't believe it to be true?

And of course, if Wright may report his experience, I have an equal right to report mine, which is that many people who *reject* the infallibility, the inerrancy, and the truth of Scripture often end up taking Scripture with very little seriousness. I find it hard to believe that this rejection and this sort of practice are never linked. Perhaps my experience is different from Wright's. But seriously, I think that both those who affirm and those who deny biblical infallibility need to attend to their practical responses to the Bible. I suspect that Wright would agree with me on this point. But then, the practical issue does not answer the question whether the Bible is a true document, or the question whether we should be concerned about its truth.

The question is simple. Given that God inspired the Bible, what effect did that inspiration have on the biblical text? Did it make that text true, reliable, even infallible, or did it leave that text as a fallible book? Wright certainly treats the Bible as a true document, and as we have seen, he even says that he is "not unhappy with what people are trying to

25. See the account of infallibility and inerrancy in my *DWG*, 167–76.
26. *LW*, 95. Cf. ibid., 91, where he challenges readers to allow the Bible to cut across their "cherished traditions."

affirm when they use words like 'infallible' . . . and 'inerrant.' "[27] But he stifles discussion of these concepts by a one-sided comment about what this discussion sometimes leads people to do. I still await a meaningful comment from Wright on this important question.

If Wright's failure to address this issue is the new feature in his "new view of biblical authority," then I confess that I prefer to stay with the old view. If he thinks this kind of talk enables us to "transcend the Bible wars," I don't believe he has succeeded. The question of the truth of Scripture will not go away. Some believe it is true; some do not. But if it is not legitimate to *contend* over this issue, if it is not worth fighting for, then I don't know what is. For if the Bible is not true, it makes no sense for us to insert ourselves into the narrative, to view Scripture as a sacramental dwelling of God, or anything else.

I realize that the difference between Wright and me is from one perspective very small. Wright has told us that in Scripture God *speaks* to us, in language. Wright is sympathetic to people who speak of infallibility and inerrancy, and his only criticism of those concepts is that they may distract us from what he thinks are more important questions. Certainly there is room in the church for people to disagree over what questions are most important.

Wright is certainly an ally in the Bible wars, even though he thinks he has gotten beyond them. I agree with him far more than I disagree. I think part of our difference stems from our different ethnicities. Wright and other European Christians are often critical of the American tendency to magnify the question of biblical infallibility. But why should anyone make a big deal of ethnicity in the church of Jesus Christ?

Yet I do think that we need to make a big deal of the truth of the text of Scripture, and that that text does not just *happen* to be true. It is true because God has inspired that text—even more, that God has *authored* that text, since it is his Word. That's what God's breathing is, his speech. It would be, perhaps, only a small step for our dear brother N. T. Wright to agree with me, to move from mere sympathy for biblical infallibility and inerrancy to affirmation of these concepts. As of

27. *SC*, 183.

now, he does not seem to see the importance of that affirmation, and this essay of mine is simply a brotherly attempt to remind him of it, and to remind all of us who respect N. T. Wright as a teacher of Scripture.

Scholarship Establishes Whether the Bible Is Historical

As our last topic, I'd like to mention one important implication of the points I have been making. It has to do with Wright's own approach to historical Bible scholarship. Since Wright prefers not to speak in traditional terms of Scripture's infallibility and inerrancy, one asks how he does evaluate its statements, particularly in historical matters. I focus on history here because of its intrinsic importance, because Wright is a biblical historian more than anything else, and because biblical history is, after all, the narrative that Wright considers so central in his theology of Scripture. He says that historicity of Scripture is important to him. Although he challenges biblical literalists to rethink their assurances, he says, this

> does not mean that I am indifferent to the question of whether the events written about in the gospels actually took place. Far from it.[28]

Now, I mentioned earlier that Wright is more conservative than many other biblical scholars in his evaluation of biblical history. As we have seen, Wright opposes the rationalist approach of the Enlightenment,[29] which led to "the muddled debates of modern biblical scholarship."[30] He is himself vitally concerned with "the question of whether the events written about in the gospels actually took place."[31] And for the most part, his judgments are that these events did take place. But why does he come to this evaluation?

The main reason he mentions is the evidence brought by biblical scholars, of whom he is, of course, a leading representative. In *SC* he summarizes his scholarly conclusions on the reliability of the

28. *LW*, 95.
29. Ibid., 87–88.
30. Ibid., 89.
31. Ibid., 95; cf. ibid., 112–13.

four Gospels[32] and on the truth of Jesus' resurrection.[33] In *LW* he says that the way to combat "modernist" views of Scripture influenced by Enlightenment rationalism is

> to go further into serious historical work than modernism (for its own reasons) was prepared to do. When we do this, we discover again and again that many of the problems or "contradictions" discovered by modernist critical study were the result of projecting alien worldviews onto the text.[34]

Today, he says, biblical scholars have better resources than the old modernists had: lexicons, ancient texts, archaeological and numismatic discoveries. So, Wright continues,

> we should gratefully use all these historical resources. When we do so . . . we will discover that quite a bit of the old "modernist" consensus is challenged on the grounds to which it originally appealed—namely, serious historical reconstruction.
>
> Christianity should be ready to give an answer about what really happened within history and how, within the historian's own proper discipline, we can know that with the kind of "knowledge" appropriate to, and available within, historical research.[35]

Note also:

> Assessing [the Gospels'] historical worth can be done, if at all, only by the kind of painstaking historical work which I and others have attempted at some length.[36]

So it appears that the scholar is the final arbiter of historical truth. Of course, according to Wright, we should not carry on this work the way the old modernists did. We can do so much better.

32. *SC*, 95–99.
33. Ibid., 112–16.
34. *LW*, 95.
35. Ibid., 95–96.
36. Ibid., 99.

But there's something wrong with this. Wright is saying that historical scholars came up with conclusions radically contrary to Scripture until, say, 1980, but now we can turn their ideas completely around with the resources we have today. But who is to say that a hundred years from now the modernists—or some new movement in the modernist tradition—might not gain the upper hand? History is a human science, and it constantly changes in its methods and conclusions. Is Wright really so sure that his own methods and conclusions will endure forever?

It is interesting that in this discussion Wright mentions that one of the problems with the adherents of modernism was their "projecting alien worldviews onto the text." Does Wright think that scholars, even conservative scholars, can entirely avoid doing this today? Is the answer to try to avoid the use of any worldview, or to read the text in the light of one true worldview? Clearly he disapproves of the modernists' use of their worldview, but he says nothing about the role of worldview, or what I would call presuppositions, in the work of historical scholarship.

I doubt myself whether anyone can read Scripture, or any other book, without any presuppositions at all. (That's the one statement in which I agree with Rudolf Bultmann.) And, to make a long story short, it seems obvious to me that Christian scholars should do their work out of a Christian worldview. So it's not just a matter of scholarship. It's not just a matter of going and looking at the facts. It is looking at the facts in the right way.

How do we find the right way to look at facts? In my judgment, that is another function of Scripture. If Scripture is our highest authority, it must determine our fundamental presuppositions, our worldview.

I think Wright does this for the most part, though he never articulates it. It is not as though the modernists imposed an alien worldview on the text and Wright reads the text with no worldview at all. It is rather that Wright reads the Scripture assuming that God exists, that miracles such as the resurrection are possible, that we live as part of the narrative of redemptive history. The Enlightenment rationalists assumed that miracles are not possible; Wright assumes that they are. If the rationalist consensus is a presupposition, then so is Wright's assumption. Wright ought to be up front about this.

And if he were to be explicit about his presuppositions, he would have to admit that we believe, say, in the resurrection not just because a new generation of historical scholars say we may, but also because the Bible says the resurrection occurred. What's missing in Wright as a historian is his reluctance to say, even though I think he believes it, that the biblical history is true because the Bible says it is.

It is significant that in 1 Corinthians 15 Paul argues the reality of the resurrection not only on the basis of historical witnesses and evidences (though he does do that), but also and primarily on the basis that the resurrection of Jesus was part of the apostolic preaching (1 Cor. 15:1–4, 11–12, 14). The Corinthians should believe in the resurrection not only because of historical evidence, but also—and primarily—because it is taught by the Word of God, by inspired apostles. For us, the equivalent point is that we should believe the resurrection because the Bible tells us to, because the Bible itself contains sufficient evidence, and because the evidence should be seen on biblical presuppositions.

If Wright understood that the Bible must control our thoughts to the deepest level, to our most fundamental presuppositions, he would not be so indifferent to questions about infallibility and inerrancy, which in the end are simply questions about the truth of Scripture. For if we embrace Scripture as our presupposition, we embrace it as our most fundamental criterion of truth. And our fundamental criterion of truth must itself be true. If Wright understood this, he would see that it is not scholarship alone that establishes the truth of Scripture, but scholarship through the lens of Scripture. Ultimately, what establishes the truth of Scripture is Scripture itself, and therefore scholarship that embraces the truth of Scripture.[37]

And that truth does not fade from age to age. "The grass withers, the flower fades, but the word of our God will stand forever"

37. Yes, in one sense that implies that it is Scripture that validates Scripture. I have discussed this kind of circularity in many places. See, for example, my *DKG*, 130–33. The fact is that any attempt to validate a final standard of truth and falsity must be circular in a sense, because it must appeal to its own standard, not some other.

(Isa. 40:8). Whatever new methods and ideas emerge among historical scholars, the Word of God remains. The church's fundamental understanding of Scripture has not changed since the time of the apostles—not because the standards of historical scholarship have remained constant over that time, for they have not; but because the church has always had the Word of God itself to stand as judge over its thinking. May God's Word continue, as he has promised, to guide us in our understanding of its truth.

17

Propositional Revelation

IN THE MID-TWENTIETH CENTURY, one of the major controversies about revelation and Scripture was whether revelation was "propositional." Evangelicals took the affirmative, and liberals (especially the "neoorthodox") the negative.

I will define *proposition* as philosophers usually define it: A proposition is a set of words that makes a truth claim, such as "the cat is on the mat." The proposition may be true or false. A true proposition is an item of "information."

So the theological question was whether revelation contained any truth claims. Orthodox Christians, of course, answered yes. The gospel, however understood, was good news, and news is propositional. The bearer of good news claims to be telling the truth. Also, orthodox Christians typically subscribe to doctrines on the basis that they are divinely revealed. So the doctrines of the creeds are propositions to be believed.

In my *DWG*, I argue that evangelicals may have put too much emphasis on the concept of propositional revelation. I emphasize in that book that the Bible is not *merely* propositional. Scripture contains not only propositions, but questions, commands, emotive expressions, and so on. And of course, Scripture is not structured as a *list* of propositions, like a doctrinal statement. It is structured mainly as a historical narrative, but also includes songs, wisdom sayings, prophecy, letters, apocalyptic. To stress propositional revelation exclusively, let alone to make that the fundamental nature of revelation, is to present the concept of revelation in intellectualist, classroom terms and to lose some of its biblical power and drama.

But Scripture most certainly contains propositions, among other things. That is to say, there are revealed narratives, revealed truths, revealed doctrines. The very first sentence of Genesis is a proposition, as is John 3:16. The propositional sentences of Scripture, to say nothing of its propositional implications and applications, are innumerable and of great importance.

So we may well ask why it was that liberal theologians (explicitly in the twentieth century, but implicitly before and after that) denied that divine revelation contained any propositions. Where did the slogan come from that "God does not reveal information; he reveals himself"?

Although I played down the concept of propositional revelation in my 2010 book, I've come to give far more importance to that concept. Indeed, I've come to see the issue of propositional revelation as the fundamental dividing line between orthodox Christianity and liberal theology.

Liberal theology is the name I use for all theology that denies the ultimate authority of Scripture over human thought. The phrase refers to the movement that began around 1650 when thinkers such as Benedict Spinoza, Thomas Hobbes, and Richard Simon sought to read the Bible as a purely human book. This movement went in tandem with the beginning of modern philosophy with Descartes. Both movements had in common a commitment to set tradition aside and make human reason the final judge of truth and falsity. This commitment is what Cornelius Van Til calls a commitment to "intellectual autonomy."

The change from a theology based on revelation and a theology based on human autonomous reasoning was very drastic. Certainly the theology of the church had never gone through such a momentous change. Before this, all branches of the church, Eastern and Western, Catholic and Protestant, traditional and sectarian, had claimed to base their teaching on Scripture. The new thinking attacked the old at its very foundations. But the new movement somehow won favor in academic circles and eventually in the church itself, as the church's ministers studied at universities. But Christian orthodoxy refused to die, and the struggle between the two movements continues today.

The liberal movement drastically revised the doctrines of the church. The doctrines of God, man, creation, fall, redemption, and consummation all had radically different content in the liberal theologies.[1] The gospel of salvation from sin by the supernatural work of Jesus Christ became a gospel of human improvement by the actualization of our own potential; the kingdom of God became the development of human culture.

But to make any of this plausible, it was also necessary to make drastic changes in the doctrine of revelation. It was necessary to exchange a doctrine of God's revealing his will to man with a doctrine of man's reasoning autonomously. Instead of man's submitting to the mind of God, it was necessary to make man's thought the final authority of truth and the definitive way to find eternal life.

In such a doctrine, propositional revelation had to go. It is not that Scripture or revelation is exclusively propositional in character; there are many other aspects of it. But of all the aspects of biblical revelation, its propositional character confronts most directly the claim of human autonomy.[2] If God reveals propositions, then he has the right to tell us what is true, and therefore what to think.

It is interesting to me that when we survey the history of liberal theology from 1650 to the present, we discover many variant ways of doing theological work. There is a great difference between Kant and Schleiermacher, and between Barth and Ritschl. But the liberal tradition is unanimous on one thing: the denial of propositional revelation. The reason is that this tradition is defined by its affirmation of human intellectual autonomy. Each theologian, to be sure, rejects propositional revelation for his own reasons; but each one certainly rejects propositional revelation. So the history of liberal theology can be understood as a sequence of different reasons for rejecting propositional revelation. In summary:

Enlightenment Rationalism (17th–18th centuries) rejected propositional revelation because it was simply incompatible with the primacy

1. J. Gresham Machen's *Christianity and Liberalism* (Grand Rapids: Eerdmans, 1923) is still the best account of the distinctives of liberalism, as opposed to those of traditional Christianity.
2. In a way, the same can be said for the character of revelation as divine *commands. Command revelation* and *propositional revelation* are in one sense interchangeable. For *propositional revelation* means that God's authority to command extends to what we think and believe. And *command revelation* means that the concepts of right and wrong are determined by divine propositions.

of human reason. These figures embraced natural revelation, but flatly denied special revelation and everything that went with it: miracles, incarnation, atonement, resurrection, and so forth. In a way, this earliest form of liberalism was the most blatant, perhaps the most honest. It showed what liberalism was at base, its strongest impulse.

G. W. Lessing rejected propositional revelation because propositional revelation in the traditional doctrine made authoritative claims about past history. But according to Lessing, past history is of its very nature uncertain and therefore insufficient to govern the religious life, which must be based on reason alone. He famously said that there was a great ditch between history and reason, and therefore between history and faith.

Immanuel Kant wrote *Religion within the Limits of Reason Alone,*[3] a book that had as its chief thesis the autonomy of reason in matters of religion. Kant used argument after argument to show that in religion, human reason must be the final judge over any purported revelation. In this book, religious liberalism makes its case for its own chief principle. Positively, Kant believed that the essence of religion was morality. A religious person was one who regarded his moral duties as divine commands. Of course, Kant did not believe that we discover our moral duties by means of divine commands. We discover them, rather, by an autonomous rational process. Then we regard them *as if* they were divine commands. So religion comes through rational morality, not by propositional revelation.

Friedrich Schleiermacher believed that feeling[4] was more fundamental than reason in religious matters. So he did not follow Kant's argumentation. But of course, propositional revelation is incompatible with autonomous feeling no less than it is incompatible with autonomous reason. Insofar as propositional revelation requires us to bypass our feelings and believe what it says, it violates Schleiermacher's principle, and Schleiermacher must reject it.

Albrecht Ritschl thought Schleiermacher's "feeling" theology was too subjective, and he claimed to have a method to overcome Lessing's

3. New York: Harper and Row, 1960.

4. There are various ways of translating Schleiermacher's *Gefühl*: *intuition* is an alternative to *feeling*. But unquestionably it is a datum of one's inner self-consciousness.

ditch and to place Christian theology on a historical foundation. But he was unwilling to surrender the autonomy of the historical scholar. So for him, faith is based not on history as such, but on the "value judgments" we make in response to the study of history. Arguably, this view is just as subjective as Schleiermacher's. In any case, it is equally far removed from any concept of propositional revelation.

Karl Barth appeared to reconstruct theology on the Word of God, rejecting the liberalism of the nineteenth century. But Barth denied even more emphatically than his predecessors the idea of propositional revelation. He used a somewhat different argument: that if propositional revelation exists, then revelation can be "possessed," "controlled," or "manipulated" by man. Of course, that is nonsense. If God reveals propositions, those propositions are precisely his means of controlling *us* and showing us that he is the Lord. But with Barth as with his predecessors, the rejection of propositional revelation allows for intellectual autonomy in the work of historical biblical scholarship.

Emil Brunner developed arguments similar to Barth's, but put more emphasis on the *personal* character of God's revelation to us. It is an *I-Thou Encounter*, not an *I-It Relationship*. So Brunner deemed propositional revelation to be impersonal and therefore inappropriate to the divine-human relation. He sometimes even argued that knowing propositional facts about a person inevitably impersonalizes the relationship. Sometimes, of course, that is true. But far more often, propositional knowledge deepens friendships.

Rudolf Bultmann distinguished between two meanings of revelation, "the communication of information by the word" (= propositional revelation) and "an event that puts me in a new situation." He assumed that these two are incompatible—that if revelation is of one sort, it cannot be of the other. He never argued that the two were incompatible, and in my judgment they clearly are not. Implicitly, what Bultmann argued was that the important thing to be gained in revelation was "a new existential self-understanding" and that propositional revelation would interfere with that. But Bultmann did not hesitate to describe the new existential self-understanding in propositions ("openness to the future," etc.), and I see no reason why God might not have done the same thing. The fact is that Bultmann did not deny propositional revelation because Scripture denied it; rather, he denied it to give to scholars the autonomy to criticize the content of Scripture.

Jürgen Moltmann rejected propositional revelation because he believed that the object of Christian hope was an entirely open future. Propositions about the future close off possibilities, and therefore, in Moltmann's view, they close off hope. On the contrary, I believe that a purely open future gives us no hope at all and that it is only God's propositional disclosure of his plan for history that gives us hope.

Wolfhart Pannenberg returned to the rationalism of the early liberals, insisting that though faith is based on history, it is based on a history ascertained by autonomous reason. Therefore, in his view, there is no place for propositional revelation, which would preclude certain conclusions of autonomous scholarship.

These are some of the most prominent figures in the history of liberal theology since the seventeenth century. It is significant that much as they differed from one another, they all rejected propositional revelation. They rejected it because it was incompatible with their fundamental assumption: that human thought must be autonomous when it considers matters of faith.

So I call on Christians who seek to be faithful to Scripture and to God to embrace propositional revelation. Propositional revelation is not all there is to revelation, of course. Scripture contains commands, questions, exclamations, poetry, parables, and other linguistic forms as well as propositions. But it most assuredly contains propositions as well. And arguably the whole Bible is propositional in a sense, for if we want to know all of God's history of redemption, all the authoritative propositional teaching God gives us, we must read the whole Bible.[5] At any rate, verses such as Genesis 1:1 and John 3:16 come to us as God's authoritative statements, given to us to be believed. If we choose not to believe them, then we have missed a fundamental principle of our life with God: that he is Lord, and we are his creatures. He has the right to tell us what to do, and that includes what to think.

---

5. It could also be argued that the whole Bible is command (because it is authoritative), that it is all interrogative (because it demands a response of its readers), that it is all exclamation (because it is all praise), and the like.

18

Meditation on Romans 11:33–36

*Delivered at a Lunch for the Trustees
of Reformed Theological Seminary,
October 6, 2011*

Oh, the depth of the riches and wisdom and knowledge of God! How
unsearchable are his judgments and how inscrutable his ways!

"For who has known the mind of the Lord,
   or who has been his counselor?"
"Or who has given a gift to him
   that he might be repaid?"

For from him and through him and to him are all things. To him be
glory forever. Amen. (Rom. 11:33–36)

This is one of my favorite passages, and I've used it in a number of
ways over the years. Today, I'd like to focus on this passage as theology,
and think of how it can serve as an example to us as we teach theology
at Reformed Theological Seminary.

The letter to the Romans is, of course, one of the most theological
books in the Bible, and more than anything else in the Bible, it resembles
a modern systematic theology. Paul here summarizes his gospel, the
basic content of his preaching. So he makes an orderly progression:
All have sinned (chaps. 1–3). So we must be justified by the work of

Christ alone, by faith alone (chaps. 3–5). Then some problems: shall we sin that grace may abound? Of course not (chap. 6). Why is it that I can't do the things I want, and I naturally do the things I don't want (chap. 7)? Then the great chapter on walking in the Spirit, chapter 8. Chapters 9–11 deal with the problem of Israel's unbelief. At the end of this comes our passage.

Although this letter is an orderly discussion of systematic theology, in some ways it is very different from modern-day systematic theologies. It is, of course, a letter, a personal communication. Theologies today follow an academic model, in which authors are not supposed to talk about themselves; personal reflections are frowned upon. Luther and Calvin were different. And Paul is more like them than like us. Paul constantly interrupts his exposition to present his personal reflections, to express his personal emotions:

> But if our unrighteousness serves to show the righteousness of God, what shall we say? That God is unrighteous to inflict wrath on us? (I speak in a human way.) By no means! For then how could God judge the world? (Rom. 3:5–6)

Paul carries on constant dialogue with imaginary, or perhaps real, opponents: "What shall we say then? Is there injustice on God's part? By no means!" (9:14).

He cries out when the truth hurts him personally: "Wretched man that I am! Who will deliver me from this body of death? Thanks be to God through Jesus Christ our Lord!" (Rom. 7:24–25).

Our passage in chapter 11 is also a personal exclamation and, like the last one, an act of worship. Paul doesn't see anything inappropriate in breaking away from his theological argument to praise, to worship God. We think maybe this is more appropriate in a letter than in a treatise. But who says so? And even if that is true, why do we so often think that theology must consist of treatises?

So Paul's theology in Romans is *personal*, and *devotional*. Further, there is a profound *humility* about it. We would certainly excuse Paul if he showed a bit of pride at being the author of Romans. Wouldn't you be just a little proud about that? So it wouldn't be hard for us to imagine a theological writer saying, "We have presented our doctrine of sin and salvation and provided adequate answers to several problems. Now we must turn to the ethical implications of what we have said." Not too much pride there, just a standard academic transition between one argument well made and the next. Now we understand this; now we will seek to understand that. But Paul pauses to note how much he *doesn't* know. "How *unsearchable* . . . and how *inscrutable* . . . . 'For who has known the mind of the Lord, or who has been his counselor?'" (Rom. 11:33–34).

That's such good theology. This is a proof text for our doctrine of the incomprehensibility of God. A proper proof text. Yet it is not set forth as a doctrine, but as an exclamation. Paul is not just saying that God is incomprehensible in general, as we might do in expounding a doctrine of analogy or accommodation. He finds God's incomprehensibility in his own teaching. He says in effect: "Folks, I've done my best to expound the gospel, to solve some problems, but I've only scratched the surface. What I've said was true, but there's so much more to it. God understands justification, sanctification, the history of redemption so much better than I do that there is no comparison. And the more we explore his plan in depth, the more we see how much we don't know, the more we are exposed to the mystery of God."

We need that in our theology, too. I'm not saying now that we need a doctrine of analogy or accommodation, though there is value in those. I'm saying that we need a specific conviction that our own formulations don't begin to encompass the mystery of God. Some theologians, in my opinion—nobody around here—speak much about the incomprehensibility of God, but they then take a cocksure and doctrinaire attitude in their polemics with other theologians, especially those of other traditions. I can't imagine Paul doing that.

But one more point. The last verse. Paul's theology here is not only personal, devotional, and humble. He is humble specifically before the sovereignty of God. He is humble because of God's sovereignty. God is incomprehensible because he is sovereign.

What do I mean by *sovereign?* All things are *from* him. He is the One who ordained eternally for the world to take the shape it has. He is the One who created the world, and who controls everything that comes to pass. All things are *through* him. Everything that happens happens because he is working in the world to bring it about. And all things are *to* him. Everything has a purpose, and that purpose is, one way or another, to bring glory to God.

That blows the mind, as we say. A God that big is certainly beyond our ability to figure him out. A God this big humbles us by his greatness, rendering trivial the partisan bickering that we theologians engage in. He bursts the academic model, challenges our pride, and makes us face the personal implications of what he says to us.

I pray that Reformed Theological Seminary will always be known for this kind of theology: theology that is personal, devotional, and humbled by the greatness of the sovereign God.

PART 3

Apologetics

19

Intellectual Repentance

I'VE WRITTEN VERY LITTLE ON this subject, but it has played a major role in my thinking about apologetic method.

Apologetics is the discipline that prepares Christian believers to "make a defense to anyone who asks you for a reason for the hope that is in you" (1 Peter 3:15). On this definition, apologetics is part of evangelism, witness to non-Christians. We should not forget, of course, that Christians also sometimes ask reasons for their hope. Apologetics evangelizes nonbelievers, but it also evangelizes the unbelief within the believer.

In both cases, apologetics, like evangelism, has the goal of repentance and faith (Acts 2:38; 16:31), with baptism as the consequence of faith in those who are not yet baptized (Matt. 28:19). Faith is turning to Christ. Repentance, the opposite side of the coin, is turning from sin. Repentance and faith designate a common movement of the soul from two perspectives, for one cannot turn to Christ without turning from sin, or vice versa.

Repentance and faith are movements of the whole soul, the whole heart, and the whole body. One who believes in God loves him with all his heart, soul, and might (Deut. 6:5; cf. Mark 12:30). Sin corrupts that wholehearted love, so as to affect everything we are, think, or do (Rom. 3:10–18). Repentance turns us away from that corruption, renewing in us the ability to say no to sin.

In many areas of life, it is not difficult to give particular examples. We should repent of worshiping false gods, disrespect for God's name,

165

dishonoring parents, murder, or adultery. We should repent of malice, lust, unkindness, gossip, or envy.

But what about the area of the mind, thought, intellect? Do we ever need to repent of the way we think?

I believe so. Our wholehearted love of God includes loving him with our "mind," which Mark 12:30 adds to the listing of Deuteronomy 6:5. Second Corinthians 10:5 urges us to "take every *thought* captive to obey Christ." Second Corinthians 4:4 says:

> The god of this world has blinded the minds of the unbelievers, to keep them from seeing the light of the gospel of the glory of Christ, who is the image of God.

Now, *mind* in Scripture is not a narrowly intellectual concept. It may often be a synecdoche for the whole life of a person. In those contexts a change of mind is a change of heart, a change in the whole person, the whole direction of his life. But to say that is not to suggest that loving God with the intellect is unnecessary. If the intellect is really part of, or an aspect of, our being, it is certainly included in the idea of a change of heart or mind.

In fact, I have argued[1] that intellect, will, emotions, intuition, and other human "faculties" are not (as some have thought) separable objects, fighting for supremacy in our heads. Rather, they are perspectives on the whole person. The intellect is the whole person thinking, the will the whole person deciding, the emotions the whole person feeling, and each of these influences the others. Repentance is repentance of the whole person, and so it includes the intellect as well as every other human capacity. The whole person is fallen; the whole person is redeemed by God's grace.

So in Scripture there is an antithesis between believing and unbelieving ways to think. When Eve chose in the garden to disobey God, her fall was not first in tasting the forbidden fruit. It was rather in her previous decision to obey Satan rather than God. This sin was a

---

1. *DKG,* 328–46; *DCL,* 361–82.

sin of the mind before it was a sin of the body. She decided that Satan, not God, was the more reliable authority for her thought. An even more profound characterization of the event is that she determined that she herself was the ultimate authority, that is, that her mind was autonomous.

All of Scripture is an exhibition of the differences, indeed antithesis, between godly thought and would-be-autonomous thought. Noah and his family believed God; but others did not, and their would-be-autonomous thinking was rebuked in God's judgment. The same for Abraham, who believed God's promise without flinching, though from a merely human point of view it appeared impossible (Rom. 4:19–21). Moses, David, Jesus, Paul—all believed God's word rather than accepting the thinking of would-be-autonomous sinners. We can generalize: all sin presupposes attempts to think autonomously. All righteousness presupposes a person's intention to think God's thoughts after him.

So Scripture does not hesitate to relate epistemological language to God's covenant lordship over us. In Psalm 111:10, the psalmist says:

> The fear of the LORD is the beginning of wisdom;
> all those who practice it have a good understanding.
> His praise endures forever!

In Proverbs 1:7, we read:

> The fear of the LORD is the beginning of knowledge;
> fools despise wisdom and instruction.

Cf. Prov. 9:10; 15:33.

In 1 Corinthians 1:18–2:16; 3:18–23; 8:1–3, Paul engages in a critique of those in the church of Corinth who considered themselves wise in the ways of the world. First Corinthians 1:20 reads:

> Where is the one who is wise? Where is the scribe? Where is the debater of this age? Has not God made foolish the wisdom of the world?

Paul tells them not to put any confidence in what the pagans considered wisdom. No tradition of non-Christian wisdom has any place for
salvation by blood atonement, or for the resurrection from the dead
(1 Cor. 15). These ideas are foolish by the world's standards. But they
are the very foundations of godly thinking.

We come to know this gospel through God's Word. Paul identifies its content with his own preaching, when he first visited Corinth
(1 Cor. 2:1–4). When he later defends the resurrection in chapter 15,
his argument rests not so much on the evidences he lists in verses 5–9
as on the fact that the resurrection of Jesus was part of the apostolic
preaching (vv. 1–3, 11–12, 14–15). And the apostolic preaching, in turn,
is the Word of God (Gal. 1:11–12).

Paul's concern is not only that the Corinthians believe in the resurrection, but that they believe it on the proper ground, the ground of
Paul's preaching of the Word of God.

To believe God on the basis of his own Word is fundamental to
biblical epistemology. This epistemology rebukes our pride as none
other. When we become Christians, we renounce claims to autonomy
and bow before God's authority. We come to believe what he says because
he says so. That is a huge change of mind and heart. It is a large change,
a turning, a repentance. To become a Christian is to repent of sin in
every area of life, including our way of thinking.

Now let us think about the implications of this fact for apologetic
method. The traditional, or classic, apologetic approach tells the non-
Christian to engage in argument using the common ground of logic and
evidence. The apologist will then try to convince the inquirer through
this method that the biblical God exists and that Christ is his Son, sent
to die for his people and rise again. If the non-Christian accepts this
argument, then the apologist will urge him to repent of his sins and
believe in Jesus.

He may indeed accept this invitation, repenting of his false worship, his unkindness, his injustice, his lusts. But one thing he is unlikely
to repent of is his false way of thinking, his claim to be autonomous in
his reasoning. For the apologist, being a classical apologist, has from
the beginning asked him to depend on precisely his autonomous rea-

soning. The apologist has not asked him to repent of that, but rather to rely on it. His apologetic presentation is inconsistent with a demand for intellectual repentance.

I am not saying that every inquirer must be confronted with his intellectual sin, for that would assume that he must be confronted with *every* sin he has committed, and nobody can accomplish that. But (1) for many inquirers, the intellect is a major stumbling block. Often it has been precisely intellectual pride that has kept someone from bowing to Christ. (2) In our present age, worship of the supposedly autonomous intellect is one of the most prevalent forms of idolatry. This is obviously true in "modern" thought, but it is also true in "postmodern" thought, for postmodern thought has never renounced the claim of intellectual autonomy. It only claims that such intellectually autonomous thought should reject overarching "metanarratives" or worldviews.

If someone professes Christ, but maintains his intellectual idolatry, there will be a major tension, a contradiction, in his heart and life.

But is there any way of presenting an apologetic that addresses intellectual idolatry, that demands intellectual repentance? I think there is.

The apologist can point out somewhere in the conversation that the inquirer needs nothing less than a new heart and life. It won't do to try to graft Christianity on to an unbelieving foundation. The Christian life is a "new creation" (2 Cor. 5:17). Old things are passed away: all things have become new. Everything must change.

Obviously, old habits must change. Evil actions and lusts have no place in the Christian life. We cannot, of course, deal with these in our own strength. God must step in and grant his grace to transform us, through Christ. He will leave us nothing to boast about. And yes, even our mind must change, our way of thinking. We need to have a new way of thinking, again by grace. For we are saved neither by our own works nor by our own wisdom. God not only gives grace to change our habits, but gives us a new mind by which to think about him and his world.

So if we have questions about God's existence, the deity of Christ, or the resurrection, we must learn to listen first to what he says about these questions. This may seem circular, but circular argument always and necessarily occurs when we try to prove an ultimate. A rationalist must use reason to prove the competence of reason. For him there is nothing higher than reason by which he can put reason to the test. A Christian must appeal to God's Word to prove God's Word, for there is nothing higher than God's Word by which to test it.

Still, the apologist can show that if God has not spoken, then reason is in a hopeless bind. Reason is not competent to guarantee itself, and if there is no God, reason cannot guarantee itself based on someone else's testimony. And if there is no personal God, there is no plan behind the universe, no reason to believe that reason can understand it.

So the inevitable consequence of such reasoning is that God does in fact exist. Not only that, but that our reason is *not* autonomous. In fact, the claim of autonomy is one thing of which we need to repent. *If God exists, the claim of intellectual autonomy is idolatrous.*

This type of apologetics, sometimes called presuppositional, leads directly to the gospel. It leads directly to repentance. It does not give the inquirer anything to boast about.

So often, apologetic debates are rather divorced from the gospel. They amount to theoretical discussions of causality, history, and so on. When they lead to God, there is an atmosphere of discovery, perhaps of pride: I have proved God! Repentance and faith come later.

Better to carry on the debate in a way that leads directly to repentance in all areas of life.

So far as I know, presuppositionalism is the only apologetic method that demands intellectual repentance and shows why it is necessary. That, I think, is a major recommendation for this approach to apologetics.

20

Intellectual Discipleship

AT SEVENTY-THREE, I am in something of a valedictory mode, and I am asking what are the most important thoughts I would like to leave to the next generation. In my festschrift,[1] I included quite a bit of grandfatherly wisdom, such as it was. There I addressed fellow believers generally. But now I want to focus on Christian intellectuals specifically. What principle do I want above all to leave with them?

It is this: Christian thinking, like everything else we do, must be servant-thinking, disciple-thinking. It is one of those things we must do to the glory of God alone (1 Cor. 10:31).

Again and again, I've seen Christians with substantial intellectual gifts, who ostensibly are spiritually solid, who have gone off into some fashionable heresy. The problem, often, is that they have not applied the lordship of Christ to their studies. They have been regular in their worship and prayer lives, meticulous in their general ethics, moving in their testimony of God's grace. But for some reason it has never occurred to them that Jesus redeems the mind as well, and that he makes substantial demands on their intellectual lives.

Typically, the way it happens is that a gifted young person (let's call him Joe) gets a scholarship to, say, Harvard. His pastor urges him to maintain his devotional life, to find a good church. But he says nothing about the specifically intellectual challenges of life at Harvard.

Joe goes there and maintains his faith in the usual areas of life. He finds a good church, reads his Bible, tries to maintain his ethical

1. John J. Hughes, ed., *Speaking the Truth in Love* (Phillipsburg, NJ: P&R Publishing, 2009).

integrity. But he majors in, say, religious studies. His professor (call him Adolf Barthmann) tells him that no educated person today can believe in a historical Adam. Joe, of course, is no match for Barthmann, either in knowledge or in intellect. Barthmann must be right, he reasons, because he is an expert and a teacher at Harvard. Certainly, he reasons, we ought to trust our teachers. And at a great institution such as Harvard, we can expect our teachers to take us to a level of truth that goes beyond what we have heard from our parents, high-school teachers, and pastors. So Joe emerges from his course not believing anymore in the historicity of Adam.

It seems to him fairly innocent, and not at all a compromise of his faith. Schooling is supposed to bring new knowledge, intellectual change. The movement from algebra to geometry in tenth grade was not any kind of crisis of faith. Why should Barthmann's religion course be a question of discipleship?

But it is. Joe should have known that. His pastor and his parents should have told him. That he didn't know is a tragedy. And it is an ignorance that must be undone.

Joe knew that majoring in religion would be a big decision. He should have brought it in prayer to God and conferred with mature Christians about his decision. He should have done some research about Prof. Barthmann and gotten to know some arguments of Barthmann's critics. He should have heard the NT passages that urge us to "test everything" (1 Thess. 5:21) and that warn us against false teaching (2 Thess. 2:11–12; 1 Tim. 4:1–7; 2 Tim. 3:1–9; 2 Peter 2; 1 John 2:18–27; 4:1–8). He should have taken pains to critically evaluate Barthmann's words by the standard of the Word of God.

That Word of God, indeed, must be the foundation of the Christian's epistemology.[2] It is not enough for Christians to determine the truth through sense experience, reason, or emotion. God must have the final word in everything. No secular philosopher admits this principle, and most Christian philosophers, together with many theologians, are

---

2. My *DKG* tries to spell out in detail what an epistemology based on the Bible might look like.

confused about it. But it is nonnegotiable for anyone who seeks to be a disciple of Christ.

If Christ is not Lord of the mind, there are two alternatives: (1) the human mind (collectively or individually) answers only to itself, and (2) there is no ultimate authority over the human mind. As Cornelius Van Til stressed over and over again, the first alternative is rationalism, the second irrationalism. But rationalism breaks down: the human mind can never do the job of God. So rationalism devolves into irrationalism. And irrationalism can be asserted only on a rationalistic basis.

Those alternatives are not open to Christians, and that is a good thing. The intellectual lordship of Christ is the only hope that we have to make progress in human learning. We can be thankful that his lordship has led us into fruitful intellectual pursuits even when we have not acknowledged him. This is his "common grace," his kindness to sinners. But that guidance is not guaranteed, and one day there will be a judgment against everyone who exalts himself against God.

The intellect is the last frontier of discipleship. It is the area least recognized as belonging to the lordship of Christ. When Christians come to recognize his lordship over the mind, they will achieve remarkable things, they will see the world rightly as God made it, and they will receive his commendation as faithful servants.

21

Review of Greg Bahnsen,
*Presuppositional Apologetics:
Stated and Defended*[1]

THERE IS A STANDARD PLOT in movies and novels, in which an ancient document or artifact, supposed lost, but found by intrepid investigators, emerges with major consequences for modern civilization. That has actually happened. Several years ago an authentic set of Bach chorales, lost for many years, was discovered in the Yale library and released to the acclaim of Bach lovers, of whom I am one. Earlier in the past century, the discovery of the Dead Sea Scrolls, and later of various Gnostic documents, came to have a great impact on academic theological discussion. And, well, imagine the commotion in the church if someone plausibly claimed to have discovered a lost letter of Paul to Corinth (he refers to two of them in 1 Corinthians 5:9 and 2 Corinthians 7:8) or an authentic ending to the gospel of Mark.

This sort of thing rarely happens with modern-day theological writings, but occasionally something will get lost in the shuffle and then be found again. So it is with the present volume, an apologetics text by the late Greg Bahnsen, one of the leading figures in the movement of presuppositional apologetics. It was likely written in the late 1970s, but for some reason was set aside. Bahnsen's untimely death in 1995, from

1. Powder Springs, GA: American Vision Press, and Nacodoches, TX: Covenant Media Press, 2008.

complications of heart surgery, doubtless made it yet more difficult for
the document to be discovered, evaluated, and published, especially since
his publishers were soon busy with another large Bahnsen manuscript,
Van Til's Apologetic: Readings and Analysis, which was published by P&R
in 1998. But recently the older document has been rediscovered, edited,
and published by American Vision, and we should be thankful to them
and to God for making this important work available.

Presuppositional Apologetics: Stated and Defended is an exposition of
and argument for presuppositional apologetics, in the form advocated
by Bahnsen's teacher Cornelius Van Til (1895–1987). Apologetics is the
theological discipline that defends the Christian faith against the objections of unbelief. It has a long history, beginning with the Bible itself, in
which God and his spokesmen frequently respond to the challenges of
sinful human beings. The apostle Paul once summarized his work as "the
defense [*apologia*] and confirmation of the gospel" (Phil. 1:7). After the
close of the biblical canon, many Christian thinkers have been famous
for their work in apologetics, such as Justin Martyr, Origen, Augustine,
Anselm of Canterbury, Thomas Aquinas, Blaise Pascal, Joseph Butler,
William Paley, F. R. Tennant, and C. S. Lewis. More recent names
include Gordon Clark, Edward J. Carnell, and Francis Schaeffer, whom
Bahnsen discusses in this volume. But Bahnsen finds all of these inadequate compared to the presuppositional apologetic method of Van Til.

Van Til immigrated to the United States from the Netherlands with
his family at the age of ten. He attended schools of the Dutch-American
Christian Reformed Church through his first year of seminary, and
then transferred to Princeton Theological Seminary in New Jersey, a
seminary of the Presbyterian Church in the USA. His Dutch-American
teachers led him to admire Abraham Kuyper, truly a renaissance man:
pastor, philosopher, theologian, journalist, educator, politician (for several years, prime minister of the Netherlands). Another towering figure
in Dutch Reformed theology was Herman Bavinck, the profound theologian whose four-volume *Reformed Dogmatics* has only recently been
translated into English.[2] At Princeton, Van Til came also to admire the

2. Grand Rapids: Baker, 2003.

formidable theological scholar B. B. Warfield, though Warfield had died several years before Van Til arrived. The Dutch thinkers emphasized that Christians and non-Christians operate according to antithetical principles of knowledge. So Kuyper had little interest in apologetics, considering it a futile attempt to construct a bridge from non-Christian to Christian thought. Warfield, however, emphasized the objective validity of the Christian faith, which in his view rendered possible and necessary its intellectual defense. Van Til sought to combine the main emphases of Kuyper and Warfield: Christianity is indeed intellectually defensible (as Warfield), but it must be defended in accord with its own distinctive principle of knowledge (Kuyper).[3]

In addition to his studies at the seminary, Van Til completed a Ph.D. in philosophy at Princeton University. In his dissertation, supervised by A. A. Bowman, he compared the God of Christianity to the Absolute of Hegelian Idealism, judging the two to be antithetical despite surface similarities. After completing his studies, Van Til taught apologetics for a year at Princeton Seminary.

In 1929, the General Assembly of the Presbyterian Church USA reorganized the seminary. Princeton had been known for its scholarly defense of Reformed orthodoxy. Under the reorganization it was forced to include faculty of "liberal" views, those who disowned or considered "unnecessary" the orthodox doctrines of the faith, such as the physical resurrection of Christ and the inerrancy of Scripture. J. Gresham Machen, a professor of New Testament at Princeton, led several conservative professors to leave there and begin Westminster Seminary in Philadelphia. Westminster's purpose was to continue the orthodox Reformed teaching of what would then be called "Old" Princeton. Like Kuyper, Machen recognized a sharp antithesis between biblical and antibiblical thinking. In his book *Christianity and Liberalism*,[4] he argued that liberalism was not a perspective or emphasis within Christianity. Rather, it was a different religion altogether. Van Til

3. Van Til's integration of these two concerns is interestingly foreshadowed in Bavinck, *Reformed Dogmatics*, 1.515: "Apologetics cannot precede faith and does not attempt a priori to argue the truth of revelation. It assumes the truth and belief in the truth" (cf. 56).
4. Grand Rapids: Eerdmans, 1923.

enthusiastically agreed with Machen's assessment, and he joined the faculty of Westminster.

Van Til's presuppositionalism begins with the antitheses of Kuyper and Machen: the content of Christian and non-Christian thought are radically opposed to one another. Christian thought is grounded on the revelation of God himself in nature and Scripture. God is *Lord*; therefore, he can speak only with supreme authority, and his Word is not to be doubted. The Word of God must be the fundamental *presupposition* of anyone who would seek to know God or his creation. To say that God's Word is our fundamental presupposition is to say that no idea from any other source can take precedence over it, or be received with more authority. We may not evaluate Scripture by submitting it to the judgment of something else. And the Word of God gives us the final word on how to make use of all other sources of knowledge. So God's lordship is the fundamental premise, the *presupposition*, of any sound Christian epistemology.

But God is not only Lord; he is also *Savior*. For Adam's sin has spread to the whole human race, and it infects human thought as well as all other aspects of human life. Fallen man resists the lordship of God and makes his own mind the ultimate standard of truth. So Scripture refers to human thought apart from God's grace as foolish, vain, and worthless. Romans 1 tells us that although God has clearly revealed himself in creation, sinful man represses that truth, does not like to have God in his knowledge, exchanges the truth for a lie. Rather than serve the Lord, he prefers to be *autonomous*, to be his own law, his own authority, his own standard of truth. The result is individual and cultural corruption: idolatrous worship, sexual license, and every other manner of wickedness. So we are unable to know God as we should unless and until God removes from us the burden of sin and stops our suppression of the truth. That he does, by sending his Son Jesus Christ to make himself an atonement for sin, and by sending his Spirit to change our hearts, so that we will trust Christ by faith. Our faith is faith in God's promise of salvation, which, like all of God's words, comes to us with absolute authority. In salvation as in everything else, God is Lord, and our knowledge of him is based on his own authority.

So there can be no sharper antithesis than between those who embrace God and those who spit on him, between those who embrace his authority and those who try to be autonomous. Thus we have seen two reasons for the necessity of presuppositional thinking: As our Lord, God has the right to demand that we think his thoughts after him. And as our Savior from sin, only he can penetrate the moral barrier that we have erected between ourselves and God's truth.

This antithesis must find expression also in apologetics. When believers bring the gospel to unbelievers, they must present it as what it is, the authoritative Word of the Lord. This does not change when the unbeliever raises objections and the conversation therefore turns apologetic. Much as the apologist may be tempted to accept the unbeliever's criteria of logical validity, truth, and ethical rightness, much as he may desire to appeal to "common ground," he must hold firm instead to God's standards, presenting arguments that themselves presuppose God's authority. He may not pretend to be neutral in order to please the unbeliever. He must present God as nothing less than the Lord, presupposing God's Word as the ultimate criterion of truth.

Many have objected that this procedure is circular, proving God's Word while presupposing the authority of God's Word. Van Til replied (1) that every system of thought is circular in a way when it tries to prove the validity of its fundamental presupposition. For not only do Christians have fundamental presuppositions, but non-Christians do as well: an ultimate commitment to the proposition that the biblical God is not Lord, which entails a commitment to some authority other than God's Word. It may be human rationality, sense experience, feeling, or some non-Christian religious or philosophical system. (Since all of these are substitutes for the true God, they fall under the biblical definition of *idols*.) But when a non-Christian seeks to prove the authority of his presupposition, he can only argue in a circle. The only way to prove an ultimate commitment to reason is to appeal to reason. The only way to prove the ultimate authority of sense experience is by appealing to sense experience. The only way to prove the ultimate authority of the Qur'an is by the Qur'an.

To the circularity objection, Van Til also replied (2) that the circularity in question does not make argument impossible. It simply means that the argument is between two entire systems, two presuppositions, rather than an argument between individual claims of one system versus those of the other. Van Til advocated that the Christian place his whole system on the table: his presuppositions, his facts (interpreted by his presuppositions), his evidences, his ethical principles, and all the rest. And he should invite the non-Christian to place his whole system on the table likewise. Then the two parties should compare each other's systems of thought, as wholes. Van Til was confident that such mutual examination would show that the non-Christian's system was unable to account for any kind of meaning, intelligibility, rationality, truth, or logic. Only the Christian presupposition could generate a system of thought that provided an intelligible account of the world and of thinking itself.

Van Til therefore advocated *transcendental argument*,[5] argument designed to show not merely that a conclusion is true, but that it must be presupposed if anything else is to be meaningful. Any lesser claim, he believed, was an insult to the Lord God. For Van Til, an apologetic must show not only that God exists, but that God is Lord, and therefore that any thinking that does not presuppose him is unintelligible, foolish, and meaningless.

Van Til's position has never been a popular one among apologists. Most apologists, even some who have studied with Van Til, have thought that it is impossible to argue with non-Christians unless there is some kind of "common ground," some premises that both positions can agree on and that can lead to the conclusion that Christianity is true. But Van Til's apologetic continues to be taught at Westminster Seminary of Philadelphia and elsewhere, and it is recognized (e.g., in Steven Cowan, ed., *Five Views of Apologetics*[6]) as one of the major movements in evangelical apologetics today. A number of writers have followed Van Til very closely. Others (such as Clark, Carnell, and Schaeffer, discussed in this volume) have echoed some of Van Til's distinctive themes, but have departed at points from his specific formulations.

5. Sometimes called *presuppositional argument* or *argument by presupposition*.
6. Grand Rapids: Zondervan, 2000.

Among the second generation of Van Tillian apologists, one of the most notable was Greg Bahnsen. Bahnsen had worked closely with Rousas J. Rushdoony, the founder of the Christian Reconstruction movement. Rushdoony maintained that all of human life, including government and culture, had to be brought under the sway of Jesus Christ. That included philosophy as well. So Rushdoony came to endorse Van Til's apologetics and wrote *By What Standard*,[7] an early popular exposition of Van Til's thought. Bahnsen agreed with Rushdoony, both on Christian reconstruction and on apologetics. At Westmont College he majored in philosophy and then (1970) came to Westminster to study with Van Til himself. During his Westminster years, Bahnsen also took several courses with me, and we were friends. His academic work was stellar, and he completed his M.Div. and Th.M. degrees in the same year (1973), which was unheard of at the time. After a brief, controversial period of teaching at Reformed Theological Seminary in Jackson, Mississippi, he completed his Ph.D. in philosophy at the University of Southern California, writing on the topic of self-deception.[8]

Following his doctoral work, Bahnsen became a pastor in the Orthodox Presbyterian Church, founded the Southern California Center for Christian Studies, and wrote a number of books and articles. Much of his writing defended the positions of Rushdoony and the Christian Reconstruction movement, particularly theonomy. *Theonomy* is the view that the laws governing Israel in the OT are normative for present-day civil governments. Bahnsen argued particularly that the penalties attached to violations of these laws (including death for adultery, homosexuality, and blasphemy) should be maintained by governments in all cultures and all ages.[9]

Through the 1980s, Bahnsen was primarily known for his defense of theonomy. But even then he continued to promote Van Til's presup-

7. Philadelphia: Presbyterian and Reformed, 1959.

8. This topic is important for apologetics. Recall from our earlier discussion that in Romans 1 Paul presents nonbelievers as self-deceived.

9. His major writings in this area are *Theonomy in Christian Ethics*, expanded ed. (Phillipsburg, NJ: Presbyterian and Reformed, 1984); *By This Standard* (Tyler, TX: Institute for Christian Economics, 1985); *No Other Standard: Theonomy and Its Critics* (Tyler, TX: Institute for Christian Economics, 1991).

positional apologetics in lectures and articles. In 1985, he debated athe-
ist Gordon Stein at the University of California at Irvine. I was there,
having driven up with a number of students from Westminster Seminary in Escondido. My testimony is that Stein was utterly unprepared
to deal with Bahnsen's "transcendental argument for the existence of
God," and most of the large audience also saw it that way.[10] After that,
Bahnsen's writings and lectures focused more sharply on apologetics,
until he died in 1995.

Very shortly after his death, his book *Always Ready: Directions for
Defending the Faith*[11] was published. This is a handbook on presuppositional apologetics, containing a great deal of biblical exegesis support-
ing this method. The early chapters are short. Many appeared earlier
as articles in *Chalcedon Reports*, published by Rushdoony's Chalcedon
Foundation. In 1998 appeared *Van Til's Apologetic*, which I referred to
earlier.

Although he had a shorter career than many theologians and apologists, Bahnsen was uncommonly productive, as the Covenant Media
Foundation catalogue indicates. His lectures and papers cover nearly
every theological and apologetic subject, together with reflections on
the history of philosophy, modern culture, and a wide range of church
issues.

Besides a remarkable work ethic, Bahnsen brought to apologetics a
new level of logical cogency. God had gifted him with a powerful intellect, which he honed through his training with Rushdoony and Van Til,
and at Westmont and USC. In his philosophical studies, he focused
(as Van Til had not) on the philosophy of language analysis, which
enabled him to dig deeply into the meanings of words and concepts and
to evaluate the logical validity and soundness of arguments. Van Til's
writing is impressive in its great knowledge of philosophy, theology, and
Scripture; but Van Til rarely put his arguments into syllogistic form,

10. I discuss my impressions at greater length in "Bahnsen at the Stein Debate," available
at http://www.frame-poythress.org/frame_articles/Bahnsen.htm. Audio of the debate and a
transcript are available at Covenant Media Foundation, http://www.cmfnow.com/index.
asp?PageAction=VIEWPROD&ProdID=5582&HS=1. Covenant Media Foundation is the major
source for many Bahnsen writings and lectures.
11. Atlanta: American Vision; Texarkana, AR: Covenant Media Foundation, 1996.

to show the precise logical basis of his conclusions. Bahnsen, however, was a master of logic, argument, and analysis. As such, he was able to add a significant dimension to Van Til's presentation.

Granted that difference in presentation, however, Bahnsen's apologetic is thoroughly and consistently Van Tillian. Though Bahnsen speaks in a style and tone different from Van Til's, the substance is almost precisely the same. I cannot think of a single point at which Bahnsen expresses criticism of Van Til, or takes a position opposed to his. In this respect, Bahnsen is different from some others. My own work follows the basic structure of Van Til's presuppositionalism, but I do differ with Van Til on some specific points.[12]

These differences can be summarized by saying that in my view Van Til often exaggerates his disagreements with others. First, he somewhat exaggerates the antithesis between believer and unbeliever. The Bible itself presents that antithesis with some qualifications. As we have seen, and as Van Til and Bahnsen acknowledge, Paul says in Romans 1 that the unbeliever has a true knowledge of God based on God's revelation in nature (Rom. 1:21). Of course, the unbeliever "suppress[es]" that knowledge in unrighteousness (v. 18). But does this suppression imply that the unbeliever can never utter a true statement, such as "the sky is blue"? If not, to what extent may the apologist agree with what the unbeliever says, and use that agreement to show the necessity of theism? At what points do such agreements become a "common ground," a false "neutrality"? On that question, I do not believe that Van Til ever arrived at a clear answer, nor did Bahnsen. Van Til himself admitted that this was a "difficult point,"[13] and that in the mind of the unbeliever "the actual situation is therefore always a mixture of truth with error."[14] But the vagueness of this formulation compromises somewhat the force of his rhetoric of antithesis.[15]

I also believe that Van Til exaggerated the differences between himself and other apologists, particularly those Bahnsen discusses in this

---

12. See my *AGG*, *CVT*, and the articles on presuppositional apologetics in Cowan, *Five Views of Apologetics*.

13. Cornelius Van Til, *An Introduction to Systematic Theology* (Nutley, NJ: Presbyterian and Reformed, 1974), 26.

14. Ibid., 27.

15. I try to analyze this problem in my *CVT*, chapter 15.

book who call themselves presuppositionalists (Gordon Clark, Edward J. Carnell, and Francis Schaeffer). At a number of points, I think Van Til and Bahnsen should have given more benefit of the doubt to those they criticize, by interpreting them in more favorable ways. I cannot take time here to explore this issue in detail.[16] Readers can compare Bahnsen's treatments of these gentlemen with mine in *CVT*. I do applaud Bahnsen for citing quotes of these apologists that affirm elements of presuppositionalism. But can it really be true, as Bahnsen suggests, that these three intelligent writers simply abandoned their presuppositional stance elsewhere in their writings and engaged in apologetic methods that flatly contradicted this stance?[17] Did they completely forget what they had said about God's authority over human knowledge? I suspect that the relationship between their presuppositional statements and their apparently anti-presuppositional "positions" is more complicated than either Van Til or Bahnsen thought.

That leads to the broader question of what precisely constitutes a transcendental or presuppositional argument. For Van Til's and Bahnsen's complaint against apologists such as the three mentioned here is that their arguments, despite their claims, are not really transcendental. Van Til and Bahnsen seemed to think, for example, that an inference from the world to God could not be properly transcendental, for such inferences imply that we can understand the world without already knowing God. So a cosmological argument, for example, which reasons from the world as an effect to God as its cause (if the world, then God), assumes that the world is intelligible apart from God and therefore denies, rather than affirms, the God of Scripture.

In my view, however, to say that "if A, then B" does not necessarily entail that we can understand A apart from B. One could indeed use that formula precisely to make the opposite point: to show

16. One example: on page 135, Bahnsen cites Clark as saying that "some corrections will be needed" to the thinking of non-Christian idealist R. G. Collingwood. Bahnsen thinks that Clark here is blind to the vastness of the antithesis between the Bible and Collingwood. I'm inclined, however, to think rather that Bahnsen here is blind to Clark's ironic understatement.

17. Bahnsen puts it thus: "Although many fine points of presuppositional character can be found scattered throughout their writings, we regretfully note that their positions as a whole are inconsistent with these points" (126).

that A makes no sense without B—a transcendental argument.[18] Indeed, this is what Bahnsen himself does in his debate with Stein: he argues, "If logic, then God"; "If scientific laws, then God"; and "If moral standards, then God." Reading him in the most favorable way, I believe that Bahnsen regarded logic, scientific laws, and moral standards as meaningless without God; so his argument is really transcendental. But if we give Bahnsen's own argument such a favorable reading, then I think we should give a similarly favorable reading to other apologists who use this procedure, such as Clark, Carnell, and Schaeffer. This is not to commend everything these men wrote. Doubtless they, like all the rest of us, failed at points to acknowledge God's lordship over our thought. But the critique of our fellow apologists ought to be precise, and we should give them the benefit of the doubt.

Bahnsen was somewhat appalled that I was willing to give such a favorable reading to apologists that he, and before him Van Til, had expelled from the presuppositional community. He criticized me on this score in lectures at Westminster Seminary (California) given in the early 1990s.[19] I replied to Bahnsen's criticisms, in effect, in the two books earlier cited.

I confess, however, that I consider it unfortunate that Van Til and his followers (including Bahnsen and me) have spent so much of their time in "movement" battles, debating who is and is not a true, authentic presuppositionalist. Apologetics should be directed toward the unbeliever, rather than primarily a matter for in-house controversy. There is a place for discussion within a movement, but in this case I think that discussion has become a tail wagging the dog. Presuppositional apologetics is a wonderful, powerful weapon in the spiritual warfare of our time. It is a tragedy that it has not been more often, and more effectively, put to use against the real enemy: unbelief.

18. The debate over the meaning of transcendental argument has continued since Bahnsen's death. See especially my "Reply to Don Collett on Transcendental Argument," http://www.frame-poythress.org/frame_articles/2003ReplytoCollett.htm; Collett's "Van Til and Transcendental Argument Revisited," in Speaking the Truth in Love, ed. John J. Hughes (Phillipsburg, NJ: P&R Publishing, 2009), 460–88; and my reply to him in the same volume (962–68).

19. Those lectures are still available in MP3 audio from Covenant Media Foundation. See http://www.cmfnow.com/index.asp?PageAction=VIEWCATS&Category=407.

I think that toward the end of his life Bahnsen came to feel that way, too. That's what I take from some of his comments to me directly and through his friends. That is why he came to give less attention to intra-presuppositional warfare and more to debates with unbelievers such as Gordon Stein and Edward Tabash. His *Always Ready* and *Van Til's Apologetic* aim to train readers to do apologetic evangelism, more than to win arguments with other apologists, though the latter emphasis is also present.

Perhaps that is part of the reason why Bahnsen did not publish the present volume, very much an in-house document, during his lifetime. One will never know for sure. Others who knew him tell me that he left this manuscript unfinished upon his departure from Reformed Theological Seminary because he needed to pursue more remunerative projects to support his family. Those friends of Bahnsen are persuaded that if he had lived, he would certainly have finished and published the present book.

In any case, this book is an important part of the historical record. It is authentic Bahnsen, vintage Bahnsen. It displays brilliantly his intellectual gifts and his devotion to the lordship of Christ in all areas of life. Some things in it, I think, do not represent Van Til or Bahnsen at their best. And the book as a whole represents, I would hope, a historical phase of the presuppositional movement that belongs to the twentieth rather than the twenty-first century. But read with some discernment, it can be a great help for those who want to witness for Christ, in Christ's way.

When he prepared to enter the hospital for the last time in 1995, I e-mailed him encouragements and reaffirmation of our friendship (which had occasionally been strained). I promised to pray for him in what I knew was a very difficult medical situation. He responded graciously, but his e-mail ended (and these were his last words to me): "I still disagree with you on the transcendental argument." That was so typical of Bahnsen: ready to defend presuppositional apologetics as he understood it right down to his last moments.

Despite my differences with Bahnsen, I revere him yet today as a great blessing of God to the church and as one of the most brilliant apologists I have known. In the present book he is young, brash, and well worth reading. He is not always right, but who among us is? He seeks to set forth the comprehensive lordship of Christ over the human mind as over everything else, and he does that effectively. In that goal we should all be in agreement, and we should seek Bahnsen's help to become more consistent in our commitment to the Lord. So I commend this book to all who seek to think God's thoughts after him.

PART 4

Ethics and Worship

22

Simple Obedience

WHEN I WAS A YOUNG BOY, the opening exercises in our Sunday school always ended with the hymn "Trust and Obey." We went home with these lines ringing in our ears:

> Trust and obey, for there's no other way
> To be happy in Jesus, but to trust and obey.[1]

So obedience to God always seemed to me to be something very basic, something fundamental, about the Christian life. *Trusting* obedience, of course. Although obedience is an obligation for everyone, we cannot rightly obey God without first trusting him for our salvation. But trust itself is an act of obedience, so in the hymn *trust* is in the imperative mood. With this agrees Psalm 37:3, which may have been the inspiration for the hymn:

> Trust in the LORD, and do good;
>   Dwell in the land and befriend faithfulness.

Of course, the necessity of obedience appears on nearly every page of Scripture. The biblical way of life is *covenantal*, which means, among many other things, that there are blessings for those who obey God,

---

1. John H. Sammis, "Trust and Obey" (1887), usually sung to the tune of Daniel B. Towner (1887).

curses for those who disobey.[2] God's basic relationship to his creation is that of covenant Lord, and that means, among many other things, that he is the One who has the right to be obeyed in all things.

The first experience of our forefather Adam was the experience of hearing the Word of God, which he knew he was to obey:

> And God said to them, "Be fruitful and multiply and fill the earth and subdue it and have dominion over the fish of the sea and over the birds of the heavens and over every living thing that moves on the earth." (Gen. 1:28)

Through Adam's and Eve's existence before the fall, there were other divine commands as well. This one was especially memorable:

> And the LORD God commanded the man, saying, "You may surely eat of every tree of the garden, but of the tree of the knowledge of good and evil you shall not eat, for in the day that you eat of it you shall surely die." (Gen. 2:16–17)

Eve, then Adam, disobeyed this command and incurred the curse of God, passed down to all of us in the human family. The Bible is the story of how God saved mankind from its sin and from the curse attached to it.

The word of God, therefore, is the driving force of the biblical narrative. Over and over again, that word comes to some human being or group of human beings. If they obey, the story moves in one direction. If they disobey, it moves in another. The Bible is the story of God's word and man's responses to that word, for better or worse. On practically every page of Scripture, God's commands are the issue, and man's obedience determines his destiny.

Over and over again, God encourages people to respond in the right way:

---

2. I have discussed biblical covenants in many places, notably the discussion of God's covenant lordship in *DG*, chapters 1–7, and the relation of God's lordship to ethics in *DCL*, chapter 3. In the latter book, note the discussion of obedience under the "normative perspective" (chaps. 9–13) and the treatment of the Ten Commandments (chaps. 22–44).

And now, O Israel, listen to the statutes and the rules that I am teaching you, and do them, that you may live, and go in and take possession of the land that the LORD, the God of your fathers, is giving you. You shall not add to the word that I command you, nor take from it, that you may keep the commandments of the LORD your God that I command you. Your eyes have seen what the LORD did at Baal-peor, for the LORD your God destroyed from among you all the men who followed the Baal of Peor. But you who held fast to the LORD your God are all alive today. See, I have taught you statutes and rules, as the LORD my God commanded me, that you should do them in the land that you are entering to take possession of it. Keep them and do them, for that will be your wisdom and your understanding in the sight of the peoples, who, when they hear all these statutes, will say, "Surely this great nation is a wise and understanding people." For what great nation is there that has a god so near to it as the LORD our God is to us, whenever we call upon him? And what great nation is there, that has statutes and rules so righteous as all this law that I set before you today? (Deut. 4:1–8)

And Moses summoned all Israel and said to them, "Hear, O Israel, the statutes and the rules that I speak in your hearing today, and you shall learn them and be careful to do them." (Deut. 5:1)

This is a major theme of Deuteronomy: cf. 6:1–25; 7:11–12; 8:1–3, 11–20; 11:1–32; 13:4; many other references. And that theme continues through Scripture.

This is not merely an OT emphasis. Some might think that since believers are saved by God's grace rather than by obeying God's law, obedience is no longer required of the NT Christian. But the mandate to obey the Lord is equally strong in the NT:

Therefore whoever relaxes one of the least of these commandments and teaches others to do the same will be called least in the kingdom of heaven, but whoever does them and teaches them will be called great in the kingdom of heaven. (Matt. 5:19)

A new commandment I give to you, that you love one another: just as I have loved you, you also are to love one another. (John 13:34)

If you love me, you will keep my commandments. (John 14:15)

Whoever has my commandments and keeps them, he it is who loves me. And he who loves me will be loved by my Father, and I will love him and manifest myself to him. (John 14:21)

If you keep my commandments, you will abide in my love, just as I have kept my Father's commandments and abide in his love. (John 15:10; cf. 1 John 2:3–4)

I have dealt with all that Jesus began to do and teach, until the day when he was taken up, after he had given commands through the Holy Spirit to the apostles whom he had chosen. (Acts 1:1–2)

But Peter and the apostles answered, "We must obey God rather than men." (Acts 5:29)

Through [Jesus Christ] we have received grace and apostleship to bring about the obedience of faith for the sake of his name among all the nations . . . . (Rom. 1:5)

But thanks be to God, that you who were once slaves of sin have become obedient from the heart to the standard of teaching to which you were committed. (Rom. 6:17)

For your obedience is known to all, so that I rejoice over you, but I want you to be wise as to what is good and innocent as to what is evil. (Rom. 16:19)

Whoever keeps his commandments abides in God, and God in him. And by this we know that he abides in us, by the Spirit whom he has given us. (1 John 3:24)

For this is the love of God, that we keep his commandments. And his commandments are not burdensome. (1 John 5:3)

Here is a call for the endurance of the saints, those who keep the commandments of God and their faith in Jesus. (Rev. 14:12)

I could not begin to list here all the biblical occurrences of *command*, *commandments*, *statutes*, *ordinances*, *obey*, *obedience*, and so on. Nobody wants to read that many proof texts. So can we not just agree that in all ages God wants his people to obey him?

More than that, he wants us to *pursue* holiness:

Since we have these promises, beloved, let us cleanse ourselves from every defilement of body and spirit, bringing holiness to completion in the fear of God. (2 Cor. 7:1; cf. 1 Peter 2:11–12; 1 John 3:3)

We are to be holy as God is holy:

But as he who called you is holy, you also be holy in all your conduct, since it is written, "You shall be holy, for I am holy." (1 Peter 1:15–16; cf. Lev. 11:44)

For just as you once presented your members as slaves to impurity and to lawlessness leading to more lawlessness, so now present your members as slaves to righteousness leading to sanctification. (Rom. 6:19)

I appeal to you therefore, brothers, by the mercies of God, to present your bodies as a living sacrifice, holy and acceptable to God, which is your spiritual worship. Do not be conformed to this world, but be transformed by the renewal of your mind, that by testing you may discern what is the will of God, what is good and acceptable and perfect. (Rom. 12:1–2)

As in Romans, Paul's other letters typically move from theology to practice. And in the "practical" sections of his letters, he exhorts his people to obey God's commands, to turn from Satan, and to seek a life worthy of the gospel (Gal. 5:16–25; Eph. 4:1–32; Phil. 3:17–21; Col. 3:1–17; 1 Thess. 4:1–12).

Paul compares the Christian life to warfare (Eph. 6:10–19) and a race:

> Do you not know that in a race all the runners run, but only one receives the prize? So run that you may obtain it. Every athlete exercises self-control in all things. They do it to receive a perishable wreath, but we an imperishable. So I do not run aimlessly; I do not box as one beating the air. But I discipline my body and keep it under control, lest after preaching to others I myself should be disqualified. (1 Cor. 9:24–27)

In seeking to be more obedient to God, we are called by Scripture to determined efforts, to struggle against the enemies of God.

Of course, we have failed to obey. So we have fellowship with God not by obeying God's law, but by receiving his free forgiveness for the sake of Jesus' sacrifice. But we should remember that even the gospel, the good news of Jesus Christ, redemption by grace alone, comes with commands attached. It calls us to repent of sin and to believe in Jesus (John 3:16; Acts 2:38; Rom. 10:9–10; 1 John 3:23). And James reminds us that a saving faith is a living faith, a faith that works (James 2:18–26). We are not saved by works, but we are saved unto good works:

> For by grace you have been saved through faith. And this is not your own doing; it is the gift of God, not a result of works, so that no one may boast. For we are his workmanship, created in Christ Jesus for good works, which God prepared beforehand, that we should walk in them. (Eph. 2:8–10)

According to this passage, good works are one of the good gifts that God gives to his people who are saved by grace through faith. But that does not make them less important. Indeed, that makes them *precious*.

Now, I have belabored what I think is obvious in Scripture: God wants us to obey him. Why, then, do I write this essay? Because I hear voices in the church calling into question this fundamental principle.[3] I won't mention names here, for I want the discussion to focus on the issues, not individuals. If you are a reader who has never heard the following arguments, feel free to stop reading at this point and consider yourself fortunate. But I think some readers, at least, will recognize the questions that I will raise and will have some interest in getting answers.

Unbelievably, some object when they hear exhortations to holiness and righteousness, encouragements to obedience. The objections, as I have heard them, are of three types:[4] (1) We can't obey, for we are too sinful. (2) Jesus was perfectly obedient, and his righteousness is imputed to believers; so we don't need to worry about obedience. (3) A passionate concern to obey God identifies you as a legalist. It shows that you are trying to please God by your works-righteousness.[5] Let's look at these one by one.

Are Believers Totally Depraved?

The doctrine of total depravity is a standard part of Reformed theology, the first of the "five points" brought in answer to the Remonstrants at the Synod of Dordt. It is the *T* in the TULIP anagram.

The Westminster Confession and Catechisms, however, do not use the phrase *total depravity*. But they speak of sin in these terms:

> By this sin they fell from their original righteousness and communion, with God, and so became dead in sin, and wholly defiled in all the parts and faculties of soul and body. (WCF 6.2)

3. In what follows I am responding in part to the essay by Timothy Kauffmann, "Sanctification, Half Full," at http://www.trinityfoundation.org/journal.php?id=282. The men he criticizes in this article are men for whom I have great respect. They are faithful and effective ministers of the gospel, and I regard them as friends. I think Kauffmann is far too negative toward them. I also think he focuses far too much on historical comparisons and too little on Scripture itself. But he raises some good questions, and I hope to shed light on those questions here. I will not be going through his essay point by point, but I will explore issues that he raises there.

4. This outline was suggested to me by a good friend who shares my concerns in this area—or, perhaps more accurately, I share hers. I urged her to write an essay on the subject, but she replied, "After you." I write mainly in the hope that she will indeed write something after I finish. Certainly she will see a need for it.

5. For triperspectival buffs: objection 1 is existential, 2 situational (redemptive-historical), and 3 normative.

From this original corruption, whereby we are utterly indisposed, disabled, and made opposite to all good, and wholly inclined to all evil, do proceed all actual transgressions. (WCF 6.4)

Wherein consisteth the sinfulness of that estate whereinto man fell?

The sinfulness of that estate whereinto man fell, consisteth in the guilt of Adam's first sin, the want of that righteousness wherein he was created, and the corruption of his nature, whereby he is utterly indisposed, disabled, and made opposite unto all that is spiritually good, and wholly inclined to all evil, and that continually; which is commonly called original sin, and from which do proceed all actual transgressions. (WLC 25)

These statements describe sin in very dark terms indeed. Many Calvinists, however, after stating the doctrine in confessional terms, are quick to qualify it: total depravity, they say, is not "absolute" depravity. Absolute depravity is the condition of the devil himself, the condition of someone who is "as bad as he can be." The distinction between *total* and *absolute* is that the former does not mean that man is as bad as he can be, but only that all our thoughts, words, and deeds are affected by sin. In my view, however, the confession's and catechism's statements quoted above seem to describe absolute rather than total depravity, given this distinction.

On these formulations, it is hard to make any room for "common grace," the possibility of unredeemed human beings' doing good. Nevertheless, the confession in chapter 16, "Of Good Works," does present some qualifications to its doctrine of depravity:

Works done by unregenerate men, although for the matter of them they may be things which God commands; and of good use both to themselves and others: yet, because they proceed not from an heart purified by faith; nor are done in a right manner, according to the Word; nor to a right end, the glory of God, they are therefore sinful and cannot please God, or make a man meet to receive grace from God: and yet, their neglect of them is more sinful and displeasing unto God. (WCF 16.7)

The Westminster divines believed that some sins were worse than others.[6] So that although unregenerate people cannot perform good works, they can perform some works that are less bad than others. Those appear to be good, and they may be called "good" because of that appearance. They externally conform to Scripture, and (in comparison with works that are even worse) they bring benefit to society. But they are not pleasing to God.

Some have suggested that we put the emphasis there. That is, we should speak not of total depravity, but of total inability—inability to please God. That is Paul's summary of the matter in Romans 8:7–8:

> For the mind that is set on the flesh is hostile to God, for it does not submit to God's law; indeed, it cannot. Those who are in the flesh cannot please God.

Total inability has a moral basis. Inability is grounded in depravity. So it is important to ground total inability in total depravity. Unregenerate human beings are not capable of doing anything genuinely good. Though they are able to do works that are less bad than others, they are never able to do anything that pleases God.

But what of the regenerate? WCF 6.5 says:

> This corruption of nature, during this life, does remain in those that are regenerated; and although it be, through Christ, pardoned, and mortified; yet both itself, and all the motions thereof, are truly and properly sin.

It may seem at first glance that there is no subjective change in the regenerate believer, for the "corruption of nature" remains and remains "truly and properly sin." But notice that through Christ, that sin is not only "pardoned" but "mortified"—i.e., put to death. How can sin be mortified while our "truly sinful" corruption continues? That is not clear in this particular confessional statement.

But again we must take account of the fact that on the Westminster view some sins are worse than others. There are degrees of sinfulness in

6. WLC 150.

the unregenerate, as we have seen in WLC 150. And we should assume that there are also degrees of sinfulness in the regenerate as well. Chapter 16 of the confession says this about regenerate good works:

> We cannot by our best works merit pardon of sin, or eternal life at the hand of God, by reason of the great disproportion that is between them and the glory to come; and the infinite distance that is between us and God, whom, by them, we can neither profit, nor satisfy for the debt of our former sins, but when we have done all we can, we have done but our duty, and are unprofitable servants: and because, as they are good, they proceed from His Spirit, and as they are wrought by us, they are defiled, and mixed with so much weakness and imperfection, that they cannot endure the severity of God's judgment. (WCF 16.5)

> Notwithstanding, the persons of believers being accepted through Christ, their good works also are accepted in Him; not as though they were in this life wholly unblamable and unreproveable in God's sight; but that He, looking upon them in His Son, is pleased to accept and reward that which is sincere, although accompanied with many weaknesses and imperfections. (WCF 16.6)

On the confession's view, regenerate good works are so mixed with sin that they "cannot endure the severity of God's judgment." None of our good works is perfectly good. This is true even though we do perform works that "proceed from [the] Spirit," and of course, the Spirit never does anything wicked. But the Spirit enables us to do good only to a certain degree. He has not chosen to enable us to do works that can endure God's judgment.

Why, then, should these works be called good at all? We learned in WCF 16.7 that the "good works" done by the unregenerate may be very impressive in some respects, but cannot please God, since they are not done with a proper motive, standard, and goal. But are regenerate good works any better? Are any of them done from a proper motive, standard, or goal? Based on WCF 16.5–6, the answer would have to be no. They are "defiled," "mixed with . . . weakness and imperfection," neither "unblamable" nor "unreproveable." So why, then, does the confession call them good works?

It seems to indicate two reasons to call them good. One is that these works are partly the work of God's Spirit: "as they are good, they proceed from His Spirit, and as they are wrought by us, they are defiled." So insofar as these works are good, they are the work of God. Insofar as they are human, they are not good. This seems to imply that we, as human beings, are not changed by regeneration. What we do as human beings is still totally depraved, no better than the unregenerate. But we may call the works of regenerate people "good" because God does good in and through them.

There is another reason, too, why we may describe works of the regenerate as good. That is indicated in WCF 16.6. Now, we know that in justification God imputes to the believer the righteousness of Christ, so that we are righteous in him. The righteousness of justification pertains to our legal standing, not our personal holiness. The righteousness of justification is our standing before God's law. Christ has taken our guilt that we may receive his righteousness. But in WCF 16.6 it almost seems as though a second imputation takes place, in the sphere of sanctification. God looks upon our defiled, imperfect works "in his Son."

In justification, God looks at the whole sinful person in his Son, and because the Son has borne that person's sins, God accepts that person as legally righteous. Now in sanctification, says the confession, God also accepts our works as righteous for the sake of Christ, not because our works merit that verdict in themselves. As in the sphere of justification, then, it can be said that our goodness is in Christ, not in ourselves.

This teaching does not encourage us to expect much of ourselves or other believers by way of practical goodness. The question, "Can I as a believer do anything good?" receives a negative answer or, at most, an ambiguous one.

But the discussion of sanctification in chapter 13 introduces more positive notes:

> They, who are once effectually called, and regenerated, having a new heart, and a new spirit created in them, are further sanctified, really and personally, through the virtue of Christ's death and resurrection, by His Word and Spirit dwelling in them: the dominion of the whole

body of sin is destroyed, and the several lusts thereof are more and more weakened and mortified; and they more and more quickened and strengthened in all saving graces, to the practice of true holiness, without which no man shall see the Lord. (WCF 13.1)

In WCF 13.2 we do read again of our moral disability:

This sanctification is throughout, in the whole man; yet imperfect in this life, there abiding still some remnants of corruption in every part; whence arises a continual and irreconcilable war, the flesh lusting against the Spirit, and the Spirit against the flesh.

But in this chapter the triumph of grace is unmistakable:

In which war, although the remaining corruption, for a time, may much prevail; yet, through the continual supply of strength from the sanctifying Spirit of Christ, the regenerate part does overcome; and so, the saints grow in grace, perfecting holiness in the fear of God. (WCF 13.3)

Is it possible to reconcile these confessional statements with one another? How can it be said that we are "perfecting holiness in the fear of God" (just above) while WLC 25 ascribes to the believer

corruption of his nature, whereby he is utterly indisposed, disabled, and made opposite unto all that is spiritually good, and wholly inclined to all evil, and that continually.

The key, I think, is to note that the confession's language of depravity pertains not to the believer as such, but to the "corruption of nature" in the believer (WLC 6.5), a corruption that is overcome by God's grace. The confession never compromises in its negative description of the corruption: "both itself, and all the motions thereof, are truly and properly sin." That corruption remains in the believer. But in the believer, the corruption is not the whole story. In WCF 13.1 quoted above, "the dominion of the whole body of sin is destroyed." The expression "body of sin" comes from Romans 6:6:

We know that our old self was crucified with him in order that the body of sin might be brought to nothing, so that we would no longer be enslaved to sin.

The corruption itself is as bad as ever, "truly and properly sin," but it is made weak by God's grace. The result is that although some corruption remains (WCF 13.3), we are no longer enslaved to sin. We have victories in the spiritual battle (13.1). The result is that "the regenerate part does overcome" (13:3), and we "grow in grace, perfecting holiness in the fear of God."

The confession, then, makes these assertions:

1. Because of the fall of man in Adam, human beings have "original corruption, whereby we are utterly indisposed, disabled, and made opposite to all good, and wholly inclined to all evil" (WCF 6.4).

2. From that corruption comes all our individual, actual transgressions (6.4).

3. Unregenerate people do nothing good. They do things that appear to be good, but are really evil, because they lack the proper goal, standard, and motive (16.7).

4. The regenerate retain their original corruption, and what it is and what it does are both properly sin (6.5).

5. Our best works cannot justify ourselves before God (16.5).

6. But God rewards our good works for the sake of Christ, though they are imperfect (16.6).

7. But besides this, God also creates in his elect a new heart and spirit, enabling us to "practice . . . true holiness" (13.1), even "perfecting holiness in the fear of God" (13.3).

8. Indeed, "through the continual supply of strength from the sanctifying Spirit of Christ, the regenerate part does overcome" (13.3).

The final word about the believer, then, is not *corruption*, but *overcoming*. As Paul says, "For sin will have no dominion over you, since you are not under law but under grace" (Rom. 6:14). The corruption of sin remains until death, but it grows weaker and weaker, through the continual strength from the sanctifying Spirit of Christ. Scripture promises victory in Jesus.

Given that pattern of biblical teaching, summarized in the confession,[7] I do not think it is helpful to speak of believers as "totally depraved." Depravity is what the confession calls "corruption," the sinful disposition that comes through Adam. But that corruption does not enslave the believer. The believer can say "no" to sin. He can "resist" the devil (1 Peter 5:8–9), and resist him successfully. And Scripture over and over again exhorts him to do that. In other words, it exhorts him to obey, as we saw at the beginning of this essay.

The biblical quotations I set forth there indicate to me that, although Scripture does teach that believers sin and continue to need forgiveness, its emphasis is on Jesus' victory over sin, and our victory in him. When Scripture exhorts us to obey, it never describes us as hopeless or desperate sinners who cannot accomplish anything good. If we are concerned about our continuing corruption and want to deal with it, God has shown us how to do that. He has given us "means of grace": the Word of God, the sacraments, and prayer. Scripture *commands* us to make use of these, and it never suggests that our corruption makes that impossible. So victory over corruption is found through obedience to God's commands.

Our continuing corruption, therefore, does not invalidate our attempts to obey God. On the contrary, for those who enjoy the saving grace of God, obedience is the way to receive his blessings.

I think, therefore, that it is unbiblical to describe believers as "totally depraved." In Scripture, the corruption of sin is a terrible thing. But through Christ we have victory over it.

I also hesitate to pray some of the traditional "prayers of confession," in which we say things such as "there is no health in us." That simply

---

7. The confession has more passages emphasizing our continuing sinfulness than emphasizing our overcoming sin through the Spirit. That in my judgment is unfortunate. Although I subscribe to the confession's teaching in both areas, I would like to see revisions here. The generally negative cast of the confession's formulations tends to discourage believers from actively waging the spiritual warfare.

is not true, given Jesus' work of redemption. Jesus has made us to be his saints, his servants, his sons and daughters. We are the "righteous man" of the Psalms. We have the "fruit of the Spirit": love, joy, peace, patience, and so on (Gal. 5:22–23). Paul says that "those who belong to Christ Jesus have crucified the flesh with its passions and desires" (v. 24). We are "not in the flesh but in the Spirit" (Rom. 8:9).

The "dead in . . . trespasses and sins" (Eph. 2:1) is in the past tense. Paul describes our present in verse 10: "For we are his workmanship, created in Christ Jesus for good works, which God prepared beforehand, that we should walk in them." So in 4:1–2 Paul calls on our obedience: "walk in a manner worthy of the calling to which you have been called, with all humility and gentleness, with patience, bearing with one another in love." Paul here has no foreboding that our remaining corruption will make it impossible for us to obey God. Rather, he believes that we have been changed, so that obedience is now second nature.

Is Imputed Righteousness Enough?

The Bible teaches that believers are justified, counted righteous, not by their own works, but by the righteousness of Christ imputed to them. This imputation is called *justification*.

> For our sake he made him to be sin who knew no sin, so that in him we might become the righteousness of God. (2 Cor. 5:21)

> We know that a person is not justified by works of the law but through faith in Jesus Christ, so we also have believed in Christ Jesus, in order to be justified by faith in Christ and not by works of the law, because by works of the law no one will be justified. (Gal. 2:16)

Justification means that Christ has taken from us the guilt and penalty of sin, so that God's law no longer condemns us. So it is a "legal" or "forensic" act on God's part. It is not an act that changes our inward ethical nature.

The fact that God imputes Christ's righteousness to believers does not in itself prejudice the moral quality of their subsequent decisions and actions. One could, with some mental exertion, imagine someone righteous by imputation who continues to live a sinful life. A righteous judicial standing, justification, is not inconsistent with some continuing sin. In fact, every believer, as we have seen, is justified, and yet commits some sins. So from a strictly logical point of view it would be possible for someone who is justified to sin all the time, to lead a life of sin.

But that mental exertion is a work of the imagination. It is fanciful, a fiction. In fact, Scripture makes plain that those who are justified in Christ are also regenerate and sanctified. Recall again Ephesians 2:8–10:

> For by grace you have been saved through faith. And this is not your own doing; it is the gift of God, not a result of works, so that no one may boast. For we are his workmanship, created in Christ Jesus for good works, which God prepared beforehand, that we should walk in them.

So Scripture, as we have seen, exhorts believers to good works, calls them to pursue holiness, and is optimistic that this pursuit will bear fruit. Although justification and sanctification are logically distinguishable, and ought not to be confused, they are never separated in the believer. If you have one, you have the other.

When Satan accuses believers, raising doubts about their salvation, it is right for them to refer to their justification. Satan has no claim on me, for I am righteous in Christ. In him, the Father accepts me as righteous. Believers should never despair that their works are inadequate to meet the Father's standards. Indeed, no one's works can make him acceptable to God. But God has accepted us because he has accepted the sacrifice of his Son. The imputed righteousness of Christ is all that we need to enter God's fellowship and all the eternal blessings of his heaven.

But in Scripture, the imputed righteousness of Christ never excuses believers from the spiritual warfare. According to Ephesians 2:8–10, we who are saved by faith alone are "created in Christ Jesus for good works," and God "prepared [them] beforehand, that we should walk in them." So our justification by faith alone is only the beginning of the Christian walk. Indeed, it motivates us to do good works:

If then you have been raised with Christ, seek the things that are above, where Christ is, seated at the right hand of God. Set your minds on things that are above, not on things that are on earth. For you have died, and your life is hidden with Christ in God. (Col. 3:1–3)

Believers have been united to Christ in his death and resurrection. In his death they have died to sin, and in his resurrection they are raised to new life (Rom. 6:1–4), so to continue in sin is an anomaly. So:

The saying is trustworthy, and I want you to insist on these things, so that those who have believed in God may be careful to devote themselves to good works. These things are excellent and profitable for people. (Titus 3:8)

The imputed righteousness of Christ is sufficient to prove that we are children of God. But it does not justify a passive attitude in the demands of the Christian life. When a believer fails to honor the Lord, he may take comfort that he is accepted in Christ. But he nevertheless needs to repent of his sin (1 John 1:9) and turn back to obey God's commandments. His very love for Christ will move him to turn from sin (which is the same as turning toward Christ). Those who love Christ, indeed, will keep his commandments (John 14:15, 21, 23; 15:10; 1 John 2:3; 5:3; 2 John 6).[8]

So preachers should never present the imputed righteousness of Christ as a furlough from the spiritual battle. Scripture makes clear that for believers that battle is strenuous and continuing (Eph. 6:10–20).

Is the Pursuit of Holiness Works-Righteousness?

It should be evident now that God deals with believers on two levels: (1) their legal standing before his court, and (2) their daily spiritual and ethical decisions. No. 1 has to do with justification, no. 2 with sanctification. No. 1 has to do with what Christ has accomplished once for all on Calvary. No. 2 has to do with what he continues to do in and

8. Compare Deuteronomy 5:10; 6:5–6; 7:9; 10:12–13; 11:13, 22.

through us as he is present through the Spirit. No. 1 has to do with what theologians call the *already*, and no. 2 has to do with what they call the *not yet*, for the perfection of holiness is yet future. No. 1 has to do with God's eternal judgment; no. 2 has to do with his fatherly discipline in this life (Heb. 12:5–17).

Believers, even theologians, are often tempted to confuse these two realms. Protestants have often accused Roman Catholics of confusing justification and sanctification. Believers sometimes confuse these when they think that some sin will damn them to hell even though they trust in Christ. As we will see, believers also make this mistake when they think their justification (no. 1) excuses them from strenuous exertions in the Christian warfare (no. 2).

Another common way of confusing these realms is when someone worries that such strenuous exertion is inconsistent with justification. So we sometimes hear one believer call another one a *legalist* if the second one is too preoccupied with obedience, especially in detail.

Now, the term *legalism* is one that we use far too vaguely in our Christian vocabulary. And when words are used without clear definition, they too often become a kind of club that we use to beat one another over the head. I think the best use of the term is to designate people like the Pharisees presented in the NT: people who seek to justify themselves by their good works. As such, they are people who put law in the place of grace. Thus, legalism is a terrible sin, and it literally brings damnation.

But legalism on this definition is very different from the pursuit of holiness. The true legalist is not at all one who pursues holiness. Rather, he avoids true holiness (obedience to God) and pursues a way of salvation of his own making.

The true pursuit of holiness (2 Cor. 7:1) is not at all legalistic and should never be described by that term. The believer's pursuit of holiness begins with the righteousness of Christ and seeks not additional justification, but sanctification through the power of the Holy Spirit.

There are problems connected with the quest for holiness. Sometimes believers adopt a mentality of moral nit-picking, claiming that it is part of the pursuit of holiness, but getting their priorities all askew, like the scribes and Pharisees who tithed "mint and dill and cumin" but neglected "the weightier matters of the law: justice and mercy and faithfulness" (Matt. 23:23). I think that should not be called legalism, unless, of course, the Pharisee-types are seeking to save themselves by all their tithes. When it is merely a matter of misplaced priorities, of course, some exhortation may be in order. But in fact Jesus does not say that the quest for detailed obedience is wrong. He even tells the Pharisaic tithers, "These you ought to have done, without neglecting the others" (v. 23). It is good to try to be obedient in matters of detail. It is even more important to be obedient in large, great matters. And it is good to know the difference. Not all matters of the law are equally weighty, but all of them make a claim on our obedience.

When a Christian is rushing around, trying to achieve perfection in every little thing, it may be appropriate for a fellow believer to remind him that his salvation is by grace through Christ, not by his own efforts to clean up his life. At the very least, this exhortation might lead him to find in Christ his *rest*. And it might lead him to a fruitful reexamination of his motives. But the best soldiers are always those who have the courage and the energy to confront the enemy. And we should honor those who fight the good fight, not seek to bring them down to a lower level.

Conclusion

So there is nothing wrong with obedience. Nothing wrong with strenuous obedience. Nothing wrong with detailed obedience. The gospel is God's free gift, but it motivates obedience. Paul says:

> Do you not know that in a race all the runners run, but only one receives the prize? So run that you may obtain it. Every athlete exercises self-control in all things. They do it to receive a perishable wreath, but we an imperishable. So I do not run aimlessly; I do not box as one beating the air. But I discipline my body and keep it under control, lest after preaching to others I myself should be disqualified. (1 Cor. 9:24–27)

And in these ways he calls us to be imitators of him, as he is of Christ (11:1).

Obedience describes the life of Christ as he came to do the work of his Father (John 5:19, 30; 8:28). It is also the broadest way to characterize the life of the believer. For everything else that God tells us to do—love, faith, hope, worship, seeking justice, spreading the good news, and so on—is a response to a divine command. Everything we do to resist Satan and to deepen our fellowship with God is a form of obedience. It is, of course, valuable to spell out the different forms that obedience can take, and to reject activities that only pretend to be obedient. But when we seek to describe in broadest terms what God expects of us, there is no better term than *obedience*. In that sense, obedience is everything. Every aspect of the faithful Christian life is obedience. Let us never discourage or mock it, or think we can substitute something else for it. Obedience is not easy, as we have seen. But it is comforting to know that our pilgrimage reduces to something so simple, amid all the complexities of life, amid all the clever schemes that promote this or that technique of spiritual growth. These schemes either are forms of obedience or are ways of avoiding obedience. We should embrace the former and turn firmly away from the latter. Just obey God.

23

Sonship

WHEN I TAUGHT at Westminster Seminary (Philadelphia) in the 1970s, I was a colleague of C. John ("Jack") Miller. Jack was unique as a seminary professor. He had considerable scholarly knowledge, but his heart was in evangelism and missions rather than academic study per se. He was also one of these people that you meet and fifteen minutes later he is dissecting your soul, as Hebrews 4:12–13 describes the work of the Word of God itself. If you would let him, he would identify your sins clearly and accurately. Eventually I saw that he could do this because he had such good discernment of his own sins and freely admitted his continuing need for God's forgiveness. And although some people resented Jack, many who sought to grow in grace were attracted to him.

In other times and places it was not uncommon for seminary professors to be pastors of churches. But at Westminster in the 1970s, with its strong emphasis on maintaining academic standards, we often heard that you could not be a professor and a pastor at the same time. Jack defied that rule, first as pastor of a little Orthodox Presbyterian Church, then as a church planter. New Life Presbyterian Church (originally Orthodox Presbyterian, later Presbyterian Church in America) began as a prayer meeting in Jack's home in Jenkintown. Jack invited Christians to come, and also non-Christians, breaking another common rule: normally, a prayer meeting is for believers only. But God reached many of the non-Christians, and the Christians received a new vision of what ministry could be like. The new church grew rapidly. Though Jack died in 1996, his influence remains powerful among those he touched personally and through his ministry. New Life Church expanded into three churches in the Philadelphia area, and many other churches acknowledge their indebtedness to Jack's work, including New Life PCA, Escondido, the church I attended in California from 1980–2000. Jack published a number of books, founded World Harvest Mission, and developed the Sonship Discipleship Course, which has been offered in many locations. World Harvest has also developed the courses Gospel Transformation and Gospel-Centered Life,[1] which stress similar themes.

In general, I am very favorable to Jack's ideas and to the Sonship course.[2] What I appreciate most about Sonship alumni is their transparency. They are quite open about their own continuing need for forgiveness, both from God and from other people. And because they have been forgiven so much by God, they do not hesitate to forgive others in the Spirit of Jesus.

They don't put on airs. Among professing Christians, they are the least likely to attract charges of hypocrisy. They don't take refuge in religious forms; they don't parade their knowledge of theology and history. I'm sure that to be so much like Jesus, you don't have to have taken the Sonship course; but that course always seems to provide a major assist toward that kind of spiritual growth.

Of course, Sonship is not perfect. In their circles one sometimes hears disparagement of those who have not taken the course or do not maintain its typical emphasis. Given their understanding that pride is a major area of sin, they understand the danger of having pride in their own movement. But of course, it is hard not to believe that Sonship people have discovered some things about God that are not widely recognized in other circles. Sonship people recognize that, too, as they should. But there is a thin line between that recognition and wrongful pride.

Sonship has tried to avoid becoming a faction in the larger Reformed and evangelical communities. But there are some tendencies in that direction because of influences within and outside the movement.

---

1. For more information on these, see the World Harvest Mission website, http://www.whm.org/who.

2. I have not taken the course itself, but have read some of the materials from it and have talked with many of its alumni.

In the remainder of this essay, I would like to present a theological commentary on Neil Williams's *The Theology of Sonship*.[3] This book presents the biblical basis for Sonship's distinctive approach to discipleship. I will offer explanations, approvals, and an occasional dissent.

Williams says, "The theological foundation for *Sonship* may be summarized by the phrase 'sanctification by faith.' "[4] He notes that Protestants are accustomed to speaking of *justification* by faith, and he concedes that the language of *sanctification* by faith is far less common. Still, he finds the basic idea in many traditions, including the Reformed. Reformed theologian Anthony Hoekema actually uses the phrase,[5] and G. C. Berkouwer devotes an entire book to the relation of faith to sanctification.[6]

To defend sanctification by faith as a biblical doctrine, Williams offers seven considerations, citing many biblical texts. In this discussion, Williams never quite defines what he means by *sanctification by faith*. From most of the seven considerations, I get the impression that his concept is fairly general and obvious: faith is trusting God, so we grow as believers as we trust him. In the Scripture passages Williams cites, that would include trusting God's Word, trusting his sovereign provision, trusting the work of Christ, trusting the presence of the Holy Spirit in our hearts, trusting that Christ is present in the Spirit, repenting of sin on the basis of Jesus' work. So far there is nothing about Sonship that is particularly new or distinctive. Every pastor I have known has taught that we grow by trusting God.

But Williams's quote from Walter Marshall suggests something more technical and precise. Marshall says:

> Some will allow, that faith is the sole condition of our justification, and the instrument to receive it . . . but they account that it is not

3. Jenkintown, PA: World Harvest Mission, 2002, available in full at http://cdn.whm.org/whmassets/eRcQPF3CTwKvMzbmcsIfdg/Theology-of-Sonship-WHM.pdf.
4. Ibid., 7.
5. Anthony Hoekema, "The Reformed Perspective," in *Christian Spirituality: Five Views of Sanctification*, ed. Donald L. Alexander (Downers Grove, IL: InterVarsity Press, 1988), 51.
6. G. C. Berkouwer, *Faith and Sanctification*, trans. John Vriend (Grand Rapids: Eerdmans, 1952).

sufficient or effectual to sanctification, but that it rather tendeth to licentiousness, if it be not joined with some other means, that it may be powerful and effectual to secure an holy practice.[7]

Marshall here draws a precise correlation between the role of faith in sanctification and its role in justification. Specifically, he says that just as faith is the *sole* condition of justification, we should accept it as the *sole* condition of sanctification. This is not only a doctrine of sanctification by faith; it is a doctrine of sanctification by faith *alone*, parallel (as Marshall goes on to explain) to justification by faith alone.

The reader unschooled in this discussion may think Williams and Marshall are advocating a passive view of sanctification: that the way to personal holiness is simple belief, without any effort or personal discipline. That would make sense of the parallel between justification and sanctification. For in justification we are indeed passive. There is no condition except the faith that receives the divine gift. But as an account of sanctification, this would not be biblical teaching, for Scripture tells us to actively pursue holiness in our lives, as in 2 Corinthians 7:1; Ephesians 4:24; 1 Timothy 2:15; and Hebrews 12:14. There is an element of human responsibility in sanctification, as well as divine sovereignty. These work together, neither compromising the other (see Phil. 2:12–13).[8]

I do not, however, accuse Marshall (and hence Williams) of holding a passive view of sanctification. Williams explicitly repudiates this idea earlier, denying what he calls "Club-Med Christianity," which says to "let go and let God."[9] As for Marshall, his view appears more complex when we note his description of faith. He denies that faith is mere intellectual assent to truth.[10] In faith, you receive nothing less than Christ himself. He says:

7. Williams, *Theology of Sonship*, 21, quoting Walter Marshall, *The Gospel Mystery of Sanctification* (Grand Rapids: Reformation Heritage Books, 1999), 43–44.

8. See my essay "Simple Obedience" elsewhere in this volume.

9. Williams, *Theology of Sonship*, 11. He is describing a view that is otherwise known as the "Keswick" view or the "victorious life."

10. Walter Marshall, *The Gospel Mystery of Sanctification* (Eugene, OR: Wipf and Stock, 2005), 50. I am using a different edition of this book from the one to which Williams refers. It is "a new version, put into modern English" by Bruce H. McRae.

This is what true saving faith is like. First, you must wholeheartedly believe the truth of the gospel and love that truth. Second, you must desire Christ and his salvation above everything else, and wholeheartedly receive him. You have to have a "spiritual appetite," which leads you to eat and drink Christ, the bread and wine of life—in the same way that a physical appetite leads you to eat real bread and drink real wine. Spiritually speaking, faith means that you feed on Christ, in the same way that you partake of a delicious meal.[11]

Marshall goes on like this for several pages, explaining that in faith we "come to a deep, heartfelt conviction of how precious Christ is,"[12] "love every part of Christ's salvation—holiness as well as the forgiveness of sins."[13]

Now, given such a rich definition of faith, we can understand why the life of faith is not passive. But that rich content does take something away from the "simplicity" that we often associate with faith. "Simple faith" is a tempting alternative to the complexities of moral effort. But on Marshall's understanding (and, I presume, that of Williams), the concept of faith incorporates much complexity within it. And if you have faith in Christ, with all that implies, then you are already engaged in moral effort. It is not difficult to understand why James goes so far as to say that works themselves are inseparable from faith, if that faith is to be a genuine, living faith (James 2:14–26). All you need is faith, if faith is rich enough to include everything else relevant to sanctification.

And on this understanding, what is the alternative to sanctification by faith? Sanctification by love? But love is part of faith, on Marshall's account. Sanctification by moral effort? But moral effort (surely part of Marshall's "spiritual appetite") is part of faith, on Marshall's account. Sanctification by works? I imagine that Marshall would repudiate this idea in his desire to make sanctification parallel to justification. But James 2:14–26 certainly defines saving faith as a working faith.

11. Ibid., 51.
12. Ibid.
13. Ibid.

Williams himself does not follow Marshall into the details of his argument. But I wonder whether for Williams, as for Marshall, this is all implicit in the doctrine that "faith is the sole condition" of sanctification as well as justification. Put it this way: definitions of faith can be minimalist or maximalist. A minimalist definition would be intellectual assent, or perhaps an "empty hand" reaching out toward Christ. A maximalist definition would be like Marshall's: a disposition that is virtually sanctified already. Theologians tend to resort to minimalist definitions in opposing works-righteousness. They tend to resort to maximalist definitions against those who are morally lazy. "Sanctification by faith alone" suggests minimalism: don't struggle, just believe. But when we define faith as richly as Marshall does, with such complexity, does the "alone" have any real force?

In section 2 of *The Theology of Sonship*, Williams speaks of the "uses" or "applications" that Sonship makes of the principle *sanctification by faith*. He insists that it is not enough to profess this principle. It must make a difference in one's life. These applications are in the areas of justification and adoption.

In regard to justification, Williams focuses on our perennial tendency to defend ourselves. We all want people to think that we are right and that we look good.

> In such a context, believing our justification has specific daily application to our lives. By virtue of our union with Christ, we are declared righteous. We do not have to gossip to show how right we are (compared with how wrong someone else is). We do not have to make excuses or run over someone to make ourselves look good and to be right.[14]

> Since the fruit of self-righteousness often looks good on the outside, *Sonship* is also concerned about this question: "What is the nature of true obedience?" What kind of fruit are we looking for? Is it merely outwardly observable "obedience"? Just because I look good, does it mean that I am obedient?[15]

14. Williams, *Theology of Sonship*, 25–26.
15. Ibid.

I noted earlier my own observation about alumni of the Sonship course: that they tend to avoid self-righteousness and hypocrisy, and that they tend to put considerable emphasis on these dangers. We can see here that this is an explicit part of their doctrinal teaching. As such, it is most praiseworthy.

But I confess that as I read this I wondered what it had to do with the doctrine of sanctification by faith (alone?). Williams has said that this is an application of his view of sanctification. I don't see the connection. It seems to me that someone who holds one of the views he rejects (either "just do it" or "let go and let God")[16] could also reject self-righteousness and hypocrisy. I think most readers will want to know what there is about *sanctification by faith* that enables us to avoid these evils, better than any other view of sanctification. Part of the problem, I think, is the difficulty Williams has (especially with Marshall's help) in *defining* sanctification by faith.

The second application Williams mentions concerns the doctrine of adoption. This is the emphasis from which Sonship gets its name: we are children of God, not orphans. This emphasis remedies the practical problem of "loving the praise of people more than the praise of God."[17] We need to remember that God our Father takes great delight in us and rejoices over us (Zeph. 3:17). God really does love us.

> Sonship endeavors to draw attention to areas where we are not believing that we are God's children—for example, anxieties regarding finances, health, marriage, children, or difficult relationships. Are not these worries related to a lack of trust in our heavenly Father? Our anxieties can reveal where our real faith is placed—where we trust in ourselves to control our world, to orchestrate peace, security, or love.[18]

So:

> We do not have to perform to earn God's acceptance and love, or the approval of others. We are already sons and daughters; now we must go and live as such.[19]

16. Ibid., 11.
17. Ibid., 27.
18. Ibid., 28.
19. Ibid., 29.

Again, I think this emphasis is a biblical one, and it ought to be found more commonly among believers. But as in the previous case, I don't understand from Williams's account how sanctification by faith relates to what he says. Again: if one holds a different view of sanctification ("just do it" or "let go and let God"), why would that prevent one from understanding the implications of adoption?

In section 3 of the book, Williams takes up criticisms that Jay Adams and Chad Van Dixhoorn have made against the Sonship course. Their criticisms center on (1) the concept of *sanctification by faith* and (2) Sonship's alleged downplaying of the law.

(1) Van Dixhoorn thinks that Sonship's doctrine of sanctification by faith undermines the church's means of grace, namely, the Word, sacraments, and prayer. Williams rightly replies that both faith and the means of grace are important: neither will accomplish their work without the other. In my judgment, little is ever accomplished in theology in arguments about what should and should not be "emphasized." When these arguments are taken seriously, and their language is clarified, they tend to end up like this one: both-and.

Adams thinks that Sonship presents "sanctification by faith" as a new insight, equivalent to "preaching the gospel to one's self as the means of sanctification."[20] Williams replies, "The phrase 'preaching the gospel to yourself' is simply a *Sonship* catch-phrase meaning to live by faith, to fix one's eyes on Jesus."[21] I note that at this point Williams plays down what many regard as the meaning of this phrase. Some think that in this phrase Sonship tells Christians to focus on the gospel as opposed to law. But if the phrase is merely a "catch-phrase," as Williams describes it, it doesn't necessarily mean that at all. But see (2) below on this.

Adams also opposes Sonship's emphasis on "leading a life of repentance." For Adams, repentance is a discrete act, renouncing a specific sin, not something that goes on all the time. He thinks repentance is an

20. Ibid., 33. Of course, as we have seen, the focus of *sanctification by faith*, according to Williams, is different. At most, "preaching the gospel to yourself" is only an aspect of sanctification by faith. But as with other aspects of this concept, I wish that Williams had more clearly shown how specifically this self-preaching is related to sanctification by faith.

21. Ibid., 33–34.

elementary principle (Heb. 5:11–6:3) from which we should move on, not a constant quality of the Christian life. Williams defends Sonship biblically by looking at the nature of the Christian life in Hebrews 7–12. Here I am inclined to think Williams has the better argument. But as with other matters in the book, I wish Williams had set forth more clearly what the life of repentance has to do with sanctification by faith.

(2) Adams also says that Sonship "downplays the law."[22] On the surface, this is an argument about emphasis, though Williams says it is really an argument about the right use of the law. He mentions a number of areas in Sonship that refer to the law as the criterion of right and wrong, the standard applied to judgments about sins. Here I think the argument comes out as a draw. But I confess that I have heard Sonship people speak negatively about the law, as if they prefer an emphasis on gospel to an emphasis on law. This debate is reminiscent of the Reformation battles over who does, and who does not, properly "distinguish law from gospel." I have taken issue with this discussion, believing that the Bible itself does not make a sharp distinction between law and gospel.[23]

So in my judgment the *Sonship* movement brings out a number of important biblical emphases, and I believe that it has encouraged a godly lifestyle in areas in which the church has had special need of growth. The theoretical exposition of these emphases, however, needs more clarification. Particularly there needs to be more careful definition on what is meant by *sanctification by faith*, its relation to justification by faith, and its difference from other views of sanctification. And then this doctrine needs to be related more clearly to the more specific emphases of Sonship, particularly justification and adoption.

22. Ibid., 35.
23. See *DCL*, 182–92, 609–16.

24

Cultural Transformation and the Local Church

I'VE BEEN ASKED whether Scripture calls the local church to the work of cultural transformation. I answer affirmatively. The church's task is to carry out Jesus' Great Commission (Matt. 28:18–20), teaching all that Jesus taught us. That teaching inevitably leads to cultural transformation. It is the gospel of the kingdom (Matt. 3:2; 4:17; Acts 8:12; 19:8; 20:25; 28:23, 31) that brings God's righteousness to bear on every aspect of human life (1 Cor. 10:31; Col. 3:17). So the gospel has led to great benefits for society, in education, government, the care of the poor, widows, orphans, the arts, philosophy, and the sciences.

So the question is not whether, but how, the local church should be involved in cultural transformation. If the issue is a failing school system, the church may encourage its members to educate their children at home, or in Christian schools. Or in some contexts it may seek to challenge the public schools to greater levels of excellence. I think that generally a local church should not seek to administer a school itself. That is usually unnecessary, and most churches are not equipped to oversee such projects. But the gospel is concerned with education (Deut. 6:6–9; Titus 2:12), and the church should encourage it to be as good as it can be. The gospel of the kingdom is comprehensive—good news for every aspect of human life.

Note (July 2012): Those who asked me to write this essay asked for something "short," and I think I managed that part of my assignment, at least. But since I have more space here, allow me to respond to a criticism of the term *transformation* that I have heard on several occasions. It is sometimes thought that if we seek to transform society, we are intending to radically change everything right away, in our lifetimes—to bring in the kingdom of God before the return of Jesus. I have never understood the term *transform* to imply all that. For those who call themselves *transformationalists*, the transformation of society is a *goal*. That goal is God's goal. He has promised that it will be achieved. When he will achieve it depends on one's millennial position. But I don't think we can accept a radical amillennialism that suggests that there will be *no* improvement in society before Jesus comes. I expect that we will not transform the earth entirely before the Lord returns. But there will be little changes, fragmentary bits of progress, the beginnings of transformation.

25

Family, Church, and State:
A Triperspectival Approach

WHEN I WAS APPOINTED to a full professorship at Westminster Seminary in California, I was asked to present an "inaugural lecture" to be given at my investiture. Given the discussions at the time about theonomy, on the one hand, and the views of Meredith Kline, on the other, I thought it would be helpful to me and my hearers if I tried in my lecture to clarify my views of the relations of family, church, and state. My lecture was published in 1989.[1]

As I began to plan my lecture, I thought that the task would not be great, because I already had some plausible categories for developing my essay. In my *DKG*,[2] I had argued that any item of human knowledge could be understood from three perspectives. The normative perspective considers everything as divine revelation, governing human thought. The situational perspective considers everything as an object of knowledge, something we can know. And the existential perspective considers everything as part of human experience.

These perspectives derive from qualities that Scripture associates with divine lordship: the normative is based on his authority, the situational on his controlling power by which he creates and directs the course of nature and history, the existential on his covenantal presence with his creatures, in their minds and hearts.

---

1. "Toward a Theology of the State," *WTJ* 51, 2 (Fall 1989): 199–226. I revised and condensed this article for my *DCL*, 595–602.
2. Especially 73–75 and 123–64.

Everything can be understood under all three perspectives. A tree, for example, can be seen from the normative perspective as part of God's general revelation, governing our thoughts about trees and their relationships to other things. Or the tree can be viewed under the situational perspective as an object of human knowledge, something available to our understanding. Or we can regard it under the existential perspective as part of human experience and therefore of human subjectivity.

Still, various things tend to focus our attention on some perspectives more than others. For example, we tend to think of the Bible as primarily normative, though it is also an object of knowledge and an aspect of experience. The Grand Canyon is more situational, dreams and imagination more existential, though they function in all perspectives.

So as I began to prepare my inaugural lecture, it appeared that I already had a promising outline to follow: Family is primarily existential, for the family nurtures and comforts us. It is home to us, our subjective center. State is primarily an instrument of power, affecting the situation in which we live, so situational. The church brings the message of God, and thus is normative.

But I have always tried to develop my theological concepts from close interaction with Scripture itself, rather than from prearranged conceptual schemes. The scheme mentioned above was one that I believed had biblical warrant. But I needed to give close attention to Scripture's explicit treatment of family, church, and state, to see whether it presented these concepts according to such a pattern, or whether it developed them differently.

The essay that emerged from this study was not particularly triperspectival. The conclusion I came to was that in Scripture family was the overarching concept, and that church and state were both forms of the family, emerging through the history of redemption and the development of civilization.

In the beginning, with Adam and Eve, there was only family. The family then performed the functions of church and state, for the family was both a worshiping community and a means of maintaining order. Eventually, however, as the (then fallen) human race became large, some differentiation in these functions occurred. In Israel, hereditary priests took the place of nuclear-family elders in bringing sacrifice to God for the people. And God raised up judges and kings to fight the nation's battles. So in Israel the functions of what we call family, church, and state became differentiated, directed by different groups of people. But these differing functions were originally and essentially functions of the family.

In the unbelieving world, there was also a differentiation of the family into church and state. But when Israel is sent into exile, and in the NT when the family of God is sent to bring its message to the pagan nations, they had to take more seriously their relationship to the pagan states. Although God called believers out of the world, they were nevertheless citizens of many nations, subject to governments that often had no regard for Christ or the gospel.

My essay presented, then, the following as the resultant pattern: The state is the governing body of the fallen family of Adam. The church is the governing body of the family of Jesus Christ. But there is no easy coexistence between these two governments. The pagan government demands worship of the pagan gods; the Christian government forbids it. The pagan government offers courts to resolve disputes between citizens. But the apostle Paul says that Christian believers are not to use those courts to resolve disputes among believers (1 Cor. 6:1–8). Rather, they are to take their disputes to church courts, to be resolved by fellow believers. In the final day, the pagan institutions will fall away, to be permanently replaced by a social order ruled by Jesus Christ.

One cannot, therefore, understand family, church, and state as three separable entities, each responsible for a well-defined segment of human life. The state has courts, but the church does, too. Paul's complaint against the state courts is not that they have overstepped the boundaries of their proper sphere of activity; it is rather that those courts are not governed by believers. Similarly, family is a nurturing body, but the church is, too, and family language (brothers, sisters, fathers, mothers) applies to the church as to the family. The NT, indeed, regards the church as an extension of the family. Rather, church and state are both extensions of the family—the former of the family of God, the latter of the family of Adam.

Lately, however, I have been giving more attention to my original idea, that family, church, and state can be seen as three perspectives on society. I have not entirely abandoned the argument of my inaugural essay, but I think that argument can be refined by a perspectival understanding of these concepts.

As I indicated, the unfallen family of Adam in the garden combined functions of family, church, and state. It was a nurturing community of love (family), a worshiping body (placed in the presence of God), and an orderly society (with the husband as the head over the wife and both partners having dominion over the animals). Here the perspectival model is appropriate. From the normative perspective the prefall society is church, from the situational perspective state, and from the existential perspective family. These functions can be distinguished, but the same people are active in all three. They are, then, perspectives on the activity of the society. The church is society in worship, the state society in ordering itself, and family the society nurturing one another.

Following the fall, and the expansion of the human race, we also see these three aspects developing, both among the believers and among the unbelievers. Noah and Abraham guided the worship of their families, bringing sacrifice on their behalf and interceding for them. They also nurtured their communities and provided order and structure. Abraham, indeed, gathered an army of 318 men to defeat a crew of thieves and kidnappers (Gen. 14:14–16).

Then, as I said before, God gave to Israel institutions of priesthood (church) and judges/kings (state). These enhanced the family, but they were extensions of powers already present in the family.

The same development took place among the pagans. Their development led not only to "states" in which kings waged war against the enemies of order, but also to "churches," in which they ordained worship, invoking gods of various kinds.

When God scattered Israel among the nations and later sent the church to bring the gospel to all the nations, then the society they encountered in each place was not simply a "state." It was also a family and a church, albeit a pagan one.

My earlier paper, therefore, was misleading to suggest that we can today distinguish church as the family of God from the state as the family of fallen Adam. It is not that the Christian family constitutes church and the pagan family constitutes state. Rather, the family of God is all three: family, church, and state (recall 1 Cor. 6:1–8), and pagan society is also family, church, and state. In each of these societies, family, church, and state are perspectives on the whole. Romans 13:1–7 is not about relations between "church" and "state" in some general way. It is, rather, about how the Christian family should behave when it finds itself under the power of a pagan state.

How, then, should we distinguish between church and state? If we could live in a Christian society, with Christian institutions, how would the church differ from the state? And how would these be related to the family?

1. First, family, church, and state would not be sharply distinguishable. The three are perspectives on the whole society.

2. The state is the society as it guards against threats to its order from within and without. In this task, every citizen, and every institution (including the church and family), cooperates.

3. The church is the society in its worship and devotion. Worship is both narrow (special meetings for honoring God) and broad (all of life as sacrifice, Rom. 12:1). It sets forth the fundamental commitments of the society. In this task as in the one above, every person and every institution (including the state) participates.

4. The family is the society seen as units of love, welfare, and nurture. The primary responsibility for nurture is the nuclear family, then the extended families, then the worship community, and then the whole society.

5. The goal of the preaching of the gospel is that all individuals become believers and that therefore all societies become like the one described above.

6. The Bible never itemizes the "proper sphere," sovereignty, or limitations of any of these three societal perspectives. In that

sense, the ongoing debate among Roman Catholics, Lutherans, Reformed, Anabaptists, and others about the "proper role" of the church, family, and state is a confusion. So is the attempt of thinkers such as Abraham Kuyper and Meredith Kline to determine the precise boundaries in which church and state can act in order to avoid "transgressing the sphere of the other."

7. There are differences between church and state, but these merely acknowledge their perspectival differences. Essentially, the church does not possess the sword, and the state does not administer the sacraments. But this is not because the two are separate and distinct spheres. Rather, it is simply that by definition the church is the society at worship, and there is no place for swords in worship except the sword of the Spirit. And by definition the state is the society defending itself against physical harm, and the sacraments are not the arsenal for such a defense.

8. Some have thought that the state governs a "nonholy" or "secular" part of reality, while the church governs a "holy" or "sacred" sphere. But nothing in Scripture suggests such a distinction. God intends that his Son Jesus Christ be recognized as Prophet (normative), Priest (existential), and King (situational) over all the earth. Therefore, he intends that societies reflect the biblical pattern that I indicated above: in each a whole people devoted to the Lord, nurturing one another in love, maintaining order and defense against evil, and worshiping Christ as King of kings and Lord of lords.

26

Might and Right

I HAVE SUGGESTED that we understand God's lordship as consisting of his control over the world, his authority over his creatures, and his presence in all parts of the universe. For now, let's look particularly at the first two of these: control and authority. These generally correlate to the concepts of might and right. God's control is his mighty power to govern all things according to his will. His authority is his right to tell all creatures what they must do. So his authority gives him the right to control, and his control gives him the power to exercise authority.

These two concepts are "perspectivally related," as I have argued. Neither exists without the other, and each presupposes the other. Control includes authority, because God's control extends to the sphere of moral obligation and, in general, to the sphere of criteria and standards. Authority includes control, because nobody can exercise authority without the power to punish, to sanction those who disobey.

It is only in God, however, that might and right perfectly coincide. God's might controls all things and his authority governs all things. When he delegates power and authority to creatures, however, they have these attributes in finite measure. Fathers have authority over their children, but civil rulers also have authority over fathers and children. The authority of the family is limited by the authority of the state, and vice versa—or, to put it better, each is limited by God's ordinance so that neither will interfere with the other.

Nevertheless, people lost in sin imagine that their authority and power are unlimited, and when they encounter limits they seek to overcome them. When their authority is challenged, they may seek to compensate with violent power. So in a sinful world, power and authority can be separated and are sometimes opposed. And sinners sometimes imagine that God is a big monster, a being with might and no right. Or they think their own moral standards can justify rebellion against God.

The most common problem today with this distinction is that people are simply ignorant of the concept of authority. So their concept of power is distorted. Children often think their parents are superior to them only in power, not in authority. They see conflict with their parents only as a contest about who is bigger, stronger, or tougher. Of course, the parent is bigger when the children are young. But that pendulum is destined to turn. Eventually the younger will prevail in a physical contest. And if physical strength is the only issue, the parent in time will be no match for the child.

Criminals typically think this way: Life is a struggle for power. The police have no authority other than their weapons and numbers. But they can be overcome, if the criminal is clever enough. Novels and movies often present pictures of societies that have lost all sense of justice, in which the "outlaws" have more justice on their side than the "authorities." So readers and viewers are made to root for the criminals. Robin Hood is the classic example. I think sometimes the so-called criminals are in the right, especially in film and novel scenarios. But real criminals often conceive of this as being the nature of all society: a struggle of power. And either they define themselves as embodying justice or they deny that there is any such thing as justice.

In tyrannical states, the ruler imagines that there is no authority over him. Either he is himself the supreme authority or he can establish authority over others by his own power.

Philosophers have often justified this criminal worldview. Thrasymachus told Socrates that justice was nothing other than "the interest of the stronger." Although Socrates went to some lengths to refute this view, Karl Marx later maintained that moral codes are nothing but rationalizations by which one economic class gained advantages over another. Friedrich Nietzsche agreed, and said the world was ready for a "transvaluation of all values." Man's most fundamental drive is his "will to power," and morality serves only to inhibit the success of superior people.

So commonly in the political discussion today, people talk as though social disputes were merely contests of wills, that there is really nothing moral going on. In many countries, when one party wins an election, the other party is unwilling to take "no" for an answer and instead takes up arms. Politics is only another form of war (as in the saying "war is politics by other means"). What was once remarkable about the Western democracies was that they governed political activity by law and accepted peaceful transitions from one regime to the next. I think this restraint cannot be understood apart from the influence in those societies of the Christian gospel. But today we see an increase in threats, mob violence, and intimidation by people who are unwilling to accept lawful developments in government/labor relations (Wisconsin), same-sex marriage (California), race relations (the George Zimmerman case in Florida). In the immigration debate, many assume that immigration law has no authority whatever, and that it is merely a matter of who is stronger: the border-crossers or the border patrol. Many object to the very term *illegal*, when it designates people who have crossed the border . . . illegally.

Nietzsche, of course, was also famous for saying that God is dead. If God is dead, indeed, it is impossible to defend the concept of just authority in society or in the cosmos. And if legal and moral authority become dead letters in society, then that society no longer regards God as alive.

27

Why I Vote Conservative

I TRY TO BASE ALL MY IDEAS, not only about theology, but about everything else, on the Scriptures. That includes politics. If I am to do "all [things] to the glory of God" (1 Cor. 10:31), that surely includes my voting behavior and my other efforts to improve the government of my country.

In theology, I typically express the uniqueness of my Christian position by sharply rejecting all the other views. I argue in my books that they are all based on autonomous human thought and are therefore both rationalistic and irrationalistic. As such, they all fall to dust, signifying nothing.

So in the same way I would like to believe that my political views are equally far removed from all the popular secular positions: a distinct "third way," beyond left and right. Today many evangelicals, especially young ones, are trying to escape from the yoke of political conservatism that has dominated evangelicalism since the days of the Moral Majority in the 1970s. They say such things as "God is not a Republican." They are trying to be radical Christians, separate from the fashionable alternatives. For that impulse I have considerable sympathy. Theoretically, I, too, want to develop a political position distinct from the cultural evangelicalism of recent generations.

I confess, however, that practically I have not attained such a position. First, I do have to do justice to common grace. *Common grace* is the traditional name in Reformed theology for the blessings that God gives to people short of salvation. By common grace, unbelievers often do good things for society, and I think those good things sometimes include good ideas. So Christians should not get into the sort of mood in which they disagree with unbelievers about every little thing.

Second, many political debates do not leave room for a third alternative. Typically we have to choose between two candidates, or two parties, or we have to vote "yes" or "no" on a proposition or bill. Often neither alternative represents an ideal Christian choice, but often one alternative is distinctly better than the other, so that the Christian would be wise to be co-belligerent with one party or other.

These two principles imply that Christians will sometimes share common ground of a sort[1] with non-Christians on some political issues.

It is not as if these considerations were unique to Christian conservatives. Christians on the political left often complain that the Bible should not be captive to the Republican Party, but their adherence to the Democrats is nothing much more than a mirror image. I honestly wish there were a third position that was truly Christian and truly distinct from the left and the right. If there were, I would join that movement immediately.

Occasionally someone will claim that there is such a position. The disciples of Herman Dooyeweerd said a lot about distinctly Christian politics a few decades ago; but although they spoke much of creation, fall, and redemption, their actual policies were not particularly distinctive. Some were very conservative (Hendrik Van Riessen), others liberal (Bob Goudzewaard). The disciples of Rousas Rushdoony claimed to have developed a political theory based on the law of Moses, but in practice their positions (except for a few that were considered peculiar) were about the same as traditional American conservatism.[2]

It may be that as of now we do not have good theological insight into what the Bible requires in our political life. Perhaps later generations will improve the church's vision in this area. But some political

---

1. I say this, aware that my mentor Cornelius Van Til abhorred the phrase *common ground*. But he was using the phrase in a deep theological sense that is not relevant here.

2. And of course, there is the view that the Bible has little or nothing to say about current politics, a view that I discussed in *The Escondido Theology* (Lakeland, FL: Whitefield Publishers, 2011). I still think that view has no credibility at all.

decisions must be made now. In William James's terms, they are "forced" and "momentous." For example, at present in America there is a national debate on whether the nation's healthcare should be managed by the federal government or not. In the upcoming elections, we must choose who will guide us most wisely on that and other issues.

My own process of deciding leads to the conclusion that of the two positions commonly argued in America today, political conservatism and liberalism, the former is far more congenial to Christian thinking. Let me list some reasons.

First, and perhaps foremost, conservatives do not generally defend abortion; liberals do. It is becoming more and more obvious to conscientious people that unborn life is human life. There is no time from conception to birth at which a nonperson becomes a person. That agrees with many representations of Scripture, such as Exodus 21:22–24; Psalm 139:13–16; and Luke 1:39–44. This fact implies that the tsunami of abortions (55 million!) performed in the last forty years or so of legalization is nothing less than a holocaust, a holocaust far worse than that perpetrated by Hitler.

Liberals not only condone these abortions, but also do everything they can to avoid any kind of restrictions on them. Abortion has become a central plank in modern liberal feminism, so that protection of this right transcends every other consideration. Liberals commonly oppose parental consent, any restriction on late-term abortions, even the preservation of babies born alive in botched abortions.

Generally I oppose "single-issue" voting, but I do not see how any Christian can vote for a candidate who condones this situation.

Second, conservatives have a decent respect for Christianity (as well as for other religions). Liberals, on the contrary, seek to erase all influence of religion from the public square. That includes symbols such as crosses in military cemeteries, plaques stating the Ten Commandments, and devotional exercises in public schools. Military chaplains are told that they may not pray in the name of Jesus, and so on. This is based on a theory that the separation of church and state in the First Amendment forbids the government to support any religious expression.

Like *Roe v. Wade*, unfortunately, this interpretation has been upheld by the Supreme Court. But that is not what the First Amendment says. The amendment merely says that Congress may not pass a law establishing a national state church, like the Anglican Church in England. It does not even forbid the establishment of churches on the state level, for at the time there were many of these, and the First Amendment was not thought to threaten them. Indeed, a chief reason for this language was to keep the federal government from establishing a church to compete with these state churches.

The current trend is to establish secularism, arguably itself a religion—at least, a movement that has all the undesirable traits of religions. Liberals support this development. Conservatives, at least, are open to questioning it.

Third, the establishment of secularism has led to a diminishing of religious liberty. Zoning ordinances have been used to stop the building of churches and the conducting of home Bible studies. Catholic hospitals and charities have been forced to include contraception (even abortive pills) in their healthcare plans. The First Amendment protections of religion have been downgraded to "freedom of worship," meaning that religious people can be free to worship in their own church buildings, but are not free to practice their convictions in the workplace. Christians cannot tolerate this. First Corinthians 10:31 commands us to do *all* things to the glory of God, and James defines *religion* not as what we do in the privacy of our church buildings, but especially in our care for orphans and widows (James 1:27). Conservatives generally support freedom of religion in this broad sense, while liberals oppose it.

Fourth, the Bible acknowledges that human beings are dead in sin, apart from the grace of God (Rom. 3:10–20; Eph. 2:1). So it gives the sword to the government to protect the people from violence coming from inside or outside the borders of the country (Rom. 13:1–7). Arguably, this is the only function of government in Scripture. But liberalism is deeply suspicious of the use of force to maintain peace, hoping that pleasant talk with our nation's enemies will solve international conflicts. Conservatism prefers a strong stance, seeking to achieve "peace through strength."

Fifth, the Bible does not assign to government the work of controlling the nation's economy, or of meeting the needs of the poor. Those responsibilities belong especially to families and to the religious community. If there is an argument for government action in some cases, then it should be a last resort.[3] But the role of government in welfare today is huge, constituting a massive share of the federal budget. Liberals favor enlarging it. Conservatives favor cutting it back.

To me these are matters of principle, matters on which I believe Scripture speaks clearly and that would prevent me from ever voting for a liberal candidate. Other issues, however, are matters of wisdom. On these there is more room for disagreement. I could not absolutely prove my views from the Bible. But they do carry weight with me as I consider candidates and political alternatives: (1) Government debt, in my view, has greatly endangered our economy. I don't believe that liberals have any idea what a great problem this is. (2) Liberals favor high taxes, especially on "the rich," not just to pay for necessary activities of government, but to equalize the rich and the poor. Attempts to equalize incomes, in my judgment, cannot be successful, and they discourage investment and hiring, both of which are sorely needed in the current economy. Conservatives resist this development, and I support their resistance.

For the most part, my politics is the same as that expounded by Wayne Grudem in his *Politics according to the Bible*[4] and the two books derived from that one, entitled *Voting as a Christian*.[5] The views presented above, then, are not unique with me. Indeed, they are standard arguments in conservative political literature. What is remarkable to me is the coherence between these positions of political conservatism and the teachings of Scripture as I understand them. This coherence is not necessarily to be expected. Conservative politics is essentially a secular movement, and many of its leading thinkers have not been Christians. Some conservative politicians and writers have been distinctly annoyed

3. See my *DCL*, 824–25.
4. Grand Rapids: Zondervan, 2010.
5. Wayne A. Grudem, *Voting as a Christian: The Social Issues* (Grand Rapids: Zondervan, 2012); *Voting as a Christian: The Economic and Foreign Policy Issues* (Grand Rapids: Zondervan, 2012).

with Christianity, to say the least—for example, the late Senator Barry Goldwater and the late pundit Christopher Hitchens. I would depart from the conservative movement in a moment if (and to the extent that) it could be shown contrary to Scripture. But as the political dialogue in America continues, and issue after issue comes up, it seems to me that the conservative position is more in line with Scripture than the alternative. Perhaps there are historical links that bring conservative politics together with the Christian faith. Perhaps the convergence is simply the providence of God, providing a way for his people to express their political voice.

28

The Bible and Joe the Plumber

IN ONE OF THE MORE MEMORABLE events of the 2008 presidential campaign, Samuel Joseph Wurzelbacher, later known as "Joe the Plumber," told candidate Barack Obama that Obama's policies would increase his tax burden. In his reply, Obama commented, "When you spread the wealth around, it's good for everybody." Most likely Obama would not have made that comment in a scripted appearance, but pundits cried "socialism." The idea of government spreading wealth suggests the slogan of Karl Marx: "From each according to his ability, to each according to his need."

The United States is usually considered to be one of the least socialist countries in the world, a bastion of capitalism or free enterprise. Capitalism teaches that market forces, not government, should allocate wealth. Aid to the poor should be given by families, churches, and charities, not by government. Totalitarianism threatens when government presumes to decide who has too much wealth and who has too little. And production declines when working people are not allowed to keep what they have earned, bringing economic hardship on the community at large. On the capitalist view, economic freedom brings economic prosperity. The extreme form of socialism, communism, has been the economic ruination of nations that have tried to implement it, such as the former Soviet Union and present-day Cuba and North Korea. Less-extreme forms of socialism, as in European democracies, tend toward economic stagnation.

All parties to the American political debate avoid extremism. Liberals such as Obama accept capitalism as a basic system, but they would use government to promote more economic equality. Conservatives usually accept the need for government intervention to help those in dire need, but they think this intervention should be rare and insist that the best general remedy for poverty is a free-enterprise economy, "a rising tide that lifts all boats."

Nobody should complain that Obama intends to *introduce* socialism to the United States. The graduated income tax, social security, and the public-school system go back many decades, as do government controls on many forms of American business. These are all inspired by the socialist vision of spreading wealth. The only legitimate complaint against Obama is that he wants to increase, perhaps considerably, the degree of socialism already present in American government.

But for now, fear of advancing socialism under Obama has been overshadowed, indeed overwhelmed, by the massive government intervention in banks and industries during the economic disaster of 2008–9. Republicans and Democrats have both used the vast power of government supposedly to avoid a total collapse, but gaining for government a stake in private industry unparalleled in American history.

Certainly that is socialism, in the historical definition—state ownership of the means of production. Moderate capitalists are willing for government to help a few, but today the largest and richest industries have become welfare recipients. One pundit observed that today about 50 percent of the nation's gross domestic product is in the hands of government—a percentage similar to the more overtly socialist countries of Europe.

In such times, Christians must ask what the Word of God says. Scripture doesn't provide anything like a detailed economic or political theory. But it does say a great deal about poverty, work, and the roles of family, church, and government. First, it affirms private property, a concept often questioned in socialist and communist theory. The eighth commandment, "You shall not steal" (Ex. 20:15), assumes that although all things belong ultimately to God, he has made a difference between what belongs to me and what belongs to you.

Second, God ordains government to maintain peace by the just use of physical force (Rom. 13:1–7; 1 Peter 2:13–17). He calls his people to pay taxes to the government (Matt. 22:17–21—here to the evil Caesar), but he never authorizes government to own a nation's means of production, or to control its economy. The ownership of resources is in the hands of individuals and families.

Third, the poor are a central concern of Scripture. While both conservative and liberal politicians today are obsessed with "helping the middle class," the Bible calls us to focus our compassion on those who are hungry, naked, homeless, dying. There are a huge number of passages about this, but read these to get started: Psalm 41:1; Proverbs 14:31; 19:17; 31:9; Isaiah 1:16–17; 3:13–15; 58:6–12. The "poor" in Scripture are not those who are lazy, however. Scripture speaks to sluggards in no uncertain terms (Prov. 6:6, 9; 13:4; 20:4; 26:15–16). Rather, those whom Scripture calls poor do what they can, but they are impoverished by famine, disease, injury. Their attempts to gain relief are frustrated by oppressors: rich people who take advantage of them, and corrupt courts biased in favor of the rich. Having no helpers in society, they cry out to God. So in the OT the "poor" are almost coextensive with the "faithful."

The Mosaic law abounds in remedies for poverty: first, a fair judicial system, not biased in favor of the rich or the poor (Ex. 23:2–3; Lev. 19:15). Then family inheritance (Lev. 25:8–17), the seventh-year release from debt (Deut. 15:1–3), interest-free charitable loans (Deut. 15:7–8), gleaning (Lev. 19:10; 23:22), and many others. The NT commends believers who made huge, sacrificial contributions to the poor (Acts 2:44–45; 4:32–37). Scripture never commands civil government to meet the needs of the poor, nor is there any suggestion that government should control the economy to benefit the poor. Indeed, we should assume that the government in general, like the courts, should not favor any economic group. Government, like all individuals and institutions, should be concerned for the poor. But the best thing that government can do for them is to be economically neutral.

Scripture, then, envisions a free economy, in which wealth is privately owned and the needs of the poor are met by the voluntary (but divinely mandated) generosity of individuals and families.

But what about true emergencies? It can be argued that an economic collapse such as that which began toward the end of 2008 is a true national security concern. Certainly in such a situation America's enemies will take advantage of our weakness. Government is charged with national security, so it should use its resources to guard against that danger. Indeed, it seems, only the government has the vast resources necessary to rescue banks, financial institutions, and other multibillion-dollar businesses, if indeed that can be done by anyone.

I am not an economist or an expert in business, so I cannot testify whether such government action is the only alternative, whether it is likely to be effective, or whether it might worsen the situation. From a biblical view, it is questionable whether government should have been allowed to accumulate the economic power that it has. But given the present centrality of government in our culture, I don't know of any biblical principle that *forbids* the use of its resources to help in such an emergency. Although God has not authorized government to take possession of a nation's resources or to spread the wealth from one group of people to another, he has not forbidden government from using what economic power it has accumulated (rightly or wrongly) to rescue the nation in time of great distress.

But what the Bible would teach us above all in this situation is this: we should not put our trust in government, private industry, or economic theory, whether capitalist or socialist. All of these have failed us miserably in the present crisis, and many times in history. We should not be looking to government to make us wealthy or to deal with the sins that have led our nation to this point in history. Now as ever, we should trust only in "the name of the Lord our God" (Ps. 20:7), the name of Jesus Christ.

29

Is America a Christian Country?

THIS IS ONE OF THOSE QUESTIONS that you hear a lot, and everyone seems to think he knows what it means. But actually, as with many other controversial questions, it can be taken in different senses, so that people talk past one another. Consider some different interpretations of the question:

1. *Did the first European settlers in America profess to be Christian?* On this interpretation, we ought to give a general affirmative. Certainly they did, overwhelmingly.

2. *Was their religion important to the first European settlers?* Certainly it was. Many came to the New World in order to practice their religion freely. The colonial charters verify this purpose, and they also state the importance of spreading the Christian faith to the native inhabitants of the continent.

3. *Did the early settlers reflect their faith in their practice?* In many ways, they did. But attendance at worship varied greatly from one place to another and one time to another. Relations between settlers and Indians varied greatly as well.

4. *Is the United States in covenant with God?* Some American writers have drawn close analogies between the United States and OT Israel. They have claimed that God would prosper the country if its people obeyed him and bring curses upon the country for disobedience. I do believe it to be a general biblical principle that

"blessed are the people whose God is the LORD!" (Ps. 144:15). In general, following the principles of Scripture does lead to prosperity, and denying them leads to curse. But the United States is different from Israel in many ways. God has not formally ratified a covenant with this country as he did with Israel from Mount Sinai in Exodus 19. He has not given us an inspired constitutional document, as he gave one to Israel in Exodus 20. And he has not given us divine title to a geographical area as he did to Israel.

5. *Were the "founding fathers" Christians?* Most all of them were professing Christians, and many spoke and wrote enthusiastically about Christ, about prayer, about the important role of the Christian religion in government and society. Doctrinal unorthodoxy, however, was common in the late eighteenth century, and many of the Founders were under the influence of deism, which denied miracle, the authority of Scripture, and the redemptive work of Christ. Thomas Jefferson was the most obvious of these, but even he often spoke (to his political advantage, perhaps) approvingly of traditional Christian faith. Benjamin Franklin was something of a skeptic, though he spoke admiringly of George Whitefield's ministry. Only Thomas Paine was a blatant unbeliever.

6. *Are the founding documents Christian?* The Declaration of Independence ascribes political rights to "nature's God," an expression that could be taken in an orthodox Christian sense or in a deist sense. The Constitution does not refer to God at all, but ascribes its provisions to the principle that "we, the people" determine to seek the blessings of government. Nevertheless, it is arguable that the political philosophy of both these documents owes much to Christian Scripture and theology. The Declaration's justification of revolution is essentially that of Calvin and Samuel Rutherford, namely, that when a king is lawless, lesser magistrates must bring him to account. George III reportedly called the American Revolution the "Presbyterian revolt." The

Constitution's doctrine of maximal individual freedom and its checks and balances on government are directly related to Scripture's recognition of the deep sin of man, its view that only God in Christ can be fully trusted. Tyrannies of the day demanded the kind of respect that in the view of the colonists belonged only to God.

7. *Does the Constitution permit the influence of religion on government?* In a word, yes. The First Amendment guarantees freedom of religion, and it does not limit that to worship services. The "separation of church and state" does not rule out government endorsement of religion. It does not even rule out European-style state churches. There were many state churches during the colonial period, and the writers of the Constitution had no intention of forbidding them. Rather, they forbade only actions by Congress (specifically mentioned) to establish its own *federal* church to compete with the other churches, state and free. So the founding documents should not be cited to require the secularity of the state. I grant that the courts have taken the Constitution to be much more restrictive of religion than in my account. I hope those court rulings can be overturned in the future.

8. *Is American culture Christian?* The influence of Christianity on American culture has waxed and waned over the years. There have been periods of revival, such as the First (early 1700s) and Second (early 1800s) Great Awakenings. Some parts of the country have been more influenced by Christianity than other parts. But Alexis de Tocqueville, a famous French visitor to the United States in the nineteenth century, author of *Democracy in America*,[1] commented with some surprise that as a general rule Americans took their religious faith more seriously than other developed nations. That has also been the case in the years since. Church attendance in America has always been greater than in Europe. And in America Christians have regularly made their case in the arts, entertainment, education, politics, government,

1. Vol. 1 (1835); vol. 2 (1840).

science, and other areas of culture. This is not to deny the general secularism that has regularly increased in its influence since the nation's founding.

9. *Is Christianity today the majority religion in America?* Yes, it is. As in no. 3 above, it cannot be said that Christians practice and promulgate their faith consistently with the teachings of Jesus and Scripture. But Christianity is still the chief religious influence in the life of the United States. And that religious influence is a powerful one. Even more than in Tocqueville's time, there is a striking difference between America in this regard and other developed nations.

So when somebody asks, "Is America a Christian country?" we should ask what is meant by that question. Interpreting it different ways will yield different answers.

30

Is Plagiarism a Sin?

MY STUDENTS at Reformed Theological Seminary regularly receive stern warnings about plagiarism. I define *plagiarism* as taking the words of someone else and including them in one's own writing or speaking without acknowledgment. In oral presentations, the acknowledgment should be oral. In written work, the author is to follow standard procedure for quotation marks and footnotes. Plagiarism is considered to be robbery of intellectual property. Penalties for plagiarism at Reformed Theological Seminary are very severe.

But the matter becomes more complicated for Christians when we note that biblical writers routinely adopt words from one another (or from third parties) without any explicit acknowledgment at all. Compare, for example, Micah 4:1–3 with Isaiah 2:2–4. These passages are nearly identical, and it is obvious that one of these prophets borrowed text from the other, or that both prophets borrowed text from a third source. Yet neither acknowledges such borrowing in any way. Or we can compare 2 Peter 2 with the letter of Jude. Although these two documents are not entirely identical, it is obvious that they have a literary kinship. Either Peter quotes Jude, making some alterations, or vice versa. Or perhaps both Peter and Jude quote from a third source.

These are only the most obvious examples. The NT abounds with quotations and allusions to OT books.[1] Sometimes the NT writer cites the OT author, but often he does not.

---

1. There is also 1 Timothy 5:18, in which, most likely, Paul quotes another NT writer, Luke.

Now, of course, in the ancient Hebrew and Greek languages in which Scripture was originally written, there were no quotation marks or paragraph indentations, and there were no conventions about identifying the sources of quotations. Yet there were ways of identifying the sources of citations, and these are sometimes used in the Bible. But they are not used regularly. Significantly, there is no indication that these writers subscribed, as an ethical principle, to the view that it is wrong to quote another author without acknowledgment.

In this respect the biblical writers had a view similar to that of some of my international students. In some parts of the world, I am told, what we might call plagiarism is accepted as a standard form of research. The teacher will ask the students to write a paper on some subject—for example, the effect of the moon's gravity on tides. The student will explore writings on the subject. When he finds a good source, he simply copies it and turns it in to his professor, who commends him. Research of this kind is a bit like a scavenger hunt. Sometimes when these students come to America, they do not understand why they can no longer use this method.

I do not find it difficult to inform these students why the scavenger method of research is forbidden at Reformed Theological Seminary. When we ask students to write papers, we want each student to submit his own work. The words must be his, so that we can evaluate him as a thinker, a scholar, and a writer. If students were free to submit the work of others, then it would be impossible for professors to evaluate a student's level of thought, research, writing, or analysis. So the ban on plagiarism is necessary for the academic functioning of the school.

To say that is not to condemn schools that permit research of the scavenger type. There is value in looking up the work of others, and there is some educational value even in copying the work of others. But at the seminary level, we expect more than that of our students. We want them to be capable of independent research, formulation, and analysis. For that purpose, scavenger research simply won't do.

But is there also a moral dimension here? Many want to say that scavenger research—what we call plagiarism—is not only inadequate for higher academic purposes, but morally wrong. On this view, it is a form of theft.

Here it is important to make some distinctions. Certainly it is theft when one author publishes the work of another in his own name for money. It is also theft, I think, when one author claims credit for the work of another in order to enhance his own reputation. In these cases there is, of course, not only robbery, but deception.

Is this not what the student scavenger does? That depends on the conventions of the class assignment. If there is general agreement between the professor and students that borrowing formulations from other authors is legitimate for the class assignment, then I don't think there is anything wrong with it. There has been no deception, since the whole class knows the rules and operates under them. And there is no theft, since the student receives no credit for being the original author of the material he submits.

But in academic courses using the Western academic system, plagiarism is wrong because it violates the rules made by the professor and by the institution. Violating these rules is morally wrong. The student is misleading the professor as to the nature of his research and the source of his writing, and he is seeking to benefit illegitimately from that research. But the moral wrong here presupposes an agreed institutional frame of reference. It is not based directly on general moral principles. Some institutions forbid plagiarism, and some institutions do not. In the former type of school, plagiarism is wrong. But in the latter, not necessarily.

When Isaiah and Malachi, or Peter and Jude, quote common sources, there is no reason to hold them guilty of any moral wrong. There is no reason to suppose that any of these is seeking to gain anything from deceiving his readers as to his authorship. There is no reason to suppose any monetary motive, or to suppose that any of these writers is trying to enhance his reputation (detracting from the reputation of the actual author).

I am making two points, then, about plagiarism: (1) Using someone else's words without acknowledgment is morally wrong in many, but not all, cases. (2) Prohibiting plagiarism is a convention of Western academic institutions with a strong pragmatic justification, and a moral justification that depends on the pragmatic.

So I would conclude that we should continue to prohibit plagiarism in Western academic institutions, but we should not bring moral condemnation on societies that fail to practice this rule.

I have not discussed in this essay the validity of intellectual property laws. I have discussed these elsewhere.[2] In the present essay, I have argued that the question of plagiarism is not a purely moral one. The issues it raises are both moral and pragmatic, and the balance of these varies with the situation. That is also my view, in the papers referenced below, of intellectual property legislation. So the present paper underscores the point made by the earlier ones, that it is important for us to make proper distinctions between the moral and the pragmatic, while recognizing their connections.

2. See "Copyright and the Reasonable Use of Technology," http://www.frame-poythress.org/frame_articles/1991OtherShoe.htm. I also suggest consideration of Vern S. Poythress, "Copyrights and Copying: Why the Laws Should Be Changed," http://www.frame-poythress.org/poythress_articles/2005Copyrights.htm. See also the secular legal paper by Stephen Kinsella, "Against Intellectual Property," published by the Ludwig Von Mises Institute, available at http://mises.org/books/against.pdf.

31

Prosperity

MANY HAVE USED the phrase *prosperity gospel* to refer to the message of preachers who promise various kinds of divine blessings to those who have faith. The phrase is usually not defined very specifically, and that is unfortunate. It seems to me that Scripture does encourage us in some situations to seek blessings from God, and it discourages this in other situations. So we must try to distinguish more carefully between biblical and unbiblical prosperity preaching, rather than to condemn all such preaching with one brush.

At the worst extreme, some prosperity preaching is quite appalling. At this extreme, a minister promises that if you want a Cadillac, say, all you need to do is visualize it and trust God for it: "name it and claim it." If you don't get it soon, it's because of your lack of faith.[1]

This is wrong. But why is it wrong? James gives us one answer:

> You ask and do not receive, because you ask wrongly, to spend it on your passions. (James 4:3)

James's point, I think, is not that we are seeking our own benefit. God wants to benefit his children; in fact, he makes all things work together for our benefit (Rom. 8:28). The "passions" here are not godly needs or even wants. The previous verses describe these passions as lusts and coveting, the sorts of desires that engender quarrels and fighting with other people:

1. Sometimes it's even worse than this: the way we show our faith is by sending money to the preacher.

247

What causes quarrels and what causes fights among you? Is it not this, that your passions are at war within you? You desire and do not have, so you murder. You covet and cannot obtain, so you fight and quarrel. You do not have, because you do not ask. (James 4:1–2)

Another argument against prosperity theology is that it encourages prayer for trivial things: parking spaces and the like. But Scripture never suggests that there is a maximum or minimum limit on the "size" of our requests. It never suggests that God is concerned only with the big things of our lives, rather than the small ones. Jesus says that God is concerned with sparrows and lilies (Matt. 10:29–31; 6:28–29), and he uses that comparison to motivate us to bring all our needs to the Father.

But the most serious consideration in the debate about prosperity theology is whether it does justice to the covenant promises of God to his people.

God's covenants typically include (1) revelation of the divine name, (2) God's previous historical blessings on his people, (3) covenant law: the ways he wants us to show our gratefulness, (4) God's promised blessings for our obedience, (5) God's promised curses for our disobedience, and (6) future administration of the covenant relationship.

The blessings of the covenant (4) are often presented in the language of prosperity:

Honor your father and your mother, as the LORD your God commanded you, that your days may be long, and that it may go well with you in the land that the LORD your God is giving you. (Deut. 5:16)

He promises to bring Israel into a land "flowing with milk and honey" (Ex. 3:8, 17; 13:5; 33:3; Jer. 11:5; 32:22; Ezek. 20:6, 15). He promises that in that land,

there will be no poor among you; for the LORD will bless you in the land that the LORD your God is giving you for an inheritance to possess—if only you will strictly obey the voice of the LORD your God, being careful to do all this commandment that I command you today.

For the Lord your God will bless you, as he promised you, and you
shall lend to many nations, but you shall not borrow, and you shall rule
over many nations, but they shall not rule over you. (Deut. 15:4–6)

The passage backtracks a bit in verses 7–11: yes, there will be poor in
the land, but those poor will benefit from the Lord, who calls their
wealthier brethren to be open-handed with them.

Israel's prosperity, therefore, is contingent on her obedience to the
covenant. And the level of Israel's obedience is a great disappointment
to the Lord. Still, there is much to be thankful for. The righteous man is

> like a tree
>   planted by streams of water
> that yields its fruit in its season,
>   and its leaf does not wither.
> In all that he does, he prospers. (Ps. 1:3)

> Yet you have made him a little lower than the heavenly beings
>   and crowned him with glory and honor.
> You have given him dominion over the works of your hands;
>   you have put all things under his feet,
> all sheep and oxen,
>   and also the beasts of the field,
> the birds of the heavens, and the fish of the sea,
>   whatever passes along the paths of the seas.

> O Lord, our Lord,
>   how majestic is your name in all the earth! (Ps. 8:5–9)

He says:

> Preserve me, O God, for in you I take refuge.
> I say to the Lord, "You are my Lord;
>   I have no good apart from you."

> As for the saints in the land, they are the excellent ones,
>   in whom is all my delight.

The sorrows of those who run after another god shall multiply;
  their drink offerings of blood I will not pour out
  or take their names on my lips.

The Lord is my chosen portion and my cup;
  you hold my lot.
The lines have fallen for me in pleasant places;
  indeed, I have a beautiful inheritance.

I bless the Lord who gives me counsel;
  in the night also my heart instructs me.
I have set the Lord always before me;
  because he is at my right hand, I shall not be shaken.

Therefore my heart is glad, and my whole being rejoices;
  my flesh also dwells secure.
For you will not abandon my soul to Sheol,
  or let your holy one see corruption.

You make known to me the path of life;
  in your presence there is fullness of joy;
  at your right hand are pleasures forevermore. (Ps. 16:1–11)

And, of course:

The Lord is my shepherd; I shall not want.
  He makes me lie down in green pastures.
He leads me beside still waters.
  He restores my soul.
He leads me in paths of righteousness
  for his name's sake.

Even though I walk through the valley of the shadow of death,
  I will fear no evil,
for you are with me;
  your rod and your staff,
  they comfort me.

You prepare a table before me
　in the presence of my enemies;
you anoint my head with oil;
　my cup overflows.
Surely goodness and mercy shall follow me
　all the days of my life,
and I shall dwell in the house of the LORD
　forever. (Ps. 23:1–6)

Now, of course, the Psalms describe curse as well as blessing. The wicked are punished severely, and even the righteous do not escape judgment, because of their own sin and because the Lord delays blessings for his own reasons. But that takes nothing away from the blessings of the covenant with God. The ambiguities of God's blessings and curses in history do not lessen our obligation to give thanks when God shows his mercy to us. There are real blessings in this life, initial installments of the fullness of blessing to be found in the life to come.

And of course, the relation of God to Israel in the Mosaic covenant was in some ways unique and different from the relation of God to new covenant believers. One of the chief blessings of the old covenant was the blessing of the land of Canaan, to which God gave title to Israel. That was the land of milk and honey, of the vine and fig tree, the land in which they were to enjoy their prosperity (Deut. 5:16). Under the new covenant, that has changed. Jesus does not promise NT believers that they will possess a specific piece of real estate, in which their prosperity is tied to their covenant obedience.[2]

But the new covenant, like all other covenants, contains a blessing promise. Jesus' Beatitudes (Matt. 5:3–11) are blessings of the new covenant, of the kingdom of God, promises to new covenant believers. These Beatitudes, like the Psalms, presuppose a context of persecution and distress. The blessed are poor in spirit, mournful, meek, hungry, thirsty, persecuted (but also merciful, pure in heart, peacemakers). Paul promises that in all things God works for the good of those he redeems

---

2. Arguably, he promised them more: dominion over the whole world (Matt. 28:18–20; 1 Cor. 3:21–23; 6:3, Eph. 6:3, Heb. 2:5–9).

(Rom. 8:28) in a context in which he describes the sufferings of this life in gruesome detail: tribulation, distress, persecution, famine, nakedness, danger, sword (v. 35). He quotes Psalm 44:22:

> As it is written,

> "For your sake we are being killed all the day long;
>   we are regarded as sheep to be slaughtered." (Rom. 8:36)

But:

> No, in all these things we are more than conquerors through him who loved us. For I am sure that neither death nor life, nor angels nor rulers, nor things present nor things to come, nor powers, nor height nor depth, nor anything else in all creation, will be able to separate us from the love of God in Christ Jesus our Lord. (Rom. 8:37–39)

There are some who discourage Christians from applying such blessing texts to our present life. One kind of amillennialism insists on regarding the present age as a time of unmitigated defeat and sorrow, and calls us to find our blessing only in the world to come. But that is not the teaching of Scripture. For one thing, Paul's statement (v. 37 above) that "we are more than conquerors" is in the present tense. And it is a description not merely of our covenant status with God, but of our actual experience. The tribulation, distress, persecution, famine, and so on of verse 35 were not hypothetical. Paul actually went through these. (He explains his personal sufferings in greater detail in 2 Corinthians 4:7–12 and 11:25–33.) Certainly Paul looked toward the resurrection as his permanent release from suffering (2 Cor. 4:13–18). But he also said that he, with us, was more than a conqueror even in this life.

In this respect, believers in the new covenant are no different from those of the old. As we have seen, the Psalms refer often to the sufferings of the righteous, but also to their blessings. Indeed, the new covenant church has often (sometimes exclusively) used the Psalms as its language of praise and prayer in public worship.[3]

As in the Psalms, new covenant believers can expect great and wonderful blessings—but "with persecutions." The most balanced NT statement of this expectation is found in Mark 10:29–30:

> Truly, I say to you, there is no one who has left house or brothers or sisters or mother or father or children or lands, for my sake and for the gospel, who will not receive a hundredfold now in this time, houses and brothers and sisters and mothers and children and lands, with persecutions, and in the age to come eternal life.

Make no mistake: this is a promise of *earthly* blessings, as well as heavenly ones.

This does not mean, of course, that every Christian will be rich in this world. As in the old covenant, there remains a paradox: there will be no poor, yet there will be poor. If God's people obey him and take care of their poor brothers and sisters, there will be no poor in the community. But there will always be people who need this compassion (Acts 2:44–45; 4:32–37; Rom. 15:26–27; 2 Cor. 8–9; Gal. 2:10).

And of course, as in the OT, there remain mysteries as to why God does not always answer our prayers for help immediately. The NT calls us to pray for earthly things as well as heavenly ones ("Give us this day our daily bread," Matt. 6:11) and promises to answer such prayers, as in Matthew 6:25–34 and Luke 11:5–13. The final answer to all the prayers of all believers will not occur until the resurrection. But this does not imply that God never answers such prayers today. Indeed, the picture we gain from Scripture in both Testaments is that such answers are the regular thing. We should expect them; and when they don't come, we should certainly ask why, as the psalmists do.

So God does promise prosperity to the believer. That is one of the benefits of living in covenant with God. It is not a "name it and

---

3. It is odd that some Reformed Christians, who recommend greater (even exclusive) use of the Psalms in worship, believe that the blessings of the Psalms do not apply to them.

claim it" prosperity, unless what we are naming and claiming is part of what God has promised, and unless our claim is part of our faithful obedience to God. Prosperity is not given to those who covet, who envy, fight, and quarrel about someone else's belongings. But it is given to those who seek their daily bread from God. God delights to bless, even to increase the wealth of those who seek to use that wealth in his service and are generous in sharing it with the poor. He is concerned with the material as well as with the spiritual, for his children need material things.

The same arguments apply to the church at the corporate level. Some have argued that in the age before Jesus returns, the victories of the church are limited to the "spiritual" sphere, so that the church does not gain any influence in society or culture. I argued above that God gives to individual believers temporal as well as spiritual blessings in this life ("with persecutions," Mark 10:30), and I think the same arguments and principles bear on the church corporate.

The church is people, of course, not buildings or abstract concepts. God's blessing of individual Christians is a blessing to the church as a whole. When one member is blessed, the whole body is blessed.

When a person is saved by God's grace, he brings his regenerate nature into the workplace with him and seeks to glorify God wherever he is (1 Cor. 10:31). Such individual witness, practiced by many people, can bring about structural change in the culture. Indeed, we have seen in history how God has used Christian witness to dramatically change the treatment of women, orphans, slaves, and the poor, and to bring change for the better to education, the arts, science, and politics. The changes that God works in individual hearts bring about changes in society and culture. And that leads to prosperity. It should not be surprising that the nations most deeply influenced by the gospel have been the most democratic, have been the most free, and have had the highest living standards.

We should be careful, then, in how we criticize prosperity theology, for such criticism risks the danger of denying God's promises of prosperity to believers today. Rather, critics of prosperity theology ought to be more specific in what they are criticizing. They should show that the preacher in question not only promises prosperity, but urges an envious spirit. The envious should repent, because they are bringing curses upon themselves, not blessings. But those who out of covenant faithfulness seek material blessings in order to advance God's kingdom (Matt. 6:33) and to show love to others should not be ashamed. Rather, they should be encouraged. Their prayers are a good thing, and the answers (however long they may be postponed) will bring glory to God and blessings to all.

32

Response to Doug Moo's Review of *Doctrine of the Christian Life*[1]

Many thanks to Ken Magnuson for organizing this meeting, and to Russ Moore and Doug Moo for their interaction with my book. I'll begin by responding to Doug.

I'm thankful, of course, for Doug's kind words about the volume. Just to mention one thing, he holds back a bit on criticisms he might have made, on the ground that he is something of an outsider to the conceptual world of the book. He does not consider himself a part of the Reformed tradition, though his soteriology is "mildly Reformed."[2] Later,[3] he wonders whether sometimes I go to Scripture "to find confirmation for an interpretive approach that he has already found in the tradition." As he says, "we all do this to some extent."[4] But this criticism of me will come as news to those in the Reformed community who think I am not "really" Reformed at all and that I refuse to read the Scripture "in the light of" the Reformed tradition. These folks think I am altogether too creative, to the extent that I have wandered far from the Reformed reservation. Thanks, Doug, for giving me some ammunition to use against that kind of criticism.

---

1. Douglas J. Moo, "A Review of John M. Frame, *The Doctrine of the Christian Life*" (paper presented at the 61st annual meeting of the Evangelical Theological Society, New Orleans, Nov. 2009).
2. Ibid., 3.
3. Ibid., 11.
4. Ibid.

I will, however, in the rest of this response focus on the three areas in which Doug has brought thoughtful criticisms of the book: on *sola Scriptura*, the law, and the Decalogue.

Sola Scriptura

On *sola Scriptura*, he raises three questions.

First Question

He thinks Romans 1–2 suggests "a more robust role for natural law" than I allow in the book. He says that "if people are condemned by natural law, then it seems that natural law must have some kind of role to play in defining good and evil."[5] In the context of Romans 1–2, I prefer to speak of *natural revelation* rather than *natural law*, given the historical use of the latter phrase. *Natural law*, as the concept has developed out of non-Christian Stoic and Aristotelian philosophy, refers to ethical principles determinable by human reason alone. That idea is problematic in Romans 1, in view of the fact that Paul speaks of the ungodly people suppressing the truth by their unrighteousness (v. 18). Obviously, if they are going to make the proper use of natural revelation, they need to stop suppressing the truth, and that change cannot come about through reason alone. In the context of Romans, that sinful suppression can be dealt with only by grace, and the message of grace comes from Scripture, not natural revelation.

But Doug is right to say that in Romans 1 the natural law/natural revelation is the ground on which the wicked are condemned. Does that imply that natural revelation plays a role in defining good and evil? That depends on what we mean by *defining*. Natural revelation is not a communication by words and sentences. It comes through nature, history, and the human conscience, and it produces within us a knowledge of good and evil sufficient to warrant judgment. But this revelation does not produce a verbal text. Further, the conscience itself is not an infallible revelation. The conscience can be wrong, can even be "seared,"

5. Ibid., 4.

as Paul describes in 1 Timothy 4:2. As Paul says, again, the unbeliever suppresses the truth by his unrighteousness.

So natural revelation does not "define" right and wrong, in the sense of producing normative verbal formulations of these concepts. If we are to define, say, abortion as good or evil, it is not enough to say that natural revelation tells us it is wrong. Natural revelation does, I believe, impress on people's consciences that abortion is wrong. But it does not provide normative verbal definitions by which we could come up with formulations and arguments to that effect. And when people argue simply from events to ethical definitions, they are likely to be caught up in naturalistic fallacies—arguments from *is* to *ought*.

The same considerations bear on the use of human reason to access natural revelation. In the natural-law tradition, ethical knowledge comes from human reason without the use of Scripture. But Scripture itself has a lot to say about the use of reason. It tells us that there is an antithesis between the wisdom of the world and the wisdom of God. It tells us that reasoning, like all other human activities, must be done to the glory of God. (Doug is right to think that Cornelius Van Til lurks behind my view of ethical epistemology.) To renounce the use of Scripture as the natural-law tradition does is to refuse to hear what Scripture says about reason.

So if natural revelation is accessible to human reason, it is accessible not to ungodly reason (the wisdom of the world, as Paul says), but to reason subject to God's spoken and written word. But then, we cannot define ethical concepts without Scripture.

Doug asks "about the implications of this claim for the participation of Christians in the 'public square.'"[6] First, the greatest need of the public square is truth. Christians believe that the Bible is truth, and it would be sinful for us to withhold that source of truth from the public. Indeed, withholding the truth from the public violates the Great Commission of Christ, the highest task of the church. It is only the gospel of Christ, found only in Scripture, that can open blind eyes to see their own sins and to turn to Christ as the only remedy.

6. Ibid.

That current social conventions exclude our truth from contemporary ethical discussion is a great evil, one that Christians ought to fight against.

Second, certainly there is no reason why Christians cannot cooperate with non-Christians in promotion of ethical causes. If atheists want to campaign against abortion, as some do, there is no reason why we should not coordinate our efforts with them. What has happened in such a case is that they have come up with the right answer on the basis of natural revelation. Their argument is doubtless inadequate, and on that account they may not continue long as our co-belligerents. But we should be thankful to God for such support, wherever it comes from.

Third, there is no rule that says we must present every argument on every occasion. Paul preached from natural revelation in Lystra and at Athens, but he preached from Scripture in the synagogues. Even when he preached from natural revelation, however, he presupposed what he knew from the Scriptures. Jesus spoke very differently to the woman of Samaria from the way he spoke to the Pharisees. So audiences are different and Christian witness is person-variable. To some audiences we might cite Scripture texts, but not to others. To some we will focus on natural revelation as it indicates what happens to people who violate biblical norms. But we should never violate the ethical principles we know to be true, and in that way Scripture controls our use of natural revelation.

And yes, Doug, I do think that all science is ideologically driven. But by common grace, God often restrains the force of false ideology and enables even unbelieving scientists to acknowledge the truth. Christians should rejoice in this fact, but should also use discernment. As President Ronald Reagan told Mikhail Gorbachev, "Trust, but verify."

Second Question

Also on the general subject of *sola Scriptura*, Doug questions my critique of the concept *adiaphora*. He says, "Yet it seems to me that there may be many occasions when we will simply not know what choice we are confronted with will bring most glory to God. And such a decision then, it seems to me, falls—from our perspective at least—into the category appropriately labeled 'adiaphora.' "[7]

Well, as I understand it, and I'm willing to be corrected, the term *adiaphora*, although as I say in the book it is used in a variety of ways, always represents something objective rather than something subjective. That is, it is about the actual ethical value of an action rather than its perceived value. So to say that, for instance, gambling is adiaphora is not to say that we cannot decide whether it is right or wrong. Rather, it is to say that by its very nature it *is* neither right nor wrong.

I agree, of course, that our ethical understanding is limited and that sometimes we have a hard time discerning whether a decision or action is right or wrong. By denying *adiaphora*, I never meant to say that ethical decision was easy; in fact, I say otherwise in the book. I only meant to say that in every case there *is* an objective right and wrong, whether or not we are able to discern which is which.

Third Question

Doug's third comment on *sola Scriptura* has to do with my brief reference to William Webb's "redemptive movement hermeneutic." I should say that perhaps I should have stayed out of this discussion. I didn't actually read the book until most of my own writing was completed. It seemed like a significant book to me, and I was impressed by Wayne Grudem's critique of it. I wanted to support Wayne's side of the debate, so I put into *DCL* a few remarks of my own. But perhaps I should have waited for an occasion when I could discuss Webb at greater length, as his work certainly deserves.

But let me jump right to Doug's question: "why, since the biblical writers explicitly speak to Christian slave owners about their responsibilities, do they not simply forbid Christians to own slaves?" I believe we ought to distinguish between different kinds of slavery. In the book I discuss the differences between the slavery of war captives and indigents, the Hebrew slavery of the OT, and the slavery of the American South. We tend today to look at all slavery through the lens of the latter,

7. Ibid., 5.

but that is not accurate. Slavery in the American South was based on kidnapping and racism, and it prevented the slaves from doing anything to advance themselves toward freedom. None of these were generally true of the Greco-Roman slavery that Paul was aware of. While I can think of nothing good to say about the slavery of the American South, Greco-Roman slavery in some contexts was, I think, superior to other possible methods of dealing with war prisoners and with debt. In some cases, the slaves benefited from the institution, especially if their masters were relatively benevolent. This is not to say that there were never abuses in the Greco-Roman form, and Paul does address these. But he does not forbid Christians to own slaves, and I think that advice was not wrong.

It is remarkable, however, that he urges masters to respect their slaves, even to "stop your threatening" (Eph. 6:9). Without threatening and its consequences, it is hard to imagine any meaningful difference between slavery and ordinary employment. Certainly, once Jesus' and Paul's concept of servant leadership is introduced into the master-slave relation, it becomes something very different. If Webb wants to call this a "trajectory" to the abolition of Greco-Roman slavery altogether, I will not object. But this qualification to the institution is not something that Scripture points to as a desirable future development. It is rather a norm that existed in Paul's own time.

The Law

So far, we have been discussing *sola Scriptura* under three subpoints. I come now to Doug's second area of concern, which he calls "Law, Grace, and Gospel." He draws our attention to the strong emphasis in the NT on the internal work of the Spirit, writing the law on our heart, giving us a renewed mind. He believes that my book should have emphasized this more fully at the expense of some of its emphasis on law.

Here I'm inclined to agree with him. As he mentions, I admit in the book some level of inadequacy in this area. Certainly the concluding chapter on "Growing in Grace" is not comparable to the rest of the book in its adequacy to its subject. But I would note that earlier in the book is a sixty-five-page discussion of the existential perspective that deals with these matters in some detail. There in chapter 18 I argue that goodness in Scripture is a characteristic of our being, not only of our actions and decisions. In 19, I discuss biblical virtues. In 20, I try to show that a godly inner character is required for ethical knowledge: that godliness and knowledge are interdependent. And in 21, I give attention to the inward "organs" of ethics, such as the heart, conscience, and emotions.

As for Doug's comment that law in the NT is secondary to inward transformation,[8] I think he is comparing apples and oranges. The law is the standard; inward transformation is the process of becoming conformed to the standard. The law defines obedience, but the Spirit's work gives us the motive to obey. I agree that the NT puts more emphasis on the latter, less on the former, than the OT. That is understandable in light of the lavish outpouring of the Spirit at Pentecost and on all believers, filling them with gifts and fruits. But of course, even in the OT the ideal was for Israel to write God's words on their heart, not just on stone tablets. And in the NT, the work of the Spirit brings about conformity to God's law.

The Decalogue

Doug's third area of concern is with my treatment of the Decalogue. He thinks I am claiming more than that "the Decalogue, as part of Scripture, remains in some sense authoritative for Christians,"[9] namely, "that all Christians recognize that the Decalogue continues to have 'normative' ethical authority over Christians." He denies that this latter view is true.

I do not find his distinction entirely clear—especially with *normative* in quotation marks. In my vocabulary, if the Decalogue is in some sense authoritative, then it is in some sense normative. *Authoritative* and *normative* are in many contexts interchangeable. Doug is not using them interchangeably, so he is assuming some distinction between them. But he doesn't define that distinction, though he implies that it is a distinction we all know about. I'm not sure that I do, but I'll try to follow his argument in any case.

8. Ibid., 8.
9. Ibid., 9.

I think what he's getting into here is the debates about covenants and dispensations. Scripture does speak of various covenants between God and Adam, Noah, Abraham, Israel under Moses, David, and Jesus. For our purposes, the most important discussion concerns the relation of the Mosaic covenant to the new covenant. The continuities and discontinuities between these are often discussed, and parties have defended such positions as dispensationalism, theonomy, Meredith Kline's covenant theology, and so on.

The NT speaks of both continuities and discontinuities between the new covenant and the old (Mosaic). Hebrews 8:13 says that the old covenant is "obsolete." But Paul in Romans 9 says that new covenant Christians are grafted into the olive tree that represents Israel. In my book, I've discussed these continuities and discontinuities in chapters 12 and 13. As is most common in my tradition, I place the emphasis on continuity. The discontinuity I find mainly in the newness of the priesthood of Christ and its implications. This newness implies that some OT statutes are no longer literally authoritative, but others continue in effect. The Decalogue contains some references to things that are not part of the new covenant, such as the promise in the fifth commandment that those who obey will prosper in the "land," that is, Canaan. But for the most part the commands of the Decalogue continue in force, owing partly to the fact that these commands republish the creation ordinances given to Adam and Eve.

If I'm right about all this (and it is a complicated area of discussion), then I think it's right to assert that, as Doug puts it, "the Decalogue continues to function for the Christian as an authoritative summary of biblical ethics."[10] I know of no discontinuity between old and new covenants that would forbid us from saying that. Doug may be right in saying that I should have argued this position more fully, taking into account the diversity on this point among evangelical, and indeed Reformed, theologians. But at any rate, I am still persuaded of it. The use of Decalogue commands by Jesus in the Sermon on the Mount and by Paul in, for example, Romans 13:9 confirms my conviction.

10. Ibid.

Doug objects especially to my treatment of the fifth commandment in which, following the example of the Westminster Larger Catechism, I find it teaching a kind of "honor" for all people. I agree that you could not draw such a conclusion from what we normally call grammatico-historical exegesis, at least from that alone. In that sense, I would agree with Doug that the commandment does not bear such an expansive interpretation. But we do need to ask what kind of exegesis Jesus assumes when he teaches that anger is a form of murder or lust a form of adultery. In these statements, Jesus is not engaging in grammatico-historical exegesis any more than were the Westminster divines.

Presuming that his use of Scripture is normative, or at least that it is not subject to criticism, I think we should see him as engaging in a kind of *application* of the precepts of the Decalogue. In that application, you read, say, the sixth commandment, and you ask what sorts of attitudes lead to murder. If you really care about avoiding murder, you will care to eliminate these attitudes in yourself. In this way, the commandment becomes more than a commandment about external behavior. It is a commandment about the heart, from which come the issues of life. And if we identify the wrong heart attitude as a certain kind of anger, then what do we replace that anger with? Love, of course. So in Jesus' meditative application, the commands of the Decalogue address the heart of man, and they proclaim an ethic centered in love. I don't know whether there is a name for this kind of "exegesis." It is not grammatico-historical, but I like the term *meditative application*.

Turning to the fifth commandment, we should certainly not deny that our literal fathers and mothers are the focus of the commandment's intention. I would not claim that "father and mother" is a phrase that by itself connotes all spheres of authority. Indeed, it is important to focus on the literal family, which is so crucial to the social nature of God's people.

But I do point out in the book that there is a structure of metaphor in Scripture, in which kings, military commanders, prophets, and even God himself are called fathers. And in that structure, the metaphorical father does claim honor for himself. God says in Malachi 1:6, "If I am a father, where is my honor?" Certainly a Jewish reader would recognize that the concept *honor* is not far from the concept *father*. Where there is metaphorical fatherhood, one would expect an obligation to honor in some sense.

Now, if we look at the fifth commandment the way Jesus looked at the sixth and seventh, we should ask what heart issue lies behind the literal commandment. Well, in this case the command itself tells us: it is the issue of the honor we show to other people, particularly those in authority. And as we study the concept of honor in Scripture, we see that it has a universal dimension. But to say that is not to equate the honor due to the police officer with the honor due to my literal father. There is a similarity between the two, so that the one can be a metaphor for the other. But they are not the same, and I have not claimed that they are. The honor we owe to God, to our fathers, and to others will differ according to the differences in the nature of the relationships. The commandment itself doesn't specify those differences, but it invites us to meditate on the metaphors it suggests. How can I claim to honor my father and mother if I have contempt for others whom God has created and ordained to watch over me? If my heart is inconsistent in that way, don't I need to ask God to change me? That is what I call *meditative application*.

Finally, Doug thinks that when I talk about the hermeneutical centrality of the Decalogue for Christian ethics, I am guilty of a "depreciation of the significance of the New Testament for the Christian's ethical reasoning."[11] Of course I don't intend that at all. I think I understand the "key new covenant realities and values" that Doug speaks about, "the fundamental values that flow from the cross and the resurrection." Perhaps my book is weak in failing to put enough emphasis on those realities, and if so I am ready to repent.

Yet the first part of the book does put considerable emphasis on redemptive history (which I discuss under the situational perspective) and the inward transformation of the believer through the indwelling of the Holy Spirit (under the existential perspective). Maybe there is not enough emphasis on that, but certainly there is some. And when I

11. Ibid., 12.

address the normative perspective, the use of the law, the main topic for discussion is the *NT* use of the law. So when we get to the Decalogue in the second part of the book, we should be prepared to look at it through a NT lens. Indeed, my treatment of the fifth commandment that Doug criticizes is an example of this. For better or worse, it's an attempt to read the Decalogue as Jesus did.

So I think we have here, perhaps, another case of apples and oranges. When Doug speaks of "the fundamental values that flow from the cross and the resurrection, the powerful transforming work of the Spirit,"[12] he is speaking not of the law itself, but of the redemption of Christ and the presence of the Spirit that enable us to keep the law. That is, of course, what redemption is. Jesus died not primarily to bring us a new law, but to bring us God's forgiveness for our transgressions against the old law, and to enable us to obey that same law. We need both, of course. But neither can simply be substituted for the other. The fundamental values of the NT are not found primarily in its moral precepts, but in the way it enables one to keep the fundamental precepts of the OT. To focus on that redemption, we must, of course, focus on the NT (which nevertheless presupposes the OT sacrificial system, priesthood, etc.). But to focus on the law, the precepts, I do not think it is wrong to concentrate on the OT, keeping in mind how these are employed in the NT.

So I still see the law itself as presented most systematically in the Decalogue. And I rejoice in the work of Jesus, through whom the law becomes no longer a terrible burden, but a blessed way of life. To appreciate the fundamental values of the NT is not to depreciate the OT, but to show how Jesus' redemption saves us from the curse of the OT law, so that we may keep it.

12. Ibid., 13.

33

Response to Russell Moore's Review of *Doctrine of the Christian Life*[1]

MANY THANKS to Russell Moore for this kind, perceptive, indeed somewhat surprising review.

When I heard that he was going to reflect on my views of the environment, I had to scratch myself a bit to try to remember what I had said on that subject. I confess that I had not expected to be praised and intelligently criticized for distinctive views of the environment. When one undertakes a book that gives the illusion of comprehensiveness, there are always some ideas that one is passionate about sharing with the public and other things that one includes simply because it is unthinkable that a comprehensive book not include them. I confess that for me the discussions of environmentalism were in the second category rather than the first. It's not that I think, or ever thought, that the environment is not a worthy object of concern. It is, instead, that I have tended to be skeptical of the rather overideologized literature on the subject, and I have not been able to do the kind of scientific research necessary to judge between the various ideological accounts. Science is my weakest suit, but it certainly seems to be among the essential skills

1. Russell Moore, "Re-Framing the Earth: Review of *Doctrine of the Christian Life*" (paper presented at the 61st annual meeting of the Evangelical Theological Society, New Orleans, Nov. 2009).

that one ought to have to enter into the contemporary discussion of the environment.

And yet now Russell Moore has done me the great favor of turning me into an environmentalist! And I am thankful and delighted. He does this by looking beyond the obvious places in my book and indeed at one point by citing another book of mine, *DG*. And I think he is right, that when you take all of this into account, a somewhat distinctive position, or at least a new perspective on the traditional Reformed accounts, emerges, and we see possibilities for applying these traditional accounts to the problems discussed today.

His account of my position is accurate: I begin with an anthropocentric account of nature, with God's creating man to be fruitful and subdue the earth. But as Russ understands, I emphasize that human beings are also part of the earth—made from dust, returning to dust, dependent on the natural world for our continued life. So there is a mutual dependence here. Our lordship over creation, then, cannot be a sheer exploitation, but must be servant leadership. Jesus taught the concept of servant leadership in Matthew 20 and presented it as something radically different from the attitudes of the kings of the Gentiles. This principle is still not understood today by the secular public. To most writers on the subject, our relation to the environment is a zero-sum game, so that human use of the environment necessarily degrades it, and any improvement to the environment must be at the expense of human beings. But in Genesis 1, for human beings to fill and subdue the earth is a good thing—for God, for man, and therefore, necessarily, for the earth as well.

The concept of competing rights—animal rights, for example—reinforces the zero-sum concept. As Russ points out, Scripture is complementarian here, as with the man-woman relationship, with each enriching the other as both fulfill their divinely given and different roles.

But we must also consider the effects of the fall, which obstructs the balance that God intended. Man became sinful, therefore selfish. And the earth received a divine curse, that it would no longer cooperate easily with human labor. So though there is still no zero-sum game, human dominion must become something of a battle. As Russell pointed out, human effort does not gradually lead to utopia. Nature resists us, and we play a role in despoiling nature.

God gave his Sabbath command to Adam and Eve as a means of rest for them and a time to acknowledge God as the source of all blessing. But after the fall, man resists God's rest. That rest remains a blessing for human beings, and it is a blessing for the earth as well. In Israel's system of sabbatical years, the earth also receives rest. But human sin resists God's rest, both for ourselves and for the earth. The rest, as Russ says, limits our economic freedom, so that we cannot spend all our time enriching ourselves. We resist that restriction. But as Russ says, it gives us a sense of the limits of our competence in proposing solutions to environmental issues. I agree with him that on "cap and trade" and other issues we need to be much more aware of our own limitations.

The one area in which Russ criticizes my approach at some length is in the areas of reproductive and genetic technology. He says:

> Frame rightly eliminates as ethical those technologies that take human life, but aren't there other issues as well: such as whether or not humanity is given dominion over human nature itself? Frame's discussion of human reproductive cloning is, I think, shortsighted to the point of being ominous in its implications. Human cloning, he writes, is "'playing God' only in the sense that we should always play God: imaging his creativity by taking dominion of natural processes for his glory."[2]

He then quotes Bill McKibben, who asks, "Whom would you worship if your genes came from Pfizer? If your daily bread came straight from a magic nanobox?"[3]

Well, I have tried hard to think this through, because I, too, find these alternatives distasteful, even rather creepy. But I'm not persuaded by the arguments usually used to prohibit all human cloning. I do say in the book that research into cloning that kills human embryos should be forbidden. And I think many of the motives that lead people to seek clones of themselves are unworthy of Christians.

2. Ibid., 15.
3. Ibid.

But, I ask, what if cloning technology progresses to the point at which there is no more danger to human life than in normal reproduction? And let's say that when that time comes, a Christian couple who cannot have children in the normal way want to have a child using the genes of one of them rather than a third party. Should we reject that desire as sinful? I cannot, I confess, understand why it should be sinful.

McKibben asks, "Whom would you worship if your genes came from Pfizer?" But in my example, the couple is not ordering genes from some manufacturer; they are using the genes that God has provided to them, from the body of one of them.

Is the point, perhaps, that our genes come directly from God, without any mediation? But they don't. My genes come from my parents, grandparents, and so on. Indeed, in various cultures and times, families encouraged their sons and daughters to choose their mates with genetics in mind, so that their children would be smart and good-looking. Does this amount to manipulation of the genome?

The role of our ancestors in contributing our genes might lead some to worship their ancestors, but not to worship Pfizer. In any case, I really can't see why involvement in this procedure would affect a person's worship at all. We know that the human genome is a special creation of God, and when we deal with the genome we should be thankful to the Creator. I know of no biblical command that says or implies that we may not make such use of the genome, so I believe that we can do this in obedience to God.

Another common argument to which Russ alludes is that cloning constitutes a "commoditization of the human species."[4] First, I think we accept a kind of commoditization in other areas. Heart transplants, for example, are very expensive. Perhaps when getting a new heart we are not exactly buying one, but the whole process is a huge commercial transaction. Are heart transplants wrong on that account? I am concerned about the possibility of premature declarations of death to facilitate transplants. That is not just commoditization; that is murder. But the fact that money is changing hands does not seem to me to be

4. Ibid., 16.

an adequate argument against such a procedure. And I don't see why cloning, given my other qualifications, should be different.

I grant that I seem to be in the minority here among Christian ethicists, and I readily grant that I may be blind to some principle that is obvious to everybody else. Part of the problem, I think, is that many (not all) who oppose cloning absolutely in every situation are governed by a natural-law type of ethic rather than a *sola Scriptura* type of ethic. For me, if cloning is wrong in all circumstances, I must see some biblical principle that makes it so.

To return to a less controversial note, I love Russ's emphasis on the need for a re-enchantment of nature. Yes, the neopagans have something here. But of course, they fail to hear the Lord speaking *in* nature because they think nature is God and God is nature. But Christians know not only that God made the natural world (creation) and that he directs it (providence), but that he is also present in it, bearing witness to himself in every event, what theologians have sometimes called *concurrence*. So it is right that we should look at the natural world in awe and wonder. Heaven is God's throne, and the earth is his footstool. And so our environmental labors are not, in the end, just a matter of self-preservation, not only obedience to the cultural mandate, but rather a form of worship.

And that awe of God's presence in the natural world will certainly, as Russ says, be a missiological point of contact. Or even more, it will be a witness to the God we proclaim. As we proclaim the gospel, this is a way in which we can display our faith to those who are listening. We are assuring all that our God is here, watching us from the perspective of every tree and field, every river and stream. As Russ says so well, "we will love and care for his wild, free, and terrible earth then, because it reminds us of him."[5]

5. Ibid., 21.

PART 5

Personal

34

A Testimony

NOTE (JULY 25, 2012): I wrote this for a volume of testimonies by Christian alumni of Princeton University.

In my grade-school years, my parents were not regular church-goers, but they took me to Sunday school at a nearby church. At first, I enjoyed Sunday school mainly for the opportunity to visit with my friends and to play pranks on the teachers. The church found it nearly impossible to find teachers willing to take the boys' class. Nevertheless, I took a church-membership class at around the age of eleven or twelve and joined the church. I understood most of the doctrinal teaching, but was still a pagan at heart. Around thirteen or fourteen, however, God confronted me. Through the youth ministry (which clearly set forth the gospel) and the music ministry (which drove it into my heart), God led me to confess from the heart that I had greatly offended him and to receive Jesus' sacrifice on the cross as my only hope and comfort.

Through junior high and high school I grew in my knowledge of Scripture and doctrine, and I learned to bring a witness to friends. But by my senior year I had settled into a kind of relativism. Troubled by Bible difficulties, I took the easy way out, regarding the Bible as a mere collection of symbols. After graduation, I spent the summer traveling through the country with some friends. We attended church only about twice the whole summer.

When I arrived at Princeton, however, I wanted to renew my relation to God, and so I visited a number of religious meetings and organizations. The one that captured my attention was the Princeton Evangelical Fellowship (PEF). That group focused on straight Bible teaching. We met twice a week with Dr. Donald Fullerton,[1] and the students met for a daily prayer meeting in someone's dorm room. We had conferences and learned to present the gospel on campus. PEF would have no part of my relativism. For them, God's Word was true, and all of it must be believed. Jesus was the only way, the only truth, the only life. Despite all the secular campus influences on the other side, God enabled me to put aside all my sophisticated reservations and embrace Christ with all my heart and mind.

When I was a freshman, I probably would have been happier to find a group with more discussion, more student input. And I didn't agree with everything that Dr. Fullerton taught. But God knew what I really needed. I needed his Word. I needed to be around people who took God at his word, who believed in prayer, who wanted to share Christ with their community and the world. By my senior year, I knew that God had led me to the right place.

I majored in philosophy, which is not what PEF would have preferred. But through PEF, and through the contrasting voices of the Princeton philosophy department, I was able to see that the Bible taught not only a way of salvation, but a distinctive worldview, different from those of non-Christian religions and of secular philosophers. I learned from the Bible that even our thought life must be brought captive to Christ (2 Cor. 10:5). Christ is Lord not only of our spiritual and moral life, but of every aspect of our existence (1 Cor. 10:31)—not only on Sunday, but on every day of the week.

That theme, the lordship of Christ over all things and over all aspects of human life, has been my great encouragement since Princeton days. I went on to Westminster Seminary, and to grad study in religion at Yale, and then returned to teach at Westminster in 1968. In 1980, I moved to California to help plant a new seminary near San Diego, and in 2000 I took a position with Reformed Theological Seminary in

1. For more about Dr. Fullerton and PEF, see my "Remembering Donald B. Fullerton," http://www.frame-poythress.org/frame_articles/Remembering_fullerton.htm.

Orlando, Florida. God has enabled me to publish a number of books and articles through this time. My series of larger books is called A Theology of Lordship, in which I have tried to show how Jesus Christ is Lord of our thinking (epistemology), of our theological method, and of our ethical choices.

I married Mary Grace in 1984, and we have five children. In California, she homeschooled our kids while ministering (with only occasional help from me) to homeless people and prisoners. She modeled, and still models, for me a level of discipleship beyond what I have attained. So God continues to challenge me to understand his lordship in deeper ways and in more dimensions. It has been a rich and wonderful journey.

I've had some major ups and downs in my life over the years, including periods of disappointment with God. But his Word and Spirit have prevailed—both for me and against me. His promises have proved true. I remain grateful for the things he taught me during my Princeton years, and I seek to continue in the directions in which he led me then.

I'm continually amazed at how events in our lives that seem to make no sense at the time turn out in the long run to form a pattern in which we can discern God's hand. The decisions I've made have not always been the right ones. Yet God has overruled and has used even my worst decisions to bring me to new levels of fellowship with himself. So I encourage my younger readers, including Princeton students, to look to the long term, for our God is the God of all history, and he sees the end from the beginning (Isa. 46:9–10).

35

Bible-Thumper

IN CHRISTIAN HOMES and Sunday schools, small children usually get their earliest instruction directly from the Bible. They hear the stories of David and Goliath and Noah and the ark. They memorize verses such as "Children, obey your parents in the Lord" (Eph. 6:1). They sing songs like the one about Zacchaeus the wee little man. Rarely do they hear about the Westminster Confession of Faith, or about St. Augustine, or John Calvin, or Friedrich Schleiermacher.[1]

This is all well and good. But when many of these children become more advanced in their education, they want to know more than they can find between the covers of Scripture. They want to learn church history and to read the works of famous Christians, past and present. This, too, is well and good. God has raised up teachers in the church not as alternatives to Scripture, but as his agents to communicate the Word of God. This is not inconsistent with the historic Protestant view of *sola Scriptura*. Scripture is our sole ultimate authority; the teachers, pastors, and writers are servants of the Word, concerned with communicating that Word and applying it. In the most important sense, they add no content to the revealed message.

There is, however, also the tendency (sometimes unconscious) to regard historical and contemporary figures as supplements to Scripture. Some of us are tempted to think that the Bible is the first level of our exposure to God, but that it is important to progress beyond it, to higher levels. There is only so much we can learn from Scripture. But

---

1. In the Orthodox Presbyterian Church, they do hear of J. Gresham Machen.

we ought to seek more, to make the best use of our intellectual gifts. To limit oneself to Scripture seems immature.

Certainly it does happen that reading Calvin, say, gives us a kind of insight that we could not have gotten from reading the Bible alone. But that is only to say that God was right in raising up teachers such as Calvin so that we can better understand the Scriptures. We need Scripture, and we also need people to teach us the Scriptures.

But sin distorts these valid considerations. So Christians who gain a sophisticated knowledge of theology often look down pridefully at those Christians who have remained focused on the Bible itself. Often those who focus on the Scripture itself are less educated and make mistakes in their exegesis. The sophisticates use that ignorance to make their case. But the unsophisticated Bible preachers also make a case against their detractors: they are ivory-tower types, and perhaps at least marginal heretics.

Such thinking exacerbates the educational and cultural divisions within the church. Nowhere are these divisions more evident than in the clashes between traditional Protestants (defenders of the "learned ministry") and Pentecostals, or between big-steeple preachers and TV evangelists. The learned ministers speak of the less learned in derogatory terms, terms such as *Bible-thumpers* and *biblicists*.

Now, I think of myself, and most other people think of me, as fairly well educated. But for some reason (I don't boast of this), I feel more affinity with unsophisticated believers than with the Christian elite. This is a feeling, not a formal declaration of allegiance. Both sides have strengths and weaknesses, and both have unjustified pride. There is truth on each side's critique of the other. I wish both sides would learn to look at themselves and their opponents more carefully and sympathetically.

So I will not try here to resolve this source of division (there are, of course, many others) in the church. But I would like to consider the bearing of this argument on theological method.

Learned ministry proponents tend to believe that theology should be an academic activity.[2] It should be the work of scholars who have

---

2. For more of my hesitations about the academic model of theology, see my *The Academic Captivity of Theology* (Lakeland, FL: Whitefield Publishers, 2012).

expertise in church history, traditional theology, and contemporary discussion. Of course, at some point, there must be reference to Scripture. Many advocates of learned ministry are also committed (often by historic confessions) to *sola Scriptura*, and so they believe that the ultimate basis for theological claims must be biblical. But they resist "too much" reference to Scripture for various reasons. I think some of those reasons include cultural prejudice. They don't want to be thought of as Bible-thumpers, spouting off Bible verses at every provocation.

But I stand with the Bible-thumpers. There are many doctrines, to be sure, that are hard to resolve by quotations of specific Bible texts. Think of the simplicity of God, the order of the divine decrees, the distinction between divine substance and divine persons. What many people fail to understand is that these doctrines are very complicated, abstract conclusions that are derived from many biblical texts and principles. Those inclined toward biblicism need to be patient with advocates of these doctrines, giving them time to work out their biblical basis. But the learned defenders of these positions also need to be more sympathetic to the demand for a biblical basis. For if these doctrines, ingenious as they are as intellectual artifacts, are not grounded in Scripture, Protestants must regard them (as David Hume said of the metaphysical speculation of his day) as sophistry and illusion, worthy only to be committed to the flames.

This is why long ago I became committed to the theological method of John Murray. Murray was as sophisticated as they come, very knowledgeable in the history of doctrine and in contemporary theology. But when it came time for him to teach theology to his students, he focused on the specific biblical texts that established each doctrine.[3]

Preparing me for Murray was my Sunday school experience at the church where I grew up, particularly one youth pastor who encouraged me to memorize about five hundred verses through the Navigators' Topical Memory System. At college, I was a member of the Princeton Evangelical Fellowship, which met twice a week for Bible study and often for prayer. At PEF, and at Westerly Road Church, you needed to know

3. See John Murray, "Systematic Theology," in John Murray, *Collected Writings* (Edinburgh: Banner of Truth, 1982), 4:1–21. See also John Frame, "In Defense of Something Close to Biblicism," http://www.frame-poythress.org.

your Bible in order to engage in doctrinal discussion. In these groups there were students of Presbyterian, Methodist, Baptist, charismatic, and independent (usually dispensationalist) convictions. When we got together, tradition counted for nothing, for we all had different traditions. The question was always: "What does the Bible say?"

When I contemplated entering seminary, my PEF friends warned me that Westminster Seminary was tradition-laden, that the school would bury me under Reformed traditions rather than grounding my ministry in God's Word. If John Murray had done that, I would not be a Calvinist today. But John Murray led us carefully through this and that passage of Scripture and made what I thought was an irrefutable case.

As things have turned out, my own theological teaching has been more philosophical than Murray's, somewhat more abstract. But my goal is to validate every one of my theological claims by God's Word. And that means, ultimately, to validate them by specific passages of Scripture.

So as it turns out, I have been a Bible-thumper: more sophisticated than most who receive that derogatory title, but with the same essential goal as any proof-texting[4] TV evangelist: to show where in Scripture my claims come from. This is why my writings contain more Bible quotations, and more chains of Bible references, than can be found in most theologies. I am not ashamed of this.

The old Bible-thumpers sometimes misconstrued the texts they quoted. But typically they defended the obvious simplicities of the biblical text against their sophisticated, modern detractors. They were firm about the creation of Adam, the virgin birth, the miracles of Jesus, his blood atonement, his bodily resurrection, and his return in glory. In my judgment, we should honor them for their stand for Christ and see their mistakes in context. I am pleased to be part of their company.

---

4. In *DKG* I offer a rationale for the use of proof texts. Although *proof-texting* is a term of opprobrium today, it has a long, distinguished theological history. The Westminster divines, for instance, added proof texts to their confession and catechisms. If a theologian claims to follow the principle of *sola Scriptura*, he obligates himself to show, or to be able to show, *where* in Scripture his doctrines are based. That biblical basis may be a broad principle, found in many places. But it must be found in *some* place. And to specify that place is to indicate a proof text. Of course, the complaint that people often use proof texts out of context must be taken seriously. But we should not assume that *every* use of a text as proof text falls to that criticism.

36

Remarks at Justin's Wedding

NOTE (JULY 25, 2012): Because of some physical problems I was unable to attend the wedding of my son Justin to Carol in Zana, Uganda, in 2010. But I provided him with a video presenting some remarks, as follows.

Justin, my wonderful son. I'm so glad that I can be with you, so sorry that I can't be with you, on this great day. Technology is wonderful, but it's no substitute for my seeing you face-to-face.

I can't begin to tell you how proud I am of you—going to a new country, reaching out to new people, seeking to glorify God, finding a wonderful lady to share God's calling and your dreams.

Carol, welcome to the family. We love you, first, because we love anyone who loves our big boy. Second, because he says that you're lovely, amazing, the most thoughtful, loving person he has met, and the biggest reason why God has called him to Uganda. Justin does not say such things thoughtlessly. Indeed, saying such things is just a bit out of character for him. When he speaks this way, we know that he speaks his true heart, and he speaks the truth. I hope I can see you soon, so that I can see firsthand what Justin sees—the goodness that our God has wrought in you for Jesus' sake.

A few words about marriage. Such a great mystery it is, according to God's Word. To participate in marriage is to participate in a drama occurring far beyond this world, beyond time and space. In Ephesians 5:22–24, we read:

Wives, submit to your husbands as to the Lord. For the husband is the head of the wife even as Christ is the head of the church, his body, and is himself its Savior. Now as the church submits to Christ, so also wives should submit in everything to their husbands.

Wives should submit not because they are lesser beings, but because Christ is Lord, and this is what Christ wants. The command comes from heaven. It is our role in the heavenly drama.

Husbands, though, have the more difficult role:

Husbands, love your wives, as Christ loved the church and gave himself up for her, that he might sanctify her, having cleansed her by the washing of water with the word, so that he might present the church to himself in splendor, without spot or wrinkle or any such thing, that she might be holy and without blemish. In the same way husbands should love their wives as their own bodies. He who loves his wife loves himself. For no one ever hated his own flesh, but nourishes and cherishes it, just as Christ does the church, because we are members of his body. Therefore a man shall leave his father and mother and hold fast to his wife, and the two shall become one flesh. This mystery is profound, and I am saying that it refers to Christ and the church. However, let each one of you love his wife as himself, and let the wife see that she respects her husband. (Eph. 5:25–33)

Here the Bible speaks of things that are profoundly mysterious and, at the same time, thoroughly practical. Again there is our role in the heavenly drama, to love our wives as Christ loved the church. But there is also the practical daily work of loving our wives as we love our own bodies. Think of what we do for our own bodies. We eat and drink, we exercise, we take supplements (inside joke), we get medical help when we need it. So each day, day by day, you need to give the same kind of attention to Carol—helping her to make it through each day, sensitive to her pains and her sorrows, thinking all the time: how can I make her happier?

But all of this is also part of that mysterious cosmic drama. Justin, you are to be Christ to Carol. In all your practical care for her, day by day, moment by moment, you are to lay down your life for her, as Christ laid down his life for us. You can't take away her sins; only Jesus can do that. And you can't even be a good husband without Jesus' help. But you must seek by Jesus' help to sacrifice yourself for your wonderful wife.

Carol, you should learn of Christ from Justin's love for you. And Justin (we often miss this), you can learn from your godly, submissive wife how God wants us to behave toward him. In the Bible, Justin, we guys at one point play a feminine role, for we are part of the bride of Christ. So both of you, Justin and Carol, will teach each other of Christ through your servant love, reflecting our great Lord, who came not to be served but to serve and to give his life for us. Learn to love one another as Christ has loved us.

37

1 Corinthians 1:9:
Remarks at Beverly Heights

NOTE (JULY 25, 2012): I attended Beverly Heights Presbyterian Church from 1945 (when I was six years old) until 1967. It was there that I first heard the gospel of grace and came to trust in Christ as my Lord and Savior. On September 18, 2010, I preached there in honor of the twenty-fifth anniversary of the pastorate of the Rev. Rick Wolling. I saw some people there that I hadn't seen in fifty years, and the church was wonderfully hospitable. Below is an edited version of my remarks.

I can't begin to tell you what a huge quantity and quality of memories came upon me when I came through the church door tonight. Beverly Heights was not only my church home, but my home away from home, from 1946 to 1967. My parents took me to Sunday school here in 1946 at the age of six, at Markham School.

The church needed more room then, but would not get it until the new addition maybe six years later. In my elementary-school years, my main interest was seeing my friends and making life hard for people. I was, frankly, a mean kid. In Sunday school and junior church we played nasty pranks on one another—stealing hymnals and piling them up, interrupting the teacher. Nobody wanted to teach our boys' class. Many teachers left us, sometimes in tears. One kid brought a penknife to class, and every time a teacher quit on us, he would put a notch in the table.

In telling you this, I'm not trying to get you to laugh or think about how cute we were, because we really hurt people, and I'm so sorry. Some of these teachers might have been your fathers, mothers, even grandparents. Some were in tears because of us. They were trying to serve the Lord, to help kids, and we didn't care. But they sowed seeds.

In my junior-high years, God got hold of me and others of my friends. I came to see that I was a sinner, and that God could be my friend only through Jesus. I heard the gospel through the church youth program, and the choir program got it into my heart.

I don't want you to look at me and say, "My, how he's improved!" When God asks, "Why should I let you into my heaven?" I will not say to him, "Look how much I've improved." I'll say, "God, be merciful to me, a sinner. My only hope is in Jesus' sacrifice on Calvary."

So my memories of Beverly Heights are qualitatively formative in my life as well as quantitatively huge.

I worked here as occasional organist, Bible teacher, youth ministry intern, through the ministries of Bill McLeister and Walter Dosch, and saw God work in the lives of lots of kids like me, and older folks, too.

My involvement pretty much ended in 1967 when I joined another church and went to teach at Westminster Seminary in Philadelphia, which was not on the approved list for Presbyterians in that day. But I kept hearing good things about what God was doing here. I worried that Beverly Heights might experience what other evangelical churches had experienced in the Presbyterian Church USA denomination—calling a liberal minister, losing the gospel.

I prayed that it wouldn't happen here, and it didn't.

Once when I was in Pittsburgh, I talked to Jack White, the president of Geneva College. He said that Beverly Heights was the place to go if you wanted evangelical teaching within the PCUSA. He knew a lot about Pittsburgh churches; he might have mentioned other churches, but he mentioned you.

So God was faithful over so many decades.

This church was founded—when? Sometime in the 1920s. It was still there in 1946 to minister to me.

And here we are in 2010, and it's still here—to bring the gospel to the community, so that kids like me can find a church home, a home away from home.

Following McLeister and Dosch, here is Rick . . .

I don't know you well, Rick, but I'm so thankful that God has used your ministry to bring to this generation the gospel as Jesus taught it, Paul, Augustine, Luther, Calvin, Edwards, McLeister, and Dosch.

And so many others: associate pastors, elders, deacons, seminarian interns, music directors, Sunday school teachers, VBS workers . . .

God says through Isaiah, "How beautiful . . . are the feet of him who brings good news, who publishes peace" (Isa. 52:7).

A long trail of beautiful feet. How wonderful it's been.

We've so far been looking at these years from a human point of view, as a succession of godly people.

But we can look at them from a higher point of view.

I want you to remember that through that whole time, God has been faithful to us. Through that time and ages past—the apostles, the prophets, Moses, Abraham, Noah, Seth—God used this vast tradition to bring the gospel to us, and all its blessings.

And he continues to do the same.

Let me share briefly one Bible passage that focuses on God's transgenerational faithfulness: 1 Corinthians 1:4–9.

The apostle Paul says this to the church in the Greek city of Corinth. As you listen, think of Beverly Heights:

> I give thanks to my God always for you because of the grace of God that was given you in Christ Jesus, that in every way you were enriched in him in all speech and all knowledge—even as the testimony about Christ was confirmed among you—so that you are not lacking in any spiritual gift, as you wait for the revealing of our Lord Jesus Christ, who will sustain you to the end, guiltless in the day of our Lord Jesus Christ. God is faithful, by whom you were called into the fellowship of his Son, Jesus Christ our Lord. (1 Cor. 1:4–9)

The church of Corinth was not a perfect church; I'm sure neither are you.

At Corinth, there were terrible things going on:

- Factions, divisions
- Sexual immorality
- Believers' suing one another in pagan courts
- Illegitimate divorce
- Believers' participating in feasts honoring idols
- Oppression of the poor at the Lord's Table
- Boasting over spiritual gifts
- Lovelessness
- Disbelief in the resurrection of the dead

Pretty big items!

But in the first nine verses, we hear none of this.

Paul agreed with my mom, who said that you should sandwich your complaints between compliments.

The climax: "God is faithful."

How can he say this, when things in the church seem to have gotten so far out of hand?

Well, who was it who called you to be a Christian?

God did. Many NT passages talk about a special "call" of God. Not as we call a kid from the backyard; God's call is more like a summons from a court. The gospel is an offer, but God's call is an offer you can't refuse.

So these people are not going to fall into the hands of Satan. Rather, God "will sustain you to the end, guiltless in the day of our Lord Jesus Christ" (v. 8).

Whatever terrible things are going on, however Satan may attack this church, if God has called you, he will sustain you to the end.

If you know Christ, you cannot lose your salvation.

On the last day you will stand guiltless—what a comfort for us who have so much to be ashamed of.

What are we called to? To heaven, to blessing, to lots of good things...

But the main thing is the fellowship of God's Son, Jesus Christ our Lord.

Jesus died, but he still lives. He is Lord of all, King of kings and Lord of lords.

And that Lord is our friend; he lives to have fellowship with us.

He lives to answer our prayers, to comfort us in trouble, to fill us with joy.

And to do that forever, and ever, and ever.

Because you are his people, you are Beverly Heights Church, and God is faithful to Beverly Heights.

From generation, to generation, to generation.

After my twenty years here, he has been faithful to this church thirty years more.

My heart is full of thanks tonight. And all of us have much to be thankful for.

38

Twenty-five Random Things
That Nobody Knows about Me

NOTE: THIS WAS a game on Facebook that my students dragged me into.

1. Around age four, when my dad took me to smoky Pittsburgh, I couldn't see all the way across the street.

2. My mom taught me to read before I went to kindergarten.

3. I was always the last guy chosen for sports teams, and with good reason.

4. We listened faithfully to Pittsburgh Pirate games from 1950–56, when the team had the worst record in baseball.

5. In high school (1955–57), I preferred listening to Sinatra, Como, Peggy Lee, Les Paul, et al., to Elvis and the new rock.

6. The Beatles first sounded to me like a lot of noise, until I heard their songs played by schmaltz orchestras like 101 Strings and Mantovani. Then I went back to the original arrangements and thought they were extraordinary beautiful.

7. In junior high I was the only boy in my church choir.

8. As treasurer in our youth group, I used to harangue the kids every week to bring a quarter for the offering.

9. In high school I was mainly known as a satirical writer, doing parodies of English classics like Tennyson's *Idylls of the King*.

10. The height of my piano study was Edvard Grieg's piano concerto. On the organ I played over half the organ works of J. S. Bach.

11. During my high-school years, I was on the verge of accepting an organ position at a Christian Science church, but chose instead a similar job at a Presbyterian church (PCUSA).

12. In my senior year of high school, I had a written theological debate with a Roman Catholic friend. We passed it back and forth, writing in it when the classes got boring. It totaled eighty handwritten pages. The summer after graduation, my Roman Catholic friend told me that he was persuaded of Protestant theology. He went to a liberal seminary, however, and became somewhat liberal in theology.

13. In late high-school years, I, too, was somewhat liberal theologically, inclined to answer every question with: "Well, it's only symbolic, after all."

14. In the summer after graduation, I traveled with some friends. We attended church only twice, and those out of sightseeing interests. But when I entered college that fall, I became deeply hungry for church fellowship.

15. I became a fundamentalist at Princeton, and more or less remain so. When I am called that, I'm not embarrassed at all.

16. At seminary I took long walks to memorize John Murray's lecture outlines.

17. My first paper for Cornelius Van Til was 125 pages. People had told me that Van Til graded by weight. So I added seventy-five pages to some material from my Princeton thesis. He gave me an A, and that is what brought me to the attention of the Westminster Seminary faculty.

18. My priorities for ministry were (a) missions, (b) pastorate, (c) academic theology. A visit to mission fields in 1960 ruled out (a). A year and two summers of pastoral experience ruled out (b). So I embraced (c) by default, as God's calling.

19. At Yale, I was bored to death by modern theologians. Still am.

20. In my early career, I felt a strong tension between my interests and my abilities. The former were focused in practical ministry; the latter were almost completely academic. God has helped me to resolve the tension by writing up academic theological theories that glorify practical ministry.

21. Norman Shepherd was the man who first hired me to teach systematic theology at Westminster Seminary.

22. The board of the Trinity Christian School of Pittsburgh hired me to go to the National Association of Christian Schools Convention at Langley, British Columbia, to oppose a motion to remove the Reformed creeds from their constitution. I did, and the motion failed.

23. I did not marry until I was forty-five. God was preparing someone special.

24. In 1999, I led a worship team of myself, a saxophonist, and a trombonist. The other two musicians were in their late seventies, but we really rocked.

25. I wrote a number of silly songs as child-rearing devices. One praised applesauce, one Kamut. One went: "Up the stairs and down the stairs to make Johnny get up." And the ever-popular reggae, "Don't Drop De Cellphone in De Tropical Smoothie."

APPENDIX

100 Books That Have Most Influenced John Frame's Thought

THE ONE HUNDRED bibliographical entries below represent the thirty-two authors who have had the most influence on John Frame's thought.[1]

Anselm. *St. Anselm: Proslogium; Monologium; An Appendix, in Behalf of the Fool, by Gaunilon; and Cur Deus Homo*. Chicago: Opencourt, 1903.

Aquinas, Thomas, and Robert Maynard Hutchins. *The Summa Theologica of Saint Thomas Aquinas*. Chicago: Encyclopedia Britannica, 1952.

Athanasius. *On the Incarnation: The Treatise de Incarnatione Verbi Dei*. Crestwood, NY: St. Vladimir's Seminary Press, 1998.

Augustine. *The City of God*. Translated by Marcus Dods. Peabody, MA: Hendrickson, 2009.

———. *On the Trinity*. Cambridge: Cambridge University Press, 2002.

Augustine, and William Benham. *The Confessions of St. Augustine*. New York: P. F. Collier & Son, 1909.

Bavinck, Herman. *Our Reasonable Faith*. Grand Rapids: Eerdmans, 1956.

———. *Reformed Dogmatics*. Grand Rapids: Baker Academic, 2008.

———. *Selected Shorter Works*. Portland, OR: Monergism Books, 2011.

1. This list, compiled by John Frame and his colleague Steve Childers, represents the historic stream of biblical and philosophical thought surveyed in the foreword of this book.

Berkouwer, G. C. *Studies in Dogmatics: The Providence of God*. Grand Rapids: Eerdmans, 1952.

Calvin, John. *Calvin's Commentaries*. 500th anniversary ed. 23 vols. Grand Rapids: Baker, 2009.

———. *The Institutes of Christian Religion*. Edited by Tony Lane and Hilary Osborne. Grand Rapids: Baker Academic, 1987.

Clark, Gordon Haddon. *A Christian View of Men and Things: An Introduction to Philosophy*. Jefferson, MD: Trinity Foundation, 1991.

Clowney, Edmund P. *Called to the Ministry*. Nutley, NJ: Presbyterian and Reformed, 1976.

———. *Christian Meditation*. Vancouver, BC: Regent College Publishing, 1979.

———. *The Church*. Downers Grove, IL: IVP Academic, 1995.

———. *How Jesus Transforms the Ten Commandments*. Edited by Rebecca Clowney Jones. Annotated ed. Phillipsburg, NJ: P&R Publishing, 2007.

———. *Preaching and Biblical Theology*. Phillipsburg, NJ: P&R Publishing, 2002.

———. *Preaching Christ in All of Scripture*. Wheaton, IL: Crossway, 2003.

———. *The Unfolding Mystery: Discovering Christ in the Old Testament*. Phillipsburg, NJ: Presbyterian and Reformed, 1991.

Edwards, Jonathan. *Freedom of the Will*. New Haven, CT: Yale University Press, 1957.

———. *The Life of David Brainerd, Missionary to the Indians, Taken from His Diary and Other Private Writings*. New York: Christian Alliance, 1925.

———. *Religious Affections*. New Haven, CT: Yale University Press, 1959.

———. *Selected Sermons of Jonathan Edwards*. New York and London: Macmillan, 1904.

———. *Sinners in the Hands of an Angry God*. Phillipsburg, NJ: P&R Publishing, 1992.

Gerstner, John H. *Jonathan Edwards: A Mini-Theology*. Wheaton, IL: Tyndale House, 1987.

———. *The Problem of Pleasure: A Primer*. Phillipsburg, NJ: Presbyterian and Reformed, 1983.

———. *Reasons for Faith*. New York: Harper, 1960.

———. *Wrongly Dividing the Word of Truth: A Critique of Dispensationalism*. Brentwood, TN: Wolgemuth & Hyatt, 1991.

Gerstner, John H., Arthur W. Lindsley, and R. C. Sproul. *Classical Apologetics*. Grand Rapids: Zondervan, 1984.

Hodge, Charles. *Systematic Theology.* Peabody, MA: Hendrickson, 1999.

Kant, Immanuel. *The Critique of Pure Reason.* New York: Cambridge University Press, 1998.

Kline, Meredith G. *Images of the Spirit.* Eugene, OR: Wipf and Stock, 1999.

———. *The Structure of Biblical Authority.* Eugene, OR: Wipf and Stock, 1997.

Kuyper, Abraham. *Lectures on Calvinism.* Grand Rapids: Eerdmans, 1943.

———. *Near unto God.* Grand Rapids: Eerdmans, 1997.

———. *Particular Grace: A Defense of God's Sovereignty in Salvation.* Grandville, MI: Reformed Free Publishing Association, 2001.

———. *Rooted & Grounded: The Church as Organism and Institution.* Grand Rapids: Acton Institute for the Study of Religion & Liberty, 2013.

———. *Sacred Theology.* Wilmington, DE: Associated Publishers and Authors, 1900.

Lewis, C. S. *Mere Christianity.* San Francisco: HarperSanFrancisco, 2001.

———. *Miracles: A Preliminary Study.* San Francisco: HarperOne, 2001.

Luther, Martin. *The Bondage of the Will.* Translated by J. I. Packer and O. R. Johnston. Grand Rapids: Baker Academic, 2012.

———. *Commentary on Galatians.* Grand Rapids: Kregel Publications, 1979.

———. *Commentary on Romans.* Translated by J. Theodore Mueller. Grand Rapids: Kregel Classics, 2003.

———. *The Freedom of a Christian.* Edited by Mark D. Tranvik. Minneapolis: Fortress Press, 2008.

———. *Luther's Large Catechism: A Contemporary Translation with Study Questions.* St. Louis: Concordia Publishing House, 1988.

———. *Luther's Ninety-five Theses.* Translated by C. M. Jacobs. Minneapolis: Fortress Press, 1957.

———. *Treatise on Good Works.* Luther study ed. Minneapolis: Fortress Press, 2012.

Machen, J. Gresham. *Christianity and Liberalism.* New York: Macmillan, 1923.

Miller, C. John. *A Faith Worth Sharing: A Lifetime of Conversations about Christ.* Phillipsburg, NJ: P&R Publishing, 1999.

———. *Outgrowing the Ingrown Church.* Grand Rapids: Zondervan, 1986.

———. *Repentance and 21st Century Man.* Fort Washington, PA: CLC Publications, 2003.

Miller, C. John, and Barbara Miller Juliani. *Come Back, Barbara.* 2nd ed. Phillipsburg, NJ: P&R Publishing, 1997.

Murray, John. *Christian Baptism*. Phillipsburg, NJ: Presbyterian and Reformed, 1980.

———. *Collected Writings of John Murray: Lectures in Systematic Theology*. Edinburgh: Banner of Truth, 1991.

———. *The Covenant of Grace: A Biblico-Theological Study*. Phillipsburg, NJ: Presbyterian and Reformed, 1987.

———. *The Epistle to the Romans: The English Text with Introduction, Exposition and Notes*. Grand Rapids: Eerdmans, 1997.

———. *The Imputation of Adam's Sin*. Phillipsburg, NJ: P&R Publishing, 1992.

———. *Principles of Conduct: Aspects of Biblical Ethics*. Grand Rapids: Eerdmans, 1957.

———. *Redemption Accomplished and Applied*. Grand Rapids: Eerdmans, 1955.

Packer, J. I. *"Fundamentalism" and the Word of God: Some Evangelical Principles*. Grand Rapids: Eerdmans, 1958.

———. *Knowing God*. 20th anniversary ed. Downers Grove, IL: InterVarsity Press, 1993.

Pascal, Blaise. *Pensées and Other Writings*. Edited by Anthony Levi. Translated by Honor Levi. New York: Oxford University Press, 2008.

Piper, John. *Desiring God: Meditations of a Christian Hedonist*. Colorado Springs: Multnomah, 2011.

Plato, and David Gallop. *Phaedo*. Oxford: Clarendon Press, 1975.

Plato, and Richard D. McKirahan. *Plato's Meno*. Bryn Mawr, PA: Thomas Library, Bryn Mawr College, 1986.

Poythress, Vern S. *Inerrancy and the Gospels: A God-Centered Approach to the Challenges of Harmonization*. Wheaton, IL: Crossway, 2012.

———. *In the Beginning Was the Word: Language—A God-Centered Approach*. Wheaton, IL: Crossway, 2009.

———. *Logic: A God-Centered Approach to the Foundation of Western Thought*. Wheaton, IL: Crossway, 2013.

———. *Philosophy, Science, and the Sovereignty of God*. Phillipsburg, NJ: P&R Publishing, 2004.

———. *Redeeming Science: A God-Centered Approach*. Wheaton, IL: Crossway, 2006.

———. *Redeeming Sociology: A God-Centered Approach*. Wheaton, IL: Crossway, 2011.

———. *The Shadow of Christ in the Law of Moses*. Brentwood, TN: Wolgemuth & Hyatt, 1991. Repr., Phillipsburg, NJ: P&R Publishing, 1995.

———. *Symphonic Theology: The Validity of Multiple Perspectives in Theology.* Phillipsburg, NJ: P&R Publishing, 2001.

———. *What Are Spiritual Gifts?* Phillipsburg, NJ: P&R Publishing, 2010.

Rushdoony, Rousas John. *The Institutes of Biblical Law.* Phillipsburg, NJ: Presbyterian and Reformed, 1980.

Schaeffer, Francis A. *Art and the Bible: Two Essays.* Downers Grove, IL: InterVarsity Press, 1973.

———. *A Christian Manifesto.* Wheaton, IL: Crossway, 2005.

———. *Escape from Reason: A Penetrating Analysis of Trends in Modern Thought.* Downers Grove, IL: InterVarsity Press, 1968.

———. *The God Who Is There: Speaking Historic Christianity into the Twentieth Century.* Chicago: Inter-Varsity Press, 1968.

———. *The Great Evangelical Disaster.* Wheaton, IL: Crossway, 1984.

———. *He Is There and He Is Not Silent.* 30th anniversary ed. Carol Stream, IL: Tyndale House, 1994.

———. *How Should We Then Live? The Rise and Decline of Western Thought and Culture.* L'Abri 50th anniversary ed. Wheaton, IL: Crossway, 2005.

———. *True Spirituality.* Carol Stream, IL: Tyndale House, 1989.

Shepherd, Norman. *The Call of Grace: How the Covenant Illuminates Salvation and Evangelism.* Phillipsburg, NJ: P&R Publishing, 2000.

———. *The Way of Righteousness: Justification Beginning with James.* La Grange, CA: Kerygma Press, 2009.

Van Til, Cornelius. *Christian Apologetics.* Edited by William Edgar. 2nd ed. Phillipsburg, NJ: P&R Publishing, 2003.

———. *A Christian Theory of Knowledge.* Nutley, NJ: Presbyterian and Reformed, 1969.

———. *The Defense of the Faith.* Edited by K. Scott Oliphint. 4th ed. Phillipsburg, NJ: P&R Publishing, 2008.

———. *Introduction to Systematic Theology: Prolegomena and the Doctrines of Revelation, Scripture, and God.* Edited by William Edgar. 2nd ed. Phillipsburg, NJ: P&R Publishing, 2007.

———. *Why I Believe in God.* Philadelphia: Westminster Theological Seminary, 1976.

Warfield, B. B. *Counterfeit Miracles.* Edinburgh: Banner of Truth, 1972.

———. *Faith and Life.* Edinburgh: Banner of Truth, 1974.

———. *Inspiration and Authority of the Bible.* 2nd ed. Phillipsburg, NJ: Presbyterian and Reformed, 1980.

———. *The Person and Work of Christ*. Phillipsburg, NJ: Presbyterian and Reformed, 1989.

———. *The Plan of Salvation*. Grand Rapids: Eerdmans, 1942.

———. *Saviour of the World*. Edinburgh: Banner of Truth, 1991.

———. *Selected Shorter Writings*. Edited by John Meeter. Phillipsburg, NJ: P&R Publishing, 2001.

Westminster Assembly. *The Westminster Standards: An Original Facsimile*. Audubon, NJ: Old Paths Publications, 1997.

Wittgenstein, Ludwig. *Philosophical Investigations*. Oxford: Blackwell, 1953.

Index of Scripture

Index of Subjects and Names